BIG
BUSH
LIES

20 Essays

and a List of the

50 Most Telling Lies

of George W. Bush

BIG
BUSH
LIES

Edited by
Jerry "Politex" Barrett

RiverWood Books
Ashland, Oregon

FIRST EDITION 2004
08 07 06 05 04   5 4 3 2 1

Cover art by Gabriel Lipper
Cover design by David Ruppe

Printed in the the United States of America

Library of Congress Cataloging-in-Publication Data

Big Bush lies : 20 essays and a list of the 50 most telling lies of George W. Bush / edited by Jerry Barrett.
     p. cm.
  Includes bibliographical references.
  ISBN 1-883991-94-3 (pbk.)
  1. United States--Politics and government--2001- 2. Political corruption-- United States. 3. Bush, George W. (George Walker), 1946- I. Barrett, Jerry, 1935-
  E902.B54 2004
  973.931'092--dc22
                              2004002680

Table of Contents

About this book

Big Bush Lies has had a gestation period of nearly a year. In May of 2003 RiverWood Books publisher Steven Scholl contacted Bush Watch Editor Jerry "Politex" Barrett with an idea to do a book on Bush lies and publish it prior to the 2004 presidential election. Barrett liked the idea and this book is the result.

The contributors to *Big Bush Lies* are nearly all full-time professionals, but all have connections to the Internet in one way or the other. A number of lawyers, quite a few academicians, and a handfull of journalists make up the diverse team of writers you'll find in this book. Most are specialists in the content area they have selected for their essay.

The table of contents notes the themes and approaches taken to the subject. The focus is on George W. Bush as a liar, and the book features essays on general political topics, both domestic and foreign. The book also indicates that Bush's lies are part of the fabric of the centuries-old clash between corporations and the state, and CEO Bush is working hard to create a state that, in one way or the other, serves the global needs and desires of corporations. The book ends with a consideration of the effects of Bush's lying upon the ideals of this country. In short, *Big Bush Lies* does not stop at exposing Bush lies, its ultimate concern is to relate them to both the history of this country and the daily lives of its citizens.

Jerry "Politex" Barrett,
April 1, 2004
Austin, Texas

Introduction: Bush Lies

BY JERRY "POLITEX" BARRETT

Definitions

In a comment that the editors of the *Washington Post* called "cavilier" and "shocking," (December 19, 2003), Bush admitted in an *ABC News* interview (December 16, 2003) that he saw no difference between Vice-President Cheney saying "there is no doubt that [Saddam] had weapons of mass destruction" and there is "the possibility that [Saddam] could acquire weapons." When Bush said, "So what's the difference?" to Diane Sawyer, he indicated that a lie and a statement of possibility are all the same to him.

This episode is an example of a Bush lie: it needn't be told directly by Bush, it could be delivered by a representative, but it is condoned by him, directly, as in this case, or indirectly, by never having it retracted. It is a lie because its intention is to deceive. While we all tell lies at one time or another, whether we are called a "liar" depends upon both the amount of lying we engage in and the seriousness of our lies. In his essay on political propaganda in this book, Ernest Partridge notes that Bush mistatements are meant to deceive because there are so many of them and they are so severe. In fact, telling them is a political way of life with Bush: his "campaign strategists feel no more obliged to tell the truth to the public than tobacco marketers feel obliged to publicize the health risks to the teen-agers they are endeavoring to 'hook.'"

How ironic that the president selected by a bipartisan *Washington Monthly* political panel of heavy hitters as the biggest liar in the last quarter century of American presidents (September 2003) ran his campaign on the promise that he would bring truth and integrity to the Oval Office. But what would you expect a liar to say? The truth? That's what tradition and the media would have us believe.

Even though we know that all American presidents lie and that Bush lies more often than other presidents and under circumstance of war similar to LBJ's and his father's, you seldom read that Bush lies in the mainstream press prior to the egregious lying that went on to convince the American people to back his desire to go to war against Iraq. As Eric Alterman has noted in *The Nation* (November 7, 2002), the deference to the office and the D.C. cant that "it is worse to call a politician a liar than to be one" provides "such complicated linguistic circumlocutions as:

Bush's statements represented 'embroidering key assertions' and were clearly 'dubious, if not wrong.' The President's 'rhetoric has taken some flights of fancy,' he has 'taken some liberties,' 'omitted qualifiers' and "simply outpace[d] the facts.' But Bush lied? Never." This is to be remembered when reporters or spinners call future Bush lies "fibs" or "technically correct." However one slices it, if the Bush statement deceives, his track record is such that it is rational to assume that it was meant to deceive, and it can be called a "lie."

Lying As A Political Way Of Life

Lying is a slippery slope, and once the politician gets on it, and they all do, to a certain extent, the question is how to stop. For instance, it's no secret that the typical joke at the beginning of the typical politician's stump speech is just that, a joke, not to be taken seriously. But what if the joke is about something that happened to the politician? Chances are pretty good that it's something embroidered, if not a total lie. Even Laura Bush is not immune to this problem.

During the 2000 campaign the typical George W. Bush stump speech began with a joke about his family, sometimes even at the twins' expense, although both Bush's told reporters that they wanted to shield them from the public limelight. As far as I know, Laura did not use the twins as joke material in any of her speeches. Since then, however, she has fallen into the trap of the little lie, and was honest enough to later admit it, reports Timothy Noah in Slate (January 5, 2004). At the National Book Festival in Washington, D.C., Mrs. Bush read 10 lines of doggerel and identified the author as her husband, George W. and herself as the "inspiration" (www.whitehouse.gov/news/releases/2003/10/20031003-22.html).

Three months later on Meet The Press Mrs. Bush said, "Well, of course, he didn't really write the poem. But a lot of people really believed that he did" (msnbc.msn.com/id/3823359).

Interestingly, Noah adds, the "White House staffer who prepared Mrs. Bush's remarks obviously strained to make the president's purported love poem sound sufficiently moronic that no one would doubt Bush had written it. [I don't] know what to make of this." Luckily, Lisa Kodanaga knows what to make of it in her essay in this book on the creating of the Bush political persona. It's just one more lie in a long, never-ending series of lies to paint Bush as something he's not to win more votes. When one fits the trivial lie into the mosaic of lies that creates the big Bush picture that the administration wants us to see, the effect is much more ominous.

Many more examples of the calculated and incessant lying that goes on as commonplace, daily activities of Bush and his administration are to be found in the various essays in this book.

How Are Lies Justified?

Lying in the name of the greater good is so prevalent throughout world history that one is not particularly surprised that Bush and members of his administration and party use lies as the coin of the realm. The problem, of course, is defining "the greater good." As you might imagine, politicians of all political stripe throughout the word interpret this concept in ways that will suit their own particular political needs and ideologies, rather than the needs of their listeners and opponents.

In Bush's case, Leo Strauss an influential political philosopher who has sometimes been called the father of supply side economic theory, which is presently being practiced by Bush, has been pointed to as an influence upon Bush's conservative administration, and Strauss has actually defended lying as an ethical tool to be used in one's fight for what's ideologically right. In an Open Democracy interview of Shadia Drury, interviewer Donny Postel notes, that Strauss' "disciples include Paul Wolfowitz and other neo-conservatives who have driven much of the political agenda of the Bush administration." Drury, professor of political theory at the University of Regina in Saskatchewan and author of several books on Strauss, says:

> "The effect of Strauss's teaching is to convince his acolytes that they are the natural ruling elite and the persecuted few. And it does not take much intelligence for them to surmise that they are in a situation of great danger, especially in a world devoted to the modern ideas of equal rights and freedoms. Now more than ever, the wise few must proceed cautiously and with circumspection. So, they come to the conclusion that they have a moral justification to lie in order to avoid persecution. Strauss goes so far as to say that dissembling and deception—in effect, a culture of lies—is the peculiar justice of the wise" (www.opendemocracy.net/debates/article-3-77-1542.jsp).

Given Bush's previous predilections as a political liar in the 2000 campaign and as the governor of Texas, as well as his view of himself as a corporate CEO, the Strauss moral view must have been icing on the cake when he stepped into the presidency.

Of course, Christian Conservatives ask, how can Bush be a liar if he's doing what God wants him to do? As Bush is quoted as saying prior to entering the White House, "I feel like God wants me to run for President....I know it won't be easy on me or my family, but God wants me to do it" (*Observer,* November 2 2003). When Bush moves into the White House and decides to go to war against Iraq, longtime close friend and Secretary of Commerce Don Evans tells *USA Today* that Bush believes he was called by God to lead the nation at this time (April 2, 2003). Are we to believe that God allows Bush to lie for the "greater good?"

The Ultimate Lie

The ultimate lie by the Bush Republican Party and conservative journalists who preach the party line is that all who accuse Bush of being a liar are "Bush haters." According to Ed Gillespie, chairman of the GOP, as quoted by Geoffrey Nunberg in the *New York Times* on December 28, 2003, Democratic attacks on Bush contain "political hate speech," "harsh, bitter personal attacks...unprecedented in the history of presidential politics." It appears that this defense of Bush lying is, in itself, a lie, given that two journalists on the Right, Robert Samuelson (*Washington Post,* December 30, 2003) and Matt Bai (*New York Times,* December 14, 2003) have described the "hate" directed against Bill Clinton as "just as vicious" and lasting much longer.

As for the actual issue of the use of the word "hate" to describe one's concerns over the fact that Bush and his administration have lied to the American people, as Bai and others have done, Stanford linguist Nunberg describes the twisting of language that has gone into that appellation: "The association of 'hate' with unacceptable forms of intolerance and bigotry tends to color the other uses of the word as well; 'political hate speech' conveys the sense of dark and irrational passions that should be ruled out of political discourse...If you said that a lot of Democrats detest Bush...it would be hard to summon up the same sense of alarm about their attacks on him." It's absolultely necessary that in a democracy the leader provides the voters with correct and accurate information and facts needed to reach a decision. Bush isn't doing that. As Gordon Livingston wrote in the *Baltimore Sun* (June 2, 2003), "A complex society, no less than a family, functions on the basis of trust. If we cannot depend on each other to obey the law, we risk chaos and there is no number of police that will save us...As the result of being lied to, we lose trust in those who govern . . ."

Reading the essays in this book, we are obviously at that point with Bush.

Part One
The Bush Corporate Presidency

Can Corporations Become Enlightened?§

BY DAVID LOY

We have given corporations dominion over the sustaining of our lives. They have become sovereign citizens and we have become consumers. They concentrate power and wealth. They design and shape our society and world. They carve our goals and aspirations. They shape our thoughts and our language. They create the images and metaphors of our time, which our children use to define their world and their lives. In other words: what corporations do well, what corporations are designed to be, is the problem. RICHARD GROSSMAN[1]

W HAT IS GLOBALIZATION, and what does it mean for our lives? There is no simple answer to these questions because there is no such "thing" as globalization. Globalization is a complex set of interacting developments: economic, political, technological and cultural. This essay presents a perspective on what is probably the main agent of globalization, on an institution which has more day to day influence on our lives than any other except governments: corporations, especially transnational ones. Despite their enormous and increasing impact upon all of us, we know surprisingly little about them—that is, about what they really are and why they function the way they do. In 1995, only 49 of the world's 100 largest economies were nations; the other 51 were corporations. Malaysia was number 53, bigger than Matsushita (54) but somewhat smaller than IBM (52); Mitsubishi, the largest corporation on the list, was number 22. Total sales of the top 200 transnational corporations were bigger than the combined GDP of 182 countries—of all except the top nine na-

§ Appeared as "Can Corporations Become Enlightened? A Buddhist Critique of Transnational Corporations" in *Butterfly: The Journal of Contemporary Buddhism* © 2001 and as Chapter 4 of David R. Loy, *The Great Awakening: A Buddhist Social Theory* (Boston: Wisdom Publications, © 2003), reprinted with permission.

tions. That is about thirty percent of world GDP. Yet, those corporations employed less than one-third of one percent of the world's population, and that percentage is shrinking.[2] In the United States, the largest 100 corporations buy about 75% of commercial network time and over 50% of public television time as well.[3] This means that they decide what is shown on television and what is not; it has become their "private medium". Corporate mergers and buyouts also mean that the nation's radio stations, newspapers, and publishing houses are owned by a decreasing number of conglomerates increasingly preoccupied with the bottom line of profit margins. In short, corporations control the U.S. "nervous system", and increasingly our international one as well. It is amazing, then, that we hear relatively little about what corporations do—which seems to be the way they like it. Newspapers and television news are full of the speeches and meetings of government leaders, even as globalization of the world economy reduces their power to direct their peoples' destiny. The main point of this paper can be summarized very simply: today, thanks to spreading ideals of democracy, states are increasingly responsible to their citizens, but whom are transnational corporations responsible to?

One of our problems today is that, in our preoccupation with present consumption and future possibilities, we tend to lose the past— that is, our sense of history. If you want to understand something, one of the first places to look is at its history, which can illuminate aspects that we otherwise overlook or misunderstand. What does history teach us about corporations and their responsibilities? Incorporated business enterprises, with legally limited economic liabilities, began in Europe. The earliest record I have found of such a corporation is from Florence, Italy, in 1532. Both the date and place are very interesting. Columbus had "discovered" America in 1492; just as important, Vasco da Gama had sailed around Africa to India in 1498 and returned with cargo worth sixty times the cost of his voyage. A profit of 6000%! You can imagine what affect that had on the dreams of Italian merchants. However, there were some problems. First, it was extremely expensive to outfit such an expedition, so very few people could afford to do so by themselves. Second, such voyages were extremely risky; the chance of a ship sinking in a storm or being taken by pirates was considerable. Third, there were debtor's prisons—not only for you but also for your family and your descendants—if you lost your ship and could not pay your debts. The solution to these problems was ingenious: legally limited liability. Unlike partnerships, where each partner is legally responsible for all business debts, limited liability meant you could lose only the amount you invested. Such an arrangement required a special charter from the state—in Renaissance

Italy, from the local prince. This was convenient not only for the investors but for the prince, because a successful expedition increased the wealth of his territory—and because he got a big cut of the profits for granting the charter.

What is the relevance of all that now? It shows us, first, that from the very beginning corporations have been involved in colonialism and colonial exploitation—a process that continues today under a 'neocolonial' economic system that continues to transfer wealth from the South to the North. Although they have plenty of help from the World Bank and the IMF, corporations continue to be the main institutions that supervise that process.

Second, it shows us that from the very beginning corporations have also had an incestuous relationship with the state. In the sixteenth century nation-states as we know them did not exist. Rulers generally were too limited in resources to exercise the kind of sovereignty that we take for granted today. The state as we know it today—politically self-enclosed and self-aggrandizing—developed along with the royally chartered corporation; you might even say they were Siamese twins inescapably joined together. The enormous wealth extracted from the New World, in particular, enabled states to become more powerful and ambitious, and rulers assisted the process by dispatching armies and navies to 'pacify' foreign lands. As this suggests, there was a third partner, which grew up with the other two: the modern military. Together they formed an 'unholy trinity,' thanks to the new technologies of gunpowder, the compass (for navigation), and this clever new type of business organization which minimized the financial risk.

In short, the modern nation-state and its military grew by feeding on colonial exploitation, in the same way that chartered corporations did.[4] This incest needs to be emphasized because we tend to forget it. We distinguish between government and the economy, but at their upper levels, there is usually little effective distinction between them. Today governments still get their royal share of the booty—now it is called taxes. On the one side, states today need to promote corporate business because they have become pimps dependent upon that source of revenue; on the other side, transnational corporations thrive on the special laws and arrangements with which states promote their activities. As Dan Hamburg, a former Democratic representative from California, concluded from his years in the U.S. Congress: "The real government of our country is economic, dominated by large corporations that charter the state to do their bidding. Fostering a secure environment in which corporations and their investors can flourish is the paramount objective of both [political] parties."[5] The same is true internationally. Almost everywhere, globalization means that the interests of politicians who control nations are increasingly intimately entwined with those who control corporations. In most countries the elite move back and forth quite easily from one to the other, from CEO to cabinet position and back again; naturally they identify with each other's interests. Think, for example, how much U.S. foreign policy today is determined by the desire to open foreign markets (and raw materials, cheap labor, etc.) to U.S. corporate penetration. Occasionally there have been exceptions to this cozy relationship—genuinely populist leaders, for example—but they tend not to last very long.

This brings us back to the question of corporate responsibility. A royal charter listed a corporation's privileges and responsibilities. It has been said that the history of corporations since then is a history of their attempts to increase their privileges and reduce their responsibilities. One important step in reducing that responsibility was the introduction of the joint stock company; the first English one was chartered in 1553. One's shares in a corporation could now be bought and sold freely, even to someone in a foreign country. The stock market has since become an essential feature of every developed economy, of course, and of most developing ones. Consider, however, the effects of this development on responsibility—on the ethical consequences of business activities. Legally, the primary responsibility of a corporation is not to its employees nor to its customers but to its stockholders; after all, they own it. What does it mean, then, when those stockholders are anonymous, scattered here and there, most living far away and with no interest in the corporation's activities except insofar as they affect its profitability?

Compare the situation of a smaller, locally owned business. Suppose you are a master carpenter living in 16th-century Italy. If business is good you might employ several other carpenters and apprentices. You may treat them badly—long hours, low wages—but it will be difficult to escape all the consequences of that. You and your family live above the workshop, or around the corner; your wife sees the wives of your senior workers, may socialize with them; your children probably play with their children, perhaps take lessons from the same teachers. You worship in the same church, participate in the same festivals. My point is that in such a situation economic responsibility is local and not so easily evaded. Everyone in the town knows how you treat your workers, and that affects your reputation—what other people think about you and how they respond to you.

Contrast that with what happened, say, at Bhopal, India in 1984, where it is now believed that up to 10,000 people died and another 50,000 permanently injured in the world's worst chemical disaster, when a Union Carbide plant leaked toxic gases. Although we do not know who they are, it's safe to say that the stockholder owners of Union Carbide were elsewhere, living in various places around the world; and that (although, exceptionally, a few were outraged enough to protest) the large majority felt no responsibility for what happened. The people responsible for managing Union Carbide also live and work far away.

Whatever legal liability a corporation may have—usually only financial—is quite different from having to live with the consequences, and this difference has a great impact upon the way that impersonal institutions like corporations can conduct their business. It is important to understand that the Bhopal problem was not primarily a technological one, as we tend to think (one of the 'inescapable dangers' of modern life), but one of responsibility—of corporate immorality. The gas that escaped is so volatile and dangerous that normally it is not stored but immediately made into a more stable compound. It was stored improperly, without being refrigerated. The emergency release valve was not working.

There had been prior problems and accidents but recommendations resulting from those incidents had not been implemented. There were no plans or exercises for emergency evacuation; no training or information had been provided to the municipality about the gas and how to respond to such an accident... Now consider: if the CEO of Union Carbide had been living next door to that plant, with his family, would those conditions have been permitted to continue?

Moreover, Union Carbide never apologized for the accident, evidently because there were some legal implications at stake. Instead, company executives in India spread rumors that a disgruntled employee had caused the disaster, but no evidence to support this were ever provided. This inability to apologize is precisely my point: it is intrinsic to the nature of large corporations that they cannot be responsible in the way that you and I can be. Dr. Rosalie Bertell, who directed the International Medical Commission to Bhopal in January 1994, was asked how the Bhopal disaster has changed the way multinationals operate abroad. Her reply is sobering: "I don't think it has, and that's scary. I think that most of them think that Union Carbide got away with it, and maybe they could get away with it. I think the effect has been minimal." The accident cost Union Carbide nothing: it settled all claims for $470,000,000.00, which was covered by its insurance.[6]

We begin to understand how "a principle purpose of corporations is to shield the managers and directors who run them, and shareholders who profit, from responsibility for what the corporation actually does."[7] We also begin to understand why we should speak of transnational corporations rather than multinational ones. Early corporations transcended local communities; today the largest, most powerful corporations transcend responsibility even to nation-states and their citizens. In their preoccupation with profitability, they have learned to play off nations and communities against each other in order to obtain the most favorable operating conditions—the biggest tax breaks, the least environmental regulation, and so forth.

This is a significant development: although corporations and nation-states grew up together, in some important respects they have become de-linked. Today corporations are freer than nation-states, which remain bound by their responsibilities to their own borders and peoples. Corporations have no such fixed obligations. They can reinvent themselves completely, in a different location and even in a different business, if it is convenient for them to do so.

So, then, what is a corporation? To become incorporated (from the Latin corpus, corporis 'body') does not mean, of course, that a corporation gains a material body. You cannot point at a corporation, because it has no physical location. In principle, at least, corporations are immortal. You can point to a building that is owned or used by a corporation, yet that building can be sold without affecting the legal status of the corporation. Everything can be replaced—all the people working for it, all the material resources owned by it, the type of activities it engages in, even its name—while it remains essentially the same corporation. That is because a corporation is not a thing but a process.

Like the physical bodies of living things, a corporation is a dissipative system. That is, it must take in energy from the outside (e.g., raw materials), which it processes in various ways (e.g., manufacturing). In order to continue "living" indefinitely its income must equal its expenditures. In addition, like other living things, this process is subject to the law of entropy: although value-added products may be produced (e.g., manufactured goods, or, for humans, a cultural product such as a book or work of art), energy is consumed in the process.

This similarity between corporations and people—both being 'empty' dissipative systems that nonetheless have a life of their own—raises the question whether corporations are subject to the same type of problems. If the primary cause of our problems is greed, ill will and delusion (the three roots of evil, according to Buddhism), is that also the problem with corporations? As our minds now work, we are rarely satisfied with what we have, but always want more. The tendency of corporations to grow and seek ever greater profits implies a similar problem.

The difference is that corporations are legal fictions. Their 'body' is a judicial concept—and that is why they are so dangerous: without a body, they are essentially ungrounded to the earth and its creatures, and to the pleasures and responsibilities that derive from being manifestations of the earth. You may prefer to say that corporations are unable to be spiritual, for they lack a soul; but I think it amounts to the same thing. As the example of Bhopal shows, a corporation is unable to feel sorry for what it has done (it may occasionally apologize, but that is public relations, not sorrow). A corporation cannot laugh or cry; it cannot enjoy the world or suffer with it. Most of all, a corporation cannot love. Love is realizing our interconnectedness with others and living our concern for their well-being. Such love is not an emotion but an engagement with others that includes responsibility for them, a responsibility that if genuine transcends our own selfish interests. If that sense of responsibility is not there, the love is not genuine. Corporations cannot experience such love or live according to it, not only because they are immaterial, but also because of their primary responsibility to the shareholders who own them. A CEO who tries to subordinate his company's profitability to his love for the world will lose his position, for he is not fulfilling that financial responsibility to its shareholders.

Despite the talk we occasionally hear about 'enlightened' corporations, a corporation cannot become enlightened in the spiritual sense. For example, Buddhist enlightenment includes realizing that my sense of being a self apart from the world is a delusion that causes suffering for the world and me. To realize that I am the world—that I am one of the many ways the world manifests—is the cognitive side of the love that such a person feels for the world and all its creatures; that realization and that love are two sides of the same coin. Legal fictions such as corporations cannot experience this any more than computers can.

That sums up the tragedy of economic globalization today: increasingly, the destiny of the earth is in the hands of impersonal institutions which, because of the way they are structured, are motivated not by concern for the well-being of the earth's inhabitants but by desire for their own growth and profit. "We are calling upon [those who wield corporate] power and property, as mankind called upon kings of their day, to be good and kind, wise and sweet, and we are calling in vain. We are asking them not to be what we have made them to be."[8] It is intrinsic to the nature of corporations that they cannot be responsible in the ways that we need them to be; the impersonal way they are owned and organized guarantees that such disappear. One might argue, in reply, that there are good corporations which take good care of their employees, are concerned about their products and their effect on the environment, etc. The same argument can be made for slavery: there were some good slave owners who took good care of their slaves, etc. This does not refute the fact that the institution of slavery is intolerable. The analogy is not too strong. "It is intolerable that the most important issues about human livelihood will be decided solely on the basis of profit for transnational corporations."9 And it is just as intolerable that the earth's limited resources are being allocated primarily based on profit for transnational corporations.

Transnational corporations are by their very nature problematical. We cannot solve the problems they create by addressing the conduct of this or that particular corporation; it's the institution that's the problem. I do not see how, given their present structure, we can repair them to make them more compassionate. Therefore, we need to consider whether it is possible to reform them in some fundamental way or whether we need to replace them with better economic and political institutions: better, because they are responsible not to anonymous investors but to the communities they function in, and better because are motivated not by profit, but by service to the earth and the beings who dwell on it. As long as corporations remain the primary instruments of economic globalization, they endanger the future of our children and the world they will live in.

NOTES

1. Richard Grossman, "Revoking the Corporation," *Journal of Environmental Law and Litigation* v. 2 (1996): p. 143.

2. "Corporate Empires," *Multinational Monitor* v. 17, no. 12 (December 1996). The information is from *Forbes Magazine* and the World Bank's World Development Report for 1996.

3. Jerry Mander, "Corporations as Machines," in Jonathan Greenberg and William Kistler, eds., *Buying America Back*. Council Oak Books (1992), p. 295.

4. The United States was born of a revolt against corporations, which had been used as instruments of abusive power by British kings. The new republic was deeply suspicious of both government and corporate power. Corporations were chartered by the states, not the federal government (the U.S. Constitution does not mention them), so they could be kept under close local scrutiny. The length of corporate charters was limited, and they were automatically dissolved if not renewed, or if corporations engaged in activities outside their charter. By 1800, there were only about 200 corporate charters in the U.S. The next century was a period of great struggle between corporations and civil society. The turning point was the Civil War (1861-65). With huge profits from procurement contracts, corporations were able to take advantage of the disorder and corruption of the times to buy legislatures, judges, and even presidents. Lincoln, is purported to have, complained shortly before his death: "Corporations have been enthroned... An era of corruption in high places will follow and the money power will endeavor to prolong its reign by working on the prejudices of the people... until wealth is aggregated in a few hands... and the republic is destroyed." Rutherford Hayes, who became president in 1876 due to a tainted election and back-room corporate-dominated elections, later declared: "this is a

government of the people, by the people and for the people no longer. It is a government of corporations, by corporations, and for corporations." Corporations gradually gained enough influence to rewrite the laws governing their creation: state charters could not be revoked, corporations could engage in any economic activity, etc. Their biggest success was in 1886, when the Supreme Court ruled (in Santa Clara County vs. Southern Pacific Railroad) that a private corporation is a "natural person" under the U.S. Constitution and thus entitled to all the protection of the Bill of Rights, including free speech. Given the vast financial resources of corporations to defend and exploit these rights, this meant, in effect, that corporations today are more free than any citizen. In sum, during and after the Civil War there was a coup d'etat in the United States—not a military takeover, but an illegal perversion of the institutions of state power. Except for a temporary setback during Roosevelt's New Deal (the 1930's), the United States has been governed by a corporate-state alliance since then.

5. "Inside the Money Chase," *The Nation*, (May 5, 1997): p. 25.

6. Information about the Bhopal disaster is from "The Bhopal Legacy: An Interview with Dr. Rosalie Bertell," *Multinational Monitor* 18, no. 3 (March 1997).

7. Richard Grossman, *Corporations' Accountability and Responsibility*, (unpublished.)

8. Henry Demarest Lloyd, *Wealth against Commonwealth* (New York: 1894), p. 517.

9. Herman E. Daly and John B. Cobb, Jr., *For the Common Good* (Boston: Beacon Press, 2nd ed. 1994), p. 178.

Corporate Lying
Applied to Public Policy:
An Interview with Trevor Rednow

Trevor Rednow is a pseudonym for a senior business executive for a Fortune 500 company. If Bush thinks of himself as a CEO running a giant corporation, how does such a person work, what is the place of lying as part of that person's corporate strategy, and what kinds of outcomes result? Rednow answers those questions. From the inside. JERRY "POLITEX" BARRETT

POLITEX: This interview is the result of months of conversations on the subject of Bush as a corporate liar. Would you provide an overview.
REDNOW: It is a well known fact among participants in large for-profit corporate organizations that corporations engage in lying and manipulation of facts to help enable their market success. This credibility gap between fact and manufactured truth is standard operating procedure in many American corporations. Only recently, due to the "outing" of the most egregious players of this style of corporate behavior have corporations made more than a token effort to clean up their act. The Bush administration, stocked full of this kind of crony corporate executives, exhibits the same sort of behaviors for which some of their former business partners are now under indictment. However, under the mask of US Government policy, the same kind of back-room dealing that is the hallmark of the most egregious type of corporate cronyism has become the operational policy of the Bush Administration.

POLITEX: Should this come as a surprise to those who knew Bush before he became President?
REDNOW: Not at all. Well before Bush was selected by the Supreme Court as the 43rd President, people that knew George Bush and his closest advisors, both in the business world and politically during his term as Governor of Texas, have not been surprised at the manner in which his administration has effectively lied to achieve their ends. In the part of the corporate world from which Bush & Co emerged, the motto that the "ends justify the means" is a tacit belief. As in business, when your market competitors take actions in an attempt to block your quest for market

power, you utilize all means at your disposal to defeat them, including misrepresentations of fact, confusing language to deflect criticism of your actions to cover up what is taking place, and the manipulation of media forms to get messages across to less informed people of why your products or services and your actions in the market are the best thing for people, even if they are not. The Tobacco companies were masters at this approach for decades. In some intellectual circles, this type of corporate behavior is called amoral capitalism. Under the Bush Administration, it has become Public Policy.

POLITEX: Is this kind of corporate government behavior on the presidential level isolated to Bush?
REDNOW: The only President who comes to mind that behaved in a similar fashion is Ulysses S. Grant, whose post Civil War administration was known for its unprecedented cronyism and insider corruption, especially with respect to the awarding of lucrative reconstruction contracts and the influx of carpet-baggers into the south to enrich themselves with the natural resources of the South at the expense of the defeated southerners. George W. Bush and his corporate political cronies are modern day carpet-baggers, pillaging America's future.

POLITEX: What about the world's future?
REDNOW: Bush and Company are solidifying their control of worldwide natural resources, at the expense of Americans safety and the international and political support of our friends and allies around the world. America itself is no longer large enough to satisfy the greed and avarice that has become embodied in our current US policy. The terrorism launched against the United States was unique in that it succeeded by utilizing the same system used by corporations to achieve their ends; namely, the ability to move capital across borders easily and the ability to manipulate foreign markets and infrastructure with a high degree of freedom. It is ironic that the very system which was intended to be used by corporations to grow their access to markets and enable more profits, was used punitively against the premier example of western capitalism. What made 9/11 such a terrifying event to those in power was that one man and a small group of radical cronies with a anti-western terrorist agenda and the attitude that the "ends justify the means" could wreak such havoc on so many people and economic institutions with no significant barriers to stop them. These terrorists simply exploited the fact that globalization had enabled them to fund and carry out their attacks quite easily. America gained a lot of sympathy in the international arena initially, but that good will has now been lost forever because another

man and a small group of radical cronies with their own radical agenda, backed up by the resources of a global superpower, have created unstable domestic and geopolitical conditions that have de-stabilized the global economic and social order with no real idea on what the social, political and economic outcomes will be. The arrogance and ignorance of both groups is what all of us have to fear.

POLITEX: Why don't corporate CEO make good Presidents?
REDNOW: Corporate CEOs of public companies operate primarily from the perspective of maximizing profits for their investors and share-holders. They are not prone to make decisions based on statesman-like principles such as the common good, civil liberties, the will of the people, and other abstract liberal democratic ideals. CEOs are for the most part autocrats who run plutocracies. Their incentives are in the form of various kinds of tax avoiding compensation and are contingent on a perception, sustained over some time period, that the company is doing well, even if it is not really. Some CEOs play the game very well and as a result enrich themselves and the investors and board members to whom they owe the quarterly renewal of their term as CEO. Most CEOs are self-serving individuals who seek power and control in order to ensure their positions of high status in society. They rely on a cadre of executives to assist them in operating a business entity such that it ob-tains at least a paper profit. Autocratic CEOs rely on a close-knit circle of trusted officers who are paid well for their loyalty. Individuals that break from the ranks or don't follow the party line are not treated kindly. This is all well-known and the subject of much recent public discussion given the kind of fiscal chicanery, with direct CEO knowledge and Board of Directors complicity, that has recently been uncovered in some of the largest blue chip corporations in America. Large companies are often unwieldy to manage, and CEOs and their closest advisors are careful to isolate any opposition within the corporation and neutralize them to the effect they can. This kind of control is necessary in order to ensure that autocratic actions can occur without interference. The outcome of all of this is a question for Americans to ask themselves: Is this the character profile of the kind of person that we want as our President?

POLITEX: Could you say more about this phenomena of corporate lying?
REDNOW: Misinformation is also used, both internally with employ-ees and externally with investors and customers, to give the appearance that the corporation is healthy and is being well managed. In the case of internal communication, the messages are usually carefully crafted and

reviewed by public relations professionals to ensure the right overt and covert psychological messages are being delivered. Such messages commonly require absolute loyalty and strict adherence to the companies' mission, and a high degree of secrecy so as not to tip off competitors, who represent the opposition to the leadership of the company and their quest for market dominance and profits. Likewise, external market and investor communication is carefully scripted and packaged so that any inner turmoil, dissent, or failures are hidden from in-depth public scrutiny. Red-herrings are often used to divert focus from real problems onto non-problems that are easily dealt with. This is all standard operating procedure for most medium to large corporations. Whistle blowers are treated harshly when they attempt to expose the misinformation and purposeful campaigns of deceit that are in play. Bush, Cheney and others in the Bush Administration are products of this type of corporate environment and they are well practiced in this style of "governance." The tactics of the Bush Administration in all spheres of public and foreign policy that have offended members of Congress, elements of the press, career government officials, and our allies, are exactly the tactics that some CEOs and their inner circle use to conduct themselves in a "I win, you lose" competitive business environment.

POLITEX: How long do such tactics last?
A: REDNOW: In the corporate world, you can achieve an inflated short-term result by instilling fear in your employees to achieve short-term productivity gains, playing hardball with your partners to force them to conform to your agenda, brow beating weaker competitors through aggressive market behavior and vicious tactics, and using clever language and inflated marketing messages to deceive your customers. These are exactly the tactics used by the Bush Administration as part of both their domestic and foreign policies, mixed with a tincture of radical right-wing ideology driven more by lust for power than by business or political skill. And of course, the means are justified by the ends because the people defining the ends know how it will benefit them first and foremost.

POLITEX: Isn't this type of corporate lying standard operating behavior in the age of mass media and anti-globalism?
REDNOW: Yes. What is so offensive to so many in the arena of public service, both domestic and foreign, is how unabashedly Bush and his administration go about undermining the very foundations and methodology of how things are typically done in the public arena. When you have no negotiation skills, no patience with due process, no respect for differ-

ent points of view, and no trust in others except people who think just like you, all that is left is shrewd manipulation through distortion, misrepresentation, and what is commonly know as "lying." As in the corporate environment, it is deemed "too inefficient" to spend time engaging in political dialogue, reaching compromise through negotiation, and working towards the best possible win-win scenario for all parties involved. It is much easier to bypass all of that when you know what YOU want, and you can manipulate the power structure to achieve your goals. And as with the mediocre CEO, there is little concern for the long-term consequences, because your focus is the short-term gain you can get. You can simply lie about the long-term consequences, because you and your cronies will have exited with the loot well before then and someone else will be left holding the bag. That is the end for which the means are in service. That is what a modern carpet-bagger is all about.

POLITEX: How do you explain the paradox that many Americans believe that George Bush represents their values?
REDNOW: REDNOW: We have a long tradition in this country, and in the countries from which many Americans immigrated, of relinquishing social and political responsibility to people that the majority of us think of as more successful than ourselves, or smarter than the average person, but with whom they can identify under a simplistic notion of trust or have some psychological projection that is satisfied by the image of a person they believe to represent them, when in fact that person does not represent them or their interests. This attitude goes back to the Romans, where political society was divided up into patricians and plebeians. The patricians were the wealthy families of Rome and they elected senators to serve their political, social and business interests. The plebeians included all the free citizens of Rome. A tribune of ten men represented the plebeians. The senators ruled on the affairs of state, but the tribunes protected the civil rights of the plebeians. Tribunes could veto a law if it was deemed onerous towards the plebeians. In America's political system, we have patricians and plebians, but no tribunes. The President is supposed to act as tribune on behalf of the American people, but in fact the President is one of the patricians, and uses his veto to ensure that those patricians that support him are handsomely rewarded. Hence, he uses his veto only to block laws that are meant to favor plebians at the expense of those favored patricians.

POLITEX: And that relates to the present in that...
REDNOW: ...In America today, the political system is primarily composed of people who are effectively selected by corporate patricians. The

plebians are modern day consumers and the role of the patricians is to ensure that the plebians work and consume while the patricians are mostly exempt from the laws that apply to the plebians. There is no tribune to veto such laws on behalf of the plebians. And so the current political system is ripe for a CEO-like President, who knows how to extract the maximum profitability for a small group of patricians at the expense of a large group of plebians, who have no effective veto to such actions. For the most part, plebians are so busy working so they can continue consuming, they have very little attention span or time to really think about what the patricians are up to, which is the perfect situation.

POLITEX: Why isn't the media establishment doing more to highlight the kind of malfeasance that is occurring?
REDNOW: Some print media figures are in fact doing just that, but very few, if any, television personalities have taken that kind of professional risk-after all they work for large corporations and are themselves patricians who are compromised by their need to have the special access to the political circles to maintain their celebrity status (and income) as television personalities. The ones that come to mind in the mainstream print media are Herbert and Krugman at the New York Times. But they have run afoul of the smear campaigns just like corporate whistle blowers, particularly Krugman. They have some autonomy in that they are associated with well-established and powerful media institutions that are sometimes participants in the distortions of fact and, though less common, sometimes illuminate fact from all the fiction. With the expansion of the Murdoch global news empire and the present desires of the Barclay twins, more and more news networks are being taken over by those with a conservative point of view, with newspaper and television outlets throughout the U.S. and other western countries. The only real hope for obtaining a distortion-free view of events is the availability of informed opinion via the Internet, and to a limited extent, elements of the international press. I think history will harshly judge the way the U.S. mass media have distorted facts, misrepresented reality, and manufactured stories to serve a radical political agenda. Unnfortunately, we are going through one of those socially regressive periods dominated by a narrow-minded jingoistic ideology that always leads to misery before it is finally washed away, historically with blood, into the sewers of history.

POLITEX: What will be George Bush's legacy?
REDNOW: George Bush is like the young emperor in the film Galdiator, showing up late and ill-prepared for battle and taking credit for victory. The young emperor then degrades the compassionate gover-

nance legacy of his more noble father, misuses his power to intimidate, abuses the political system, passes onerous laws, and falsely professes to wear the cloak of a great man of the people. The emperor is eventually shamed and dethroned by the former general and enslaved gladiator Maximus, because he represents the real values of the plebians. The mob is never kind to an autocrat in the end. Thomas Jefferson understood this socio-political phenomena, Ulysses S. Grant did not. George Bush's legacy will be similar to that of Grant-one known for cronyism, corruption through misuse of power, and short-sighted malfeasance in the face of what could have been a defining moment for the future of the world. Unfortunately, it will take a long time for America, and the world, to recover from such actions.

Before The Presidency:
The CEO of Deception

BY JERRY "POLITEX" BARRETT

As both the Loy essay and the Rednow interview suggest, the corporate CEO traditionally puts his company's bottom line before the truth, and deception is the order of the day. However, the trick is not to lie in so blatant a fashion that you go beyond the limits of the law or strain the credulity of your listeners. So truth is shaved, facts are distorted, non sequitur responses to questions are lies implying truth. During the 2000 campaign Bush told reporters that he would run his administration the way CEO's ran their corporations. By now, CEO deception is often the order of the day in Corporation U.S.A. As Phillip Bobbitt, a former White House adviser on foreign policy and intelligence wrote in *USA Today* (November 18, 2003): "President Bush is not a simpleton and he is not greedy for his country's wealth. Rather, he sees himself as a CEO, as a businessman, running a competitive firm. The law is merely a set of obstacles to be overcome, to be evaded, to be repealed." To accomplish these aims, Bush, like most other CEO's, practices deception, a skill that he had perfected long before becoming president. Here are just a few examples, in chronological order:

Drugs (Age 18-28?)
During his presidential campaign, one of Bush's themes was that he was going to bring morality and ethics back to the White House, so, like the defense that puts its accused on the stand, that gave reporters permission to ask questions about Bush's private morality and ethics. Back in 1999, a national reporter quizzed Bush on drug use, and vague answers led to more questions, and before long it morphed into this Richard Cohen headline in the *Washington Post*: "Bush is a Fifth-Amendment Cokehead" (August 19, 1999). After the original questions were asked, Bush spinners spent each day trying to get out ahead of the story. Here's what I wrote in summary:

> According to *Washington Post* reporter Dan Balz, "Bush has privately reassured some top supporters that his 'youthful mistakes' did not in-

volve hard drugs and would not disqualify him to be president, according to several sources." If that's really the case, why can't Bush assure the American people? Is it because the only people that really count in Dubya's world are people with big money? Why can't Bush tell the average citizen that "his 'youthful mistakes' did not involve hard drugs?". . . With respect to his drip-feeding of cocaine facts to the American people, few TV talk show reporters have addressed Bush's reason for providing information as he did. Those who have addressed that topic suggest that the Bush temper took over his common sense, and once the original "Not in 7 Years" story was out of the bag, Bush and the spinners spent the next 48 hours revising the story, eventually turning it into "Not in 25 Years."

One scribe suggested that's what can happen at any time when Bush makes a campaign stop without one of his press spokespersons nearby. Another factor was that Bush was being pressed for an answer by the reporters and he grew angry. According to Balz, Bush's original "7 years" response was in answer to a question about what he would do as President, not what he had done in the past, and Bush decided that it was relevant. By the following day, his spinners evolved the answer to cover the last 25 years, but Bush never said that, which is why the *New York Times* headline read that Bush "implied" 25 years. Wednesday and Thursday were filled with many statements, clarifications, and contradictions by Bush and his spinners, indicating how the game of "Obfuscation" is played in Texas. However, the final obfuscation is that Bush finally never really addressed his own question: could he pass the current White House test? Based on what Bush has said thus far, the answer is, no: Further, Bush has never addressed the specific question reporters have been asking for months: Did he ever use cocaine? "Yes" or "no" would suffice (<www.bushwatch.com/bushcoke.htm>).

Two questions remain in the present: Can Bush fill out his present White House job application required of senior government officials in his own administation, and did Bush use hard drugs between, 18 and 28? Neither of these questions have been answered to this day.

AWOL (Age 26]
During the Democrat primaries in January of 2004, Michael Moore called Bush a "deserter" while introducing Dem candidate Wesley Clark, and for over a month the issue of Bush's service to the Guards was renewed in the press. As the pressure for full disclosure increased, Bush released individual documents that did not satisfy the questions report-

ers were asking, leading to Bush's promise to TV journalist Tim Russert to release all of his military records. The White House claimed this was done 5 days later in a Friday evening "document dump" on the evening of February 13, but, as the *Washington Post* noted the following day, the "released papers do not document [Bush's] Alabama service." On the other hand, they did document that Bush had been "suspended from flying status" for "failure to accomplish his annual medical examination," and that his commanding officers at Houston's Ellington Air Force Base were unable to evaluate his performance between May 1, 1972 and April 30, 1973 because "Lt. Bush has not been observed at this unit during the period of report."

One week from the day Bush promised Russert he would release all of his military records, syndicated columnist Bill Press noted in the *Tallahassee Democrat* that "evidence on Bush adds up to AWOL." Press wrote that according to the White House documents:

> Bush was not paid at all between April 1972 till October 1972. Which means even the White House admits he did not report for duty in Alabama, as required, for at least six months. Second, that Bush was paid for nine appearances, a total of 25 days, between October 1972 and April 1973, but they don't say where. Third, that Bush received a dental exam at Dannelly Air National Guard Base in Montgomery on Jan. 6, 1973.

This new dental record doesn't account for the six month AWOL gap in the Bush military White House records, from April 16, 1972 through October 27, 1972. Neither does the dental record prove Bush was paid for service in the Alabama guards on January 6,1973. (Previously released White House documents do not support that he did.) What we do know for a fact is Bush went to Alabama to work in a political campaign which ended in November of 1972 (and those political operatives remember him well), and by January of 1973 he had no reason to be serving in any Alabama guard unit and was supposed to have reported back to his home base in Houston months prior to that date but, according to his commanding officers, did not.

Further, if Bush could go to an Alabama military base and have his teeth examined, why could't he have taken his physical, including a drug test, rather than allowing himself to be disciplined and grounded from flying for not taking the required exam in Alabama in August? We do know that in early 1973 Bush was working full-time for PULL a minority children's program in Houston, having returned to Houston after the November election in Alabama. Josh Benson, writing in the *New Republic* (February 12, 2004), comments:

George W. Bush has a stock response to questions surrounding his service in the Texas Air National Guard in the 1970s: "I did report," he has said. "Otherwise, I wouldn't have been honorably discharged." . . .

A cursory survey shows plenty of examples of servicemen with questionable--and occasionally criminal--histories who have nonetheless collected honorable discharges from the military. . . . John Allen Muhammad, convicted last November for his participation in the D.C. sniper shootings, served in the Louisiana National Guard from 1978-1985, where he faced two summary courts-martial. In 1983, he was charged with striking an officer, stealing a tape measure, and going AWOL. Sentenced to seven days in the brig, he received an honorable discharge in 1985.

DUI (Age 30)

During the 2000 presidential campaign Bush told the *Washington Post* and other reporters traveling with him, "I do not have a perfect record as a youth. When I was young, I did a lot of foolish things." How would you define "young"? Fifteen? Twenty? Twenty-five? How about 30? When Bush was 30, in 1976, he was arrested for drunk driving. Here's how Bush described it to reporters when the event bubbled to the surface in 2000:

> Bush: There's a report out tonight that 24 years ago I was apprehended in Kennebunkport, Maine, for a DUI. That's an accurate story. . . . I was pulled over. I admitted to the policeman that I had been drinking. I paid a fine. . . .
> Reporter: Governor, was there any legal proceeding of any kind? Or did you just —
> Bush: No. I pled—you know, I said I was wrong and I . . .
> Reporter: In court?
> Bush: No, there was no court. I went to the police station. I said, "I'm wrong.". . .
> Bush: No, none at all. None whatsoever. As a matter of fact, I, you know, I tried —I mean, I—listen, I told the guy I had been drinking and what do I need to do? And he said, "Here's the fine." I paid the fine and did my duty.
> Reporter: Is there any action that you or your family took after that night?
> Bush: No, there's not. I mean, none. . . .
> Reporter: Governor, are there any more mistakes of this kind or similar awaiting to be discovered?
> Bush: No.
> (Source: www.dir.salon.com/politics/feature/2000/11/03bush_
> transcript/index.html).

According to Docket #76/7-02342, which was originally posted at CNN, Bush pleaded guilty to the charge and paid a $150 fine. But Bush lied to the reporters three times, if the docket record is to be believed. He implied that he paid the fine at the police station. The docket record says he paid the fine over a month later, on October 15, 1976. He said that there were no legal proceedings of an kind, but the docket says he was scheduled for hearings on September 16, 1976 and October 15, 1976 and was given two continuances along the way, one to September 30, 1976, the other to October 25, 1976. The October 15, 1976 hearing coincides with the date the fine was paid. He said there was no court hearing. The docket record indicates two hearing dates. He said neither he nor his family took any action after that night. Action of some sort had to be taken with respect to the continuances, the hearings, the paying of the fine, and the return of the $500 bond which one supposes must have been provided so Bush would not have to spend time in jail (<www.bushwatch.org/dwi2.htm>).

What Bush withheld from the reporters was that his right to drive in Maine was suspended, and this is a summary of a relevant story that appeared in the *Boston Globe* after the DUI news broke:

> *Boston Globe* reporters Stephen A. Kurkjian and David Armstrong imply that Bush lied another time when he participated in a hearing with Maine officials in a successful attempt to regain his right to drive in Maine, two years after the DUI infraction. [Bush told Maine authorities, that, since he lived in Texas, he was unable to take a driver rehabilitaion course.] Bush's 'comments, made in a 1978 hearing conducted by telephone, clash with the presidential candidate's more recent recountings of his drinking habits at that time in his life.' Another point made in the story continues to baffle us. People who lived in Maine in the '70's indicate that Bush's infraction would not have been taken as seriously then as it would be taken today. Having said that, why was Bush given such a lengthy suspension of his license for a fist-time DUI? [Suspension then was 30 days, Bush's suspension was "indefinite"] (See Maine DMV record at <www.thesmokinggun.com/archive/bush dmv1.html>).

Even today, a first-time DUI only merits a 90-day suspension. Also, in 1976 would a first-time DUI be forced to complete a driver rehabilitation course prior to having his suspension lifted? Nothing in Maine's 1997 laws indicates such a requirement (<www.bushwatch.org/-dwi2.htm>).

In 1999 Bev Conover, publisher and general editor of Online Journal, and Linda Starr, an editor for that Internet political magazine, discovered that in 1995 Governor Bush had his drivers' licence changed to #0000000005 and his previous license destroyed, along with the relevant records. When news of the Bush DWI arrest broke five days before the election, the Online Journal story was taken nationwide:

> Sources told MSNBC.com's Jeannette Walls that Bush associates had been worried for several years about his arrest record and had hoped that because it was in Maine, and not Texas, it wouldn't surface. The sources said Bush took one step to keep it under wraps in March 1995, when his driver's license number was changed. Walls first reported this in August 1999 in The Scoop, an MSNBC.com column. At the time, the sources told Walls that Bush got his license number changed because he was worried about an arrest record surfacing. "He has an arrest record that has to do with drinking," a source said then. "He's worried it will come out, but his handlers keep assuring him it won't" (MSNBC, November 3, 2000).

Harken Energy Stock (Age 44)

After the Enron bubble burst and its officials headed for the hills, Bush came on strong as the man who would clean up this corporate mess. But reporters discovered that the very deceptions that Bush proposed to root out from corporate America's way of doing business were those he appeared to have used when he was, what he calls, an "entrepreneur." This line of questioning naturally led to a revisit of the allegations that Bush was involved in illegal behavior while an official at Harken Energy Corporation.

In answer to the most serious charge, that Bush was involved in insider trading, he replied at a July 8, 2001 news conference, "The SEC fully looked into the matter. They looked at all aspects of it, and they did so in a very thorough way. And the people that looked into it said there is no case." But a *Washington Post* editorial (July 12, 2002) written to defend Bush's Harken behavior describes the SEC decision with a different emphasis: ". . .the Securities and Exchange Commission investigated the case and did not take action, apparently because it could not find firm evidence of wrongdoing." In a letter to Bush's lawyers, "Career SEC Officials" went further: "In the letter, the SEC emphasized that the decision not to charge Bush "must in no way be construed as indicating that (Bush) has been exonerated" (*The Daily Enron*, July 3, 2002).

Clearly, the career SEC officials who authored the letter to Bush's lawyers were in some degree of conflict with the higher officials at the SEC, many of whom had direct political ties to then-President Bush and his administration. For example, the head of the SEC was a Bush appointee.

The facts of Bush's alleged insider trading have been reported:

In June of 1990, Bush sold two-thirds of the Harken stock he had received in the Spectrum 7 deal—and collected $318,430 more than it was worth when he first obtained it. Get low, sell high? Anything wrong with that? The month before this sale, Harken appointed Bush to a committee to determine, as Ivins and Dubose put it, "how restructuring [of the firm] would affect ordinary shareholders." According to Ivins and Dubose, who note the previous reporting work of *U.S. News and World Report*, when Bush served on this committee, he was privy to information indicating the company was in trouble. He then dumped his stocks before this news became public. "U.S. News" concluded that at the time of the sale there was 'substantial evidence to suggest that Bush knew Harken was in dire straits'" (*The Nation,* February 2, 2002).

When President Bush sold more than 200,000 shares in Harken Energy Corp. in June 1990, he said he did not know the company was in bad financial shape. But memos from the company show in great detail that he was apprised of how badly the company's fortunes were failing before he sold his stock—and that he was warned by company lawyers against selling stock based on insider information (Salon, July 12, 2002).

"One week before George W. Bush's now-famous sale of stock in Harken Energy Corp. in 1990, Harken was warned by its lawyers that Bush and other members of the troubled oil company's board faced possible insider trading risks if they unloaded their shares." (*Boston Globe*, October 30, 2002).

The editor of The Truth About George web site writes, "According to SEC reporting requirements, Bush had to file an insider trading form — known as Form 4 — by the 10th day of the month following the sale [of Harken stock.] Although Bush was about eight months delayed in filing this form, it was and still is common for insiders to file this form late" (September 6, 2002). A link on the site is headlined, "Bush Violated Security Laws Four Times, SEC Report Says." The Truth About George editor adds, "It may seem that filing this form is inconsequential, but this is the mechanism that helps alert the SEC to the possibility that a corporate insider has bought or sold stock based on non-public information.

Through this form, the SEC can deter insider trading and prosecute its perpetrators." The effect of delaying sending the form to the SEC, then, if one were an inside trader, would be to attempt to cover one's tracks.

Bush has conflicting answers about the delay in reporting the transaction:

> A decade ago, Mr Bush blamed the SEC, which he said had lost the forms he had filed. When the story resurfaced last week, the White House admitted that this had not been the case. Instead, White House spokesman Ari Fleischer blamed the delay on "a mix-up with the attorneys", but could not shed light on how the confusion arose (*Guardian*, July 30, 2002).

However, in a White House press conference on July 8, 2002, Bush simply gave no helpful answer: "As to why the Form 4 was late, I still haven't figured it out completely."

In the Court (Age 50)

As a resident of Travis County, living in Austin, Texas, I have been called for jury duty on a number of occasions, and have served more than once. A jury form in Travis County, Texas, looks like a folded postcard and, in order to speed things up, the person called is asked to answer a number of quesions in advance of actually reaching the court house at the requested time. Bush filled out the form, but according to CNN, left a number of spaces blank, including spaces for answers about his criminal record. When you get to the court house a clerk collects the questionnaires and gives them to the lawyers to look through as a preliminary way of weeding out applicants with criminal records, among other things. Since Bush had previously pleaded guilty to a Class D misdemeanor in Maine, some might conclude that his unwillingness to fill out the relevant spaces on the questionnaire indicated he didn't desire to have that part of his background made public.

> Mr. Bush was called for jury service in a 1996 drunken-driving case in Austin but was dismissed from the panel before the potential jury members were questioned about their histories of drinking and driving. P. David Wahlberg, the defense attorney who struck Mr. Bush from the 1996 jury panel, said Thursday that he did so after the governor and the governor's lawyer asked the judge to excuse Mr. Bush. Mr. Bush had initially said he would perform jury service, Mr. Wahlberg said. But, he said, on the eve of trial, the governor's lawyer, Al Gonzales—later appointed by Mr. Bush to the Texas Supreme Court

[and now is the White House lawyer, with a good shot at the Supreme Court]—asserted that it would be improper for a governor to sit on a criminal case in which he could later be asked to grant clemency (*Dallas Morning News*, November 3, 2000).

After the jury dismissal, Texas reporters asked Bush if he ever had been arrested for drunk driving. Bush replied: "I do not have a perfect record as a youth. When I was young, I did a lot of foolish things" (*Washington Post*, November 3, 2000).11/3/00) [Note: As noted above, the DUI arrest happened when Bush was 30 years old.]

The deception is pretty obvious, but Bush didn't stop there, he didn't leave well enough alone. "Bush told Wayne Slater of the *Dallas Morning News*, 'I'm glad to serve.' Bush added, 'I think it's important. It's one of the duties of citizenship.' He also told KVUE-TV in Austin, 'I'm just an average guy showing up for jury duty.' And in video footage shown by KVUE in 1996, Bush had some additional comments on his feelings regarding the case. The KVUE reporter asked Bush if he didn't 'really just want to give the guy a pardon and go home?' Bush, who has presided over a staggering 145 executions as governor, answered, 'No, I probably want to hang him and go home.' Travis County's lead prosecutor on the case was quoted as saying that Bush "directly deceived" him to avoid jury duty. (<www.dir.salon.com/politics/feature/2000/11/05/jury_duty/index.html>).

Fallout (Age 51)

In 1998, *Dallas Morning News* reporter Wayne Slater specifically asked Bush about his arrest record after information surfaced that he was arrested for disorderly conduct in 1966 when, as a student at Yale, he was busted for snatching a Christmas wreath in New Haven, Conn. Asked whether he had been arrested on anything 'after 1968,' Slater wrote, the governor replied, 'No.' Slater recalled that Bush seemed ready to change his response when Karen Hughes, his spokeswoman, stopped the conversation. After a Maine TV reporter broke the DUI story Thursday, Bush initially questioned the story's timing before Hughes stepped in to tell reporters that Dubya had been totally open about his past and hadn't spoken of this bust because he wasn't asked (Carlos Guerra, *San Antonio Express-News*, November 5, 2000).

Slater emphasized the context of the conversation, however, and his gut feeling now that Bush was on the brink of disclosing the 1976 drunken-driving arrest to him. "When he said the word 'no,' clearly he wasn't telling the truth," Slater said. But, Slater said, he then asked

Bush if "had he ever been arrested before 1968, and he said, 'Well …,' and I felt he may have been ready to correct what he had just said, but [Bush spokeswoman] Karen Hughes stepped in and stopped the interview (Jake Tapper, Salon, November 3, 2000).

Two years later on Bush's campaign plane, Slater is telling other reporters about the Hughes interruption and Hughes appears:

'That conversation was off the record, wasn't it, Wayne?' she said.

"Slater said it wasn't. The mood grew even tenser. The crowd increased in size."

"So Hughes tried again, explaining why she had cut off the 1998 conversation, which had left Slater with the impression that Bush was on the brink of correcting his lie before Hughes abruptly ended the conversation."

Bush 'was hinting that something had happened, that's why I stepped in and stopped the conversation," she said....

"Hughes was asked again about Bush's 'No.'"

"'The governor disagrees with that,' she said. 'The governor does not believe he said that. He has not addressed that issue'" ("Busted!" Salon, November 3, 2000)

In the Governor's Office, Part I (Age 51)

At the 2000 Democratic Convention Al Gore honored the memories of two 1998 hate crime victims, Matthew Shepherd, the gay man from Wyoming, Mr. Cheney's "home" state, who was beaten to death while tied to a fence, and James Byrd, Jr., the black man from Texas who was dragged to death from a chain behind a pick-up truck. Dennis and Judy Shepherd, Matthew Shepherd's parents, and Renee Byrd Mullins, James Byrd, Jr.'s daughter, were members of a panel devoted to crime and victim's rights, an issue that Gore promised to focus on if he became president.

Shepherd and Byrd have been linked together as victims of hate crimes ever since their killings. In April of this year, Shepherd and Byrd survivors met at the Millenium March on Washington for Equality, a civil-rights demonstration. But one year earlier, Renee Byrd Mullins observed first-hand that the well-publicized talk of Governor George W. Bush's "compassionate conservatism" is a sham, a political play on words that has little meaning in the real world of Bush politics.

At the time of her ten-minute meeting with Bush in the solemnity of the Governor's Office in the Texas State Capitol, Mullins had come to Austin to lobby for a hate crimes bill that had been proposed by a Democratic legislator. Although the bill had passed the Democratic House,

Mullins had the opportunity to visit with Bush prior to a vote in the Republican Senate. Texas had a vague, toothless hate crimes law passed by a previous Democratic legislature and signed into law by Bush's Democratic predecessor, and Bush was determined that if he couldn't eliminate it, at least he could prevent if from being strengthened. First, the Governor let it be known in the Senate that he did not want the bill to reach his desk. (Republican senators who had previously voted for hate crimes legislation were told that the Governor wanted a "no" vote.) Then Bush did what he often does in such instances, he told the press that since the matter is being considered by the legislature, in order to be fair he would not comment upon it until it reached his desk. Given Bush's willingness to get behind bills that benefit his corporate friends, it's clear that his "fairness" is as selective as his "compassion."

Bush wanted to kill the proposed hate crimes bill, which was more specific about penalities as well as groups covered, such as homosexuals. First, he thought of the bill as affirmative action legislation, and he was on record as being against affirmative action bills. Secondly, for the first time a proposed bill of its kind specifically included gays, and his Christian Coalition backers were against that. Looking ahead to his run for president, it made good political sense to Bush not to rile his limited number of African-American backers by reminding them of his position on affirmative action. Later, after the bill was killed by the Senate, it became convenient to have his spokesmen in the Lege report that the bill would have passed if not for the inclusion of homosexuals in its language. This was a calculated, convenient excuse. Remember, though, when Byrd's daughter visited Bush, the Senate had not had its way with the hate crimes bill passed by the Dem House, and Bush was anxious to get it killed.

A pregnant Renee Byrd Mullins was able to get a short meeting with Bush through the help of Texas Rep. Senfronia Thompson (D-Houston), who accompanied her to the meeting. Later, the specifics of the meeting were reported by Mullins to *Newsday* columnist Marie Cocco, whose story of the meeting was published in the *Austin American-Statesman* on February 14, 2000: "It didn't feel [like] a good greeting I had a very short handshake. In essence, he was saying, 'OK, tell me what you want and get out.'... He's a very hard person. He had a wall built up before I even got in there."

Byrd's sister Harris was further offended that Bush acted as if he had much to do with the swift, Texas-style prosecution the killers went through. "To me it was a show for the people," she says, "but the people who live in Texas know the kind of governor he is and the type of liar he is. . . ."

The chasm between the Byrd family and the governor began right after Byrd's murder, when Bush said he wouldn't attend Byrd's funeral because he thought the atmosphere would be too "politically charged"— even though Senator Hutchison, Transportation Secretary Rodney Slater and other officials had no problem attending. Bush spokeswoman Karen Hughes said that Bush's no-show at the funeral was at the Byrd family's request, but no one in the Byrd family knew about such a request.

"Nobody told him to stay away," says Mullins.

The family also disputed Bush's claim that he called the Byrds to offer his condolences, saying that not one of them could recall ever speaking to him. Although Bush cannot recall whom he supposedly spoke with, a Bush spokesman produced phone records showing a two-minute phone call from the governor's mansion to a home in Jasper.

"He says that, but I don't know who he talked to," says Stella Byrd.
"He didn't talk to me" (Salon October 16, 2000).

In the Governor's Office, Part II (Age 52)

Glen Maxey is a retired gay politician who served in the Texas House of Representatives for 12 years and was well-respected on both sides of the aisle as a man of political courage. A Democrat, he is best known to many as the man who fought long and hard for affordable health insurance for children under CHIP, a national health plan. At that time, Governor Bush was on the presidential campaign trail, but the *Austin Chronicle* reported his Texas legislative activity: "After he had kicked off the session by pushing through a $45-million tax break for oil well owners and trying to bust a children's health program, the governor had disappeared into his presidential campaign."

In December of 2001 Maxey told the *Austin American Statesman* that Bush, who opposed gay adoptions and gay marriage as governor, went over to him on the floor of the Texas House: He "put his hands on my shoulders and he pulled me in where almost our noses were touching, It's almost an uncomfortable level where he gets really close and personal, nose to nose. And he says to me, 'I value you as a person and I value you as a human being, and I want you to know, Glen, that what I say publicly about gay people doesn't pertain to you,'" Bush has yet to deny Maxey's report, but Bush spinner Scott McClellan claims it never happened: "He congratulated him on passing the Children's Insurance bill. That was the extent of the conversation." I'm inclined to believe Maxey's version of the story, not McCellan's denial on Bush's behalf, because Maxey has created a record of credibility, and Bush has not. Further, Bush's double-speak is typical of the man, as observers, both right and left, have pointed out. Bush's comment to Maxey would be just one more instance of the longtime gap between what Bush says and what he does.

On the Campaign Trail (Age 53)

Apart from the previously reported events that took place earlier in Bush's life but were commented upon during the campaign, I find these two events, which took place on the same day during the campaign, both relevant and amusing:

> Reuters, Monday October 30, 2000: Former President George Bush sought to solidify support for his son in Republican-leaning Louisiana on Monday by promising that a vote for George W. Bush was a vote for dignity in the White House. . . .The former president spoke to about a thousand supporters in this affluent and largely white New Orleans suburb.

> AP, Monday October 30, 2000: Appearing on the Jay Leno show this evening, George W. Bush told Leno . . . that surrogates are irrelevant. "Bush said . . . he didn't think Clinton would necessarily help Gore by campaigning because he said people will make up their own minds."

The Bush deceptions during the 2000 campaign are too numerous for this humble essay. Perhaps a cottage industry will evolve covering Bush prior to his selection as President as The CEO of Deception.

Part Two
The Bush Lie Machine

"Ranch Dressing":
The Conscious Construction of George W. Bush's Image

BY LISA KADONAGA

Introduction

"You know I could run for governor but I'm basically a media creation. I've never done anything. I've worked for my dad. I worked in the oil business. But that's not the kind of profile you have to have to get elected to public office."
George W. Bush, 1989 [1]

Around the world, the most persistent image of George Walker Bush, 43rd President of the United States, is of a cowboy. News photographs may show him in a business suit, but in the editorial pages he is frequently depicted in Western gear. [2] This is done by both his supporters and his detractors, at home and abroad. The White House must surely be pleased by this, given that Bush is no cattleman, and there are more photos of him on a Segway than on horseback. Bush-as-cowboy is a marketing triumph, and living proof of the power of image-making.

Arguably, many of the techniques Bush's team have adopted to create his public persona are common in politics today. In Bush's case, what stands out is the amount of effort that's been devoted—and the extent to which this has been accepted uncritically by the mainstream media.

Why Texas?

"Actually, I—this may sound a little West Texas to you, but I like it. When I'm talking about—when I'm talking about myself, and when he's talking about myself, all of us are talking about me." George W. Bush, May 31, 2000 [3]

Bush's first foray into politics was a 1978 Congressional race in Midland, which he lost to Democrat Kent Hance. Bush was derided as an eastern preppy—after one of his campaign ads featured him jogging, Hance wondered if Bush was "trying to get away from someone." [4] Bush learned from this, and since then has identified himself as a Texan—in particular, coming from West Texas. With his background and family associations, he could have formed ties with a number of different regions—but the selection of a large, economically-powerful state with a rich cultural history was undoubtedly a strategic choice, for personal and public reasons.

Perhaps in an attempt to maintain his Texas image in voters' minds, Bush tends to avoid stating personal connections to other states. He downplays the fact he was born in Connecticut—unlike previous presidents, even after taking office his birthplace was not listed in "Who's Who in America."

A brochure produced for Bush's 1978 Congressional run read "Born July 6, 1946 and raised in Midland, Texas."[5] Bush's opponent in the Republican primary "accused Bush of omitting the fact that he was born in New Haven"—Bush's team claimed this was unintentional.[6]

While other politicians eagerly capitalize on personal connections to as many areas as possible, no matter how tenuous—Bush has gone out of his way to distance himself geographically and culturally from the east and west coasts. On many occasions, he's sneered at California or New England stereotypes ("brie and cheese," or "swilling white wine"). His liking, in his pre-teetotaller days, for B&B's—a cocktail invented by a fancy New York nightclub—is rarely mentioned.[7]

Bush gives the impression that he disdains, even fears, being seen as something other than Texan—he seems reluctant to embrace any other part of the country, as if it would negate his identity. This is at odds with his own claim of being "a uniter, not a divider"—and now that he is the American head of state, it conflicts with his obligation to lead the entire nation.

Sometimes he ends up portraying a caricature of a Texan: a TV cowboy in monogrammed boots that have never seen mud or stirrups. He has been known to serve "calf fries" (deep-fried bull testicles) at the Governor's mansion in Austin— and his use of over-the-top pseudo-Western expressions like "smoke 'em out" and "wanted dead or alive" seems calculated to make an impression. Actor Timothy Bottoms, studying Bush's accent, commented that "George is a chameleon. He'll go to Texas and it'll be quite thick, then he'll go to Washington and it drops off."[8] Bush—who accused the previous administration of constantly remaking itself in response to polls and focus groups—is as sensitive to surface appearances as Bill Clinton ever was.

Lights, Camera, Action . . .

"I do not reinvent myself at every turn. I am not running in borrowed clothes."
George W. Bush, August 3, 2000 [9]

Politicians and their aides always have been concerned about image. Since the days of Ronald Reagan, a former Hollywood actor, this has become even more pronounced in American political life. Aspiring politicians often receive professional coaching on how to dress, how to "act naturally" in front of cameras and live audiences, and how to read a speech convincingly off a Teleprompter. But the Bush presidency has taken this to a new level: "Officials of past Democratic and Republican administrations marvel at how the White House does not seem to miss an opportunity to showcase Mr. Bush in dramatic and perfectly lighted settings. It is all by design: the White House has stocked its communications operation with people from network television who have expertise in lighting, camera angles and the importance of backdrops."[10]

Costumes

People entering public office—or the professions—have to adapt to expectations about how they should dress. It's also accepted that politicians and celebrities will have to wear special clothing for particular functions: furthermore, it's customary for unions, civic organizations, government agencies, or branches of the military to present dignitaries with special monogrammed clothing—and for the visitors to be photographed in their new gear. However, Bob Somerby points out that analysts such as Howard Fineman praised Bush for his strategic selection of different outfits for campaign stops, after condemning Al Gore as indecisive and duplicitous for doing the same thing.[11]

Bush's clothing had already undergone considerable changes, as he became more involved in politics.[12] When his wardrobe was upgraded for the presidential campaign, various reporters noted that his clothes were nicer than in previous years, although *Business Week* scoffed that he seemed to have been hastily dressed in them.[13]

Since the election, Bush's wardrobe has become even more upscale—this may be why the White House takes pains to show him in running shorts or work clothes at other times.[14] His aides are indignant when a live news feed accidentally shows him having his hair groomed prior to a TV broadcast—but they encourage the presence of photographers when he is dirty and sweaty from cutting cedar at his ranch.[15] Judy Keen notes that "Bush's ranch time signals voters who don't own tuxedos and didn't go to Ivy League schools that he has something in common with them," and for this reason, Keen adds "grubby jeans, a battered cowboy hat and scuffed boots" are an essential part of his costume while in Crawford.[16] Louis Dubose observes that Bush adopted a Stetson with a "cattleman's crease" in a sort of "LBJ makeover."[17] At the ranch, his apparently-casual choice of a white cowboy hat, and a Crawford Volunteer Fire Department T-shirt, have great symbolic value.[18]

In 2003, another outfit was added to Bush's clothing selection—the flight suit he wore for a visit to the USS Abraham Lincoln. Some observers suggested that it looked "custom made;"[19] a Vietnam veteran pointed out that "his uniform is more tailored and stylized than the pilot next to him."[20] In a bizarre way, Bush's costumes are reminiscent of the Village People, the 1970s pop group whose members dressed as "All-American male myths"[21]—the cowboy, the soldier, the construction worker. At the other extreme, Bush has appeared in Yale doctoral regalia, acquired with his honorary degree at the 2001 commencement—despite protests by faculty and students that Bush had not, as yet, done enough work to warrant such an award.[22]

Sets

One particular trademark of the current White House is its emphasis on professional set design for presidential appearances. The Communications Office has created a vast number of specially-themed backdrops for Bush to stand in front of when he speaks. Often the letters are too small for the invited audience to read, but perfectly positioned for TV.[23] In order to ensure the backdrops are up to presidential expectations, the White House even designs them for institutions such as universities and government agencies, which presumably have the capability to do it for themselves.[24]

The fancier backdrops have sometimes resulted in complications. The backdrop for Bush's January 2003 speech at a St. Louis trucking company featured graphics of boxes stamped "Made in U.S.A."[25] Real boxes were to be stacked around the president's lectern, but the ones available at the company were marked "Made in China" or "Made in Taiwan." The telltale overseas labels were covered up by volunteers working for the White House.[26]

People are also used as part of the display. Carefully-selected minority groups appeared onstage at the GOP 2000 convention,[27] and Laura Bush was strategically placed with a group of female supporters across the street, while her husband was appearing on Oprah's talk show.[28]

Sometimes the audiences are appropriately dressed to convey a message, even if it means donning clothes they wouldn't normally wear. In preparation for a GOP tax cut rally in 2001, a memo circulated by the National Association of Manufacturers requested: "the Speaker's office was very clear in saying that they do not need people in suits"—adding, "If people want to participate—AND WE DO NEED BODIES—they must be DRESSED DOWN, appear to be REAL WORKER types, etc. We plan to have hard hats for people to wear."[29]

At a 2003 event in Indianapolis, "White House staff members instructed men on stage with the president to remove their ties,"[30] in order to make them appear more like "ordinary" Americans. A state

Republican legislator was seen "with a tie before the speech, tieless as he shook hands with Bush, then wearing a tie again in an interview afterward."[31]

James Zogby commented on Bush's "carefully crafted" address to "what the media described as a supportive Arab-American audience."[32] This time the president's backdrop included Arabic writing. Zogby adds: "Behind the president was seated a small group of about 40 Iraqi Americans, some Shiites and some Chaldean."[33] The group Bush was facing was unseen, "but the impression was created that it was an enthusiastic crowd representative of Michigan's 400,000 plus Arab Americans"—although "the room was only one-third full," with about 300 people. Zogby observes that the group "was carefully screened to include Republicans and supporters of the president,"[34] although this was not reported in media coverage. This type of audience screening isn't unusual—at another speech in California, while "hundreds of demonstrators" marched outside, Bush spoke to "a friendly audience of military personnel, United Defense staff and Republicans hand-picked by the California GOP."[35]

The setting which sees the most use, aside from the White House and Camp David, is "Prairie Chapel," the Bush ranch in Central Texas. In 1999, shortly before the 2000 presidential campaign, Bush purchased the Engelbrecht property near the small town of Crawford.[36] At 1,600 acres, it's smaller than a classic big Texas ranch—actually it used to be a hog farm. The administration refers to it as the "Western White House," and has put this on official signage in the press briefing room—even though large portions of the state, and the country, are further west.

The actual work of managing the property is done by foreman Kenneth Engelbrecht, the son of the previous owners—nevertheless, the ownership of "Prairie Chapel" is a key part of Bush's public persona. Bush has "downplayed his privileged upbringing and Ivy League education—and embraced the persona of a rough-hewn, back-slapping, nickname-conferring rancher."[37] To portray a rancher, obviously a ranch is essential equipment.

Bush has shown off "Prairie Chapel" in lengthy interviews with reporters, which contrast with his abrupt, even hostile manner in traditional press conferences. "Ranger George knows every inch of his acreage"[38]—he points out different species of trees, after being advised on the subject —his nickname for himself is "Tree Man."[39] "To Bush, 'liberating' his oaks from cedar is an act of environmental protection. The non-native cedar robs native oaks of water and light, he says."[40] The "cedars" he refers to, actually a species of juniper, are native to the area.[41]

Bush's cedar-clearing assumes the proportions of an elaborately staged ritual. It would be more efficient to do it by mechanical means (or even through the use of other techniques used in restoration ecology, such as controlled burns or grazing by livestock)—but his insistence that White House staff pitch in makes it "part workout, part macho competition."[42] An observer describes the proceedings: "Out here, Secret Service agents trained to take the bullet for the president ensure falling trees do not strike him. Some watch the perimeter around Bush, while those closest to him guide cedar away from his head."[43] A doctor and nurse are "close by" in case of accidents.[44]

It's interesting that, rather than returning to his childhood home in arid Midland, where Bush has allegedly stated he would like to be buried,[45] he has settled in a different part of the state, and is in effect re-creating the pastoral landscape of the Eastern parklands, where he lived for much of his adolescence. His favorite place on the property is a waterfall—he had an artificial lake installed, and spends a great deal of time clearing the cedar scrub, which he says will improve the view.[46] In 2001, the Bushs' moved into a newly-built home. Designed for them by architect David Heymann, it incorporates features such as a greaywater-recycling system, and a geothermal heat pump (the same type Al Gore had installed in the Vice President's official residence)—a perfect way to present Bush as environmentally-friendly, with considerable savings on energy bills.

Another possible reason for choosing Crawford over West Texas, and cultivating the image of the folksy gentleman rancher, is that Bush is trying to affiliate himself both with blue-collar rural Texans, and with their wealthier counterparts in Houston or Dallas who have purchased vacation homes in the central part of the state. Bush has lived most of his life in cities—Midland, Houston, the university towns of the eastern seaboard, and the Texas state capital in Austin. By choosing a property nearer to Crawford than Waco, he is hoping to lay claim to small-town America, and the "heartland" values which he and his image-makers associate with it.

Props

"Prairie Chapel" abounds with convenient items for photo-ops: for example, the white, four-door truck that Bush is seen driving around, was provided by members of the state's propane industry.[47] Bush also uses the ranch's Gator 4x4s, and the "bass buggy" that was a gift from his uncle. He has had less luck with vehicles elsewhere—while clutching a tennis racket, he was photographed falling off a Segway scooter in 2003.

The ultimate visual aid and "political prop" would be Air Force One, the president's official aircraft. Jennifer Loven observed that "Air Force One was used for dozens of landings in Bush's successful bid to strengthen Republicans' grip on congress."[48] In particular, "Events were staged so Bush would be photographed speaking—candidate at his side—with the jet filling the background."[49]

Much smaller objects can also have an impact—for example, the badge of Port Authority policeman George Howard, which Bush held up during his speech to the nation after the attacks, was given to him by Arlene Howard, the officer's mother. It had not been Mrs. Howard's idea to do this: "But when Port Authority officials asked if she'd give George's shield to George W. Bush, she couldn't refuse."[50] The gesture was well-received by the media, and by the public—although longtime columnist Jimmy Breslin could not help wondering if it had been inspired by Bush's father's highly-political use of a slain policeman's badge, during the 1988 election campaign.[51]

Script

Bush relies on a group of talented speechwriters, who at times seem to have conflicting ideas about how their man should present himself. He seems to like the poetic language of Michael Gerson, even though it doesn't really fit his established persona—many of the speeches are well-written, but vacillate between markedly different styles. What often results is "a mix of high oratory with an extremely simple vocabulary and moral themes that usually offer stark black and white choices."[52] They sound fine, yet conceal "a complete vacuum of real policy." At certain times, the speeches are "heavily edited" by Karen Hughes, to make them sound more attractive to female voters[53]—for example, by using family references such as "moms and dads" instead of more specific but less cuddly descriptors like "employees" or "taxpayers."

Cinematography

In the early days of George W. Bush's presidency, a Texas reporter noted that Bush was "scripted and coached as Ronald Reagan ever was."[54] He described an evening press conference at Governor's mansion in Austin, where Bush walked along "a path marked on the hardwood floor with masking tape and ending with a masking tape arrow that pointed to the podium before him."[55] Arrangements are considerably more sophisticated now. When Bush spoke at Mt. Rushmore in 2003, he and the camera platform were positioned so that on TV, he appeared "in profile, his face perfectly aligned with the four presidents carved in stone."[56]

These are minor things—a professionally-produced backdrop, or a quiet word to the cameraman—with a relatively small number of people involved. They didn't need a team of professionals to ensure that, when Bush sat down to announce the start of the Iraq War, the presidential flag behind him "was folded in such a way that the quiver of arrows could be seen in the eagle's clenched talon."[57] However, there are times when they do rely on just such a team. We saw glimpses of this during the 2000 election recount period, what appeared to be spontaneous local pro-GOP demonstrations were actually organized by "out-of-state paid political operatives" —arriving "from New York, Ohio and Washington D.C., many flew to Florida on expense-paid trips."[58] Some of these lobbyists were vocal participants.[59]

Bush's confidence has increased, along with the sophistication of the events. At one August 2001 trail-building photo-op in Colorado, he wore what appeared to be brand-new work clothes, and was inadvertently photographed holding a shovel with the price sticker still attached. A 10-year-old witness said: "He smelled kind of funny. Like fresh carpet."[60] Two years later, at a similar appearance, Bush felt secure enough to make a sardonic comment on "the notion that the day was staged."[61] "'This is an unstaged walk in the park,' Bush laughingly called out to reporters"— and "the group rounded a turn to see a group of volunteers shovelling dirt onto the trail under pre-positioned camera lights."[62]

The White House staff, particularly Karl Rove, have become adept at crafting apparently spur-of-the-moment events. One of the most-publicized photos taken in the painful aftermath of the WTC attacks showed Bush, bullhorn in hand, addressing a crowd of rescue workers, from atop a crushed fire engine in the rubble—Bush's climb onto the impromptu platform appeared spontaneous. It may not have been. Retired firefighter Bob Beckwith was already standing on the fire engine:

> Suddenly, a cleanly-dressed man appeared before Beckwith, whose boots, blue jeans and sweatshirt were ashen, and he asked the veteran firefighter to jump up and down on the pumper to test its safety. He was Senior Advisor to the President Karl Rove, who told him to stay there to help 'someone' up onto it but to get down afterward.[63]

The fact that Beckwith was "waiting and waiting" until Bush appeared suggests that someone had planned this action in advance.

For the highly-publicized landing on the aircraft carrier USS Abraham Lincoln, a communications staffer "embedded himself on the carrier to make preparations days before."[64] This event was an important one for the White House, since images of Bush landing on the carrier in a S-3B Viking jet allow the White House to "symbolically reconstruct a combat history that never happened"—an impression heightened by Bush's name stencilled on the plane.[65] Bush, who has not flown a military jet since the early 1970s reportedly did try out the controls, but only for part of the quarter-hour flight.[66] In their choice of words, some media accounts wrongly implied that Bush himself had landed the plane on the flight deck.

The White House had claimed that Bush chose the jet "solely to avoid inconveniencing the sailors."[67] But the USS Abraham Lincoln made faster time than expected, and "instead of the carrier being hundreds of miles offshore," it was "just 39 miles from the coast."[68] The White House then claimed that Bush decided to fly out on the Navy S-3B jet for a tail-hook landing anyway "to see it as realistically as possible," even though the carrier was well within helicopter range, and had to be slowed "when land became visible."[69] Lindlaw adds: "There was no denying the ship's movements were carefully choreographed to benefit Bush. Commanders gauged the wind and glided along at precisely that speed so that sea breezes would not blow across the ship during Bush's speech," creating "unwanted noise."[70] The carrier also was turned, in order to provide "the vast sea as his background instead of the very visible San Diego coastline," and "steamed in lazy circles during much of his visit."[71] Bush spent the night aboard, departing by helicopter before the carrier arrived in port the next day.[72]

Other aspects of the event were just as well-organized: the White House claimed that it was not a victory speech,[73] though in that setting it was difficult to avoid coming to the conclusion that the event was meant to apply not just to the homecoming of that particular carrier, but to the wider context. Bush said "Major combat operations in Iraq have ended," and "The battle of Iraq is one victory in a war on terror."[74]

Elisabeth Bumiller pointed out that the White House staff "had choreographed every aspect of the event, even down to the members of the Lincoln crew arrayed in coordinated shirt colors over Mr. Bush's right shoulder and the 'Mission Assomplished' banner placed to perfectly capture the president and the celebratory two words in a single shot. The speech was specifically timed for what image makers call 'magic hour light,' which cast a golden glow on Mr. Bush."[75] She quoted Joshua King, a former Clinton administration staffer: "If you looked at the TV picture, you saw there was flattering light on his left cheek and slight shadowing on his right. It looked great."

Months later, as American soldiers continued to die in Iraq, Bush distanced himself from the White House-produced "Mission Accomplished" banner under which he had given his speech. He passed the responsibility on to his staff, who attributed the idea to the carrier's crew. [76]

Knowing about these situations, the detailed planning behind other White House events isn't too surprising. Bush's overseas visits are preceded by a special team that arranges lighting and staging—for a speech in Romania, equipment was rented in Britain, and trucked all the way to Bucharest.[77]

Preparation also extends to Iraq War briefings—for example, the construction of a customized $200,000 set in Qatar, by the same designer who makes the backdrops which routinely appear behind George W. Bush at speeches.[78] Costuming is also used: "The background maps of the world are in pretty shades of soft blue, the better to complement the khaki uniforms [....] lighter than the usual attire of these soldiers and officers."[79] The media manipulation extends beyond the command center. There are continuing questions about the Pentagon's version of the rescue of Private Jessica Lynch—the BBC called it "one of the most stunning pieces of news management ever conceived."[80]

The Uses of Propaganda

"I asked them the other day, would it be okay if I cut a 30-minute tape, a piece of propaganda, no questions, just here—here it is, here's 30 minutes of me talking. Please run it, not only across your airwaves but run it internationally, if you don't mind." George W. Bush, November 13, 2001[81]

Shortly after the terrorist attacks, the White House set up meetings to encourage "ways that Hollywood stars and films might work in concert, in ways both formal and informal, with the administration's communications strategy."[82] One of the fruits of this was "Time of Crisis: DC 9/11" (formerly titled "The Big Dance"). Lionel Chetwynd, the writer-producer, is "among the few outspokenly conservative producers in Hollywood, and one of the few with close ties to the White House," who was appointed by Bush to the President's Committee on the Arts and the Humanities late in 2001.[83] "Time of Crisis" contains a mixture of actual news footage and re-enacted scenes.

Chetwynd calls it "a straightforward docudrama"[84]—unfortunately, in practice, it combines the worst features of documentaries and drama. Many of the re-creations are drawn-out cabinet meetings without much action, while the fictionalized scenes frequently have awkward dialogue that may leave viewers hoping things didn't unfold that way. Paradoxically, its political agenda actually got in the way of it being an effective propaganda film. "Time of Crisis" is seriously weakened by the filmmakers trying to do too much at once, rather than focusing on the strongest elements of propaganda: emotion-based storytelling, and compelling imagery. Ultimately, the best propaganda is a version of reality so attractive that the audience WANTS to believe.

In the propaganda genre, persuading the audience to accept your version of reality —in effect, winning the argument—comes ahead of historical facts, even-handed reporting, plot and character complexity. But these considerations are still important, and the administration's "carefully constructed and zealously protected portrait of Bush as the supremely decisive, intuitive commander"[85] is so simpleminded that Chetwynd's film only serves to emphasize how powerful some of the real White House's techniques are, for influencing media coverage—without being anywhere near as obvious.

Although Chetwynd claims that he wanted to create "an accurate representation," and that everything was based on "two or three sources," at times the movie diverges significantly from Bush's own accounts.[86] It doesn't address the conflicting statements he's made, about his own thoughts and actions on the day of the attacks—for example his assertion, subsequently repeated, that he saw the first aircraft crash on TV while he was still at the school.[87]

On the film's version of the Ground Zero visit, one reviewer comments: "what was a staged scene to begin with is staged to the second power."[88] According to Chetwynd, the real Bush claimed that "he was approached by a rescue worker . . . who angrily jabbed him and said, 'I'm digging for my brother here, and I didn't vote for you, but you find the people who did this, and you take care of business, you hear me?'"[89] (It's unclear why the Secret Service would allow a distraught man to make threatening moves at the president.) In the film, the worker is deferential to "Bush" (as played by Timothy Bottoms), and shakes hands with him.[90]

Another problem is that even with an admiring writer like Chetwynd, there are still times when "Bush" still comes across as distant and insincere. While meeting bereaved families, "Bush" seems to think that an autograph will reassure people more than hugs. The characterization is less than consistent—after repeated scenes where "Bush" advises calm diplomacy, he flippantly advocates bloody vengeance. There is also a revealing moment where he tells "Laura" that the upcoming speech is "no time for Dubya"—implying that the latter is a folksy persona he can slip on or shed, as the situation requires. During that speech, when the film abruptly cuts to a shot of the real Bush delivering the climax, the differences between him and the version played by Bottoms are jarring. Besides being unfair to the actors, if the intent was to transfer the audience's sympathy to the real George W., it's too clumsy to succeed.

The vignettes showing "Bush" demanding to be flown home so he can reassure the American people, and laboring over his upcoming speech, can only raise questions about the real president: Why didn't anyone listen to the Commander-in-Chief's orders? How could Bush and his competent, dedicated staff have let those flawed "16 words" on African uranium slip through?

Conclusion

"There's an old saying in Tennessee—I know it's in Texas, probably in Tennessee — that says, fool me once, shame on—shame on you. You fool me, you can't get fooled again." George W. Bush, September 17, 2002[91]

Image-making is prevalent in many aspects of our culture, to the extent that it's even used to present an individual as honest and genuine, and above that type of manipulation. Portraying Bush as a "good man" was absolutely crucial for the GOP election strategy[92]—and one which they undoubtedly intend to continue. The "regular guy" is "the essence of who Bush is and what he expects others to be. He's asking them to buy him more than any agenda."[93] Indeed, according to Carney and Dickerson, Karl Rove believes that "most people don't retain the details" of the proposals, but are more influenced by "a positive feeling about Bush."[94]

Many voters fear and mistrust Bush's policies, "but like him personally."[95] As superficial as this sounds—in a society where a significant portion of the electorate can be swayed by the comments of late-night comics, a positive personal image is a definite asset. In a close election, being seen as more trustworthy or friendlier than one's opponent could be a deciding factor, overcoming doubts about the candidate's position on important issues. Democratic Congressman George Miller notes that Bush "is essentially in a race between his personality and his policies."[96]

Politically, Bush is no fool—he "tends to his public image so assiduously, rarely letting an opportunity pass to project a down-home manner."[97] He has become an expert at hosting seemingly-casual gatherings: western-themed dinners for allies like Tony Blair and Vladimir Putin, backyard cookouts for the press corps, even the reunion for his Yale graduating class. Bush and his staff are willing to go to extraordinary lengths to create the impression of relaxed informality ... and to be ruthless about making him appear warm and jovial, such as during his famous "charm offensives." This perception resonates with so many people that the White House keep it at the heart of their image-making—with occasional detours to show Bush in academic robes at a graduation, or an Asian silk jacket for an APEC meeting, or a tuxedo for a formal dinner—but always, in the background lurks the "jolly rancher."

It's increasingly apparent that the leader has become so reliant on this type of manipulation that people notice it only when it's absent. After the 9/11 attacks, various commentators noted that Bush appeared weak and uncertain.[98] If this is the way he "really" is, minus the backdrops and adoring crowds, and no time for rehearsals—this says a great deal about his administration.

A deeper and even more troubling question is whether we the public have also become accustomed to these techniques and equate them with leadership—or are unable to distinguish between a clever public-relations offensive, and genuine grassroots activity. As Paul Krugman put it: is "man on horseback" politics becoming part of America?[99] Other commentators point out that the Republicans are not alone in this—lobbyists from across the political spectrum purposely "assemble average Americans who can convey the appropriate political message."[100]

In recent years, we've also seen the rising popularity of "reality shows" like "Survivor" and "Junkyard Wars"—supposedly spontaneous, but planned and controlled behind the scenes. "Blair Witch Project," presented as an amateur film, had a professional marketing effort behind it.

Many us are reluctant to ask questions about whose "reality" it is, and who benefits from it. Those who ask questions and look behind the curtain were formerly seen as protecting the public interest, in the tradition of investigative reporters, consumer advocates, and fraud squads. However, the same attitudes and techniques, used against someone who appears friendly and well-intentioned, are frequently perceived as mean-spirited.

Bush and his staff know this—they were counting on it, not only to deflect criticism during the election campaign, but to turn it around and portray the Democrats as bullies.

In any case, the media seem to be full of praise for the new, improved reality the White House is showing us. "Television camera crews, meanwhile, say they have rarely had such consistently attractive pictures to send back to editing rooms."[101] This seems to indicate a change in tone from the 2000 campaign, when Al Gore was derided for a canoeing photo-op which critics charged had been "helped along" by the release of water from a dam.[102] "They seem to approach an event site like it's a TV set [....] They dress it up really nicely. It looks like a million bucks,"[103] a cameraman says approvingly, of Bush's staff.

Actually the costs of the backdrops and staging are considerably more than that, given that the White House events budget in 2003 was $3.7 million—in addition, an unknown amount is covered by official hosts, such as government agencies, other levels of government, private corporations, and political parties.[103] Aside from the cost factor, there is a real danger in the media becoming a willing conduit for the White House Communications Office, broadcasting the administration's message uncritically.[105] "We are all complicit for accepting planned and staged events" observed a former photo editor.[106] He was referring to the media, but this applies to the rest of us, too.

When a staged photo-op is revealed as such, or shown to go wrong—

as when Bush's 2002 Earth Day speech was snowed out[107]—or someone notices that, as of March 2004, more than 300 American soldiers had been killed in Iraq since Bush's appearance under the "Mission Accomplished" banner[108]—cynics say, what difference does this make?

After all, everybody uses these techniques, and by shining a light on them, you're only revealing your own willing participation. Why rock the boat—just sit back and enjoy the show. It works for professional wrestling, even down to the "hand-painted" signs at rallies which are given out to the crowd.[109] Wrestling, too, is marketed on multiple levels—in dead earnest, to the people who believe it's real—and with an ironic wink, to those who are in the know (or want to see themselves as such). Don't ruin it for everyone, they warn: "You'll never be able to see politics the same way again."

One wonders—would that be such a bad thing? Because then we'd actually have to do something about it.

ACKNOWLEDGMENTS
The author thanks Jerry Barrett, Hank Blakely, Madeleine Kane, and Harry Haney for their support and encouragement—and members of Democratic Underground, for help with tracking down various sources.

NOTES
    1. At <www.dubyaspeak.com/himself.shtml>.
    2. For example, Anita Kunz's cover art for the *New Yorker Magazine* (October 13, 2003).
    3. At <www.politicalhumor.about.com/library/blbushisms2000.htm>.
    4. Lois Romano, and George Lardner, Jr., "Young Bush, a political natural, revs up," *Washington Post* (July 29, 1999).
    5. Ibid.
    6. Ibid.
    7. "The Essential Bush," *Philadelphia Daily News* (August 3, 2000).
    8. John Leland, "Questions for Timothy Bottoms of 'That's My Bush'," *New York Times Magazine* (March 25, 2001).
    9. At <www.edition.cnn.com/2000/ALLPOLITICS/stories/08/03/gw.speech/>.
    10. Elisabeth Bumiller, "Keepers of Bush image lift stagecraft to new heights," *New York Times* (May 16, 2003)
    11. Bob Somerby, "Our current howler (part II): who's changing now?" *The Daily Howler* (December 11, 2001).
    12. Romano and Lardner, "Young Bush"; and Patrick Beach, "The First Son; George W. Bush had his rebellions," *Austin American-Statesman* (June 13, 1999).
    13. Margaret Carlson, "Suffering for George W," *Time Magazine Online* (August 7, 2000); Nicholas Lemann, "The redemption," *New Yorker* (January 31,

2000); and Stan Crock, "George W., the ill-suited president," *Business Week Online* (January 30, 2001).

14. Lisa Lenoir, "Stitch in time produces new classic," *Chicago Sun Times* (May 6, 2001) and "Bush inaugurated in Oxxford!" *Oxxford Clothes* (2001).

15. Lloyd Grove, "We begin combing in five minutes!" *Washington Post* (March 21, 2003) and Associated Press, "Working on range 'helps me put it all in perspective,'" *St. Petersburg Times*, (August 11, 2002).

16. Judy Keen, "Bush escapes life in the 'bubble' at his ranch," *USA Today* (August 24, 2003).

17. Louis Dubose, "The making of a president: dressing like Johnson and acting like Reagan," *Austin Chronicle* (November 24, 2000).

18. Mike Allen, "'I am in my element here,'" *Washington Post* (August 26, 2001) and Editorial, "Presidential brush cutting," *New York Times* (August 28, 2001).

19. Ron Steinman, "Photo op," *The Digital Journalist* (June 2003).

20. David Boje, "Bush as top gun: deconstructing visual theatric imagery," June 3. Paper in preparation for the Academy of Management in Seattle (August 2003).

21. "The Best of the Village People," CD liner notes, PolyTel, 1994.

22. Louise Story, "Protests planned for Bush's graduation visit," *Yale Daily News* (May 19, 2001).

23. Bumiller, "Keepers of Bush image."

24. Ibid.

25. Katy Textor, "American-made mystery," *ABC News* (January 22, 2003).

26. Bumiller, "Keepers of Bush image."

27. James Carney and John F. Dickerson, "The selling of George Bush," *CNN* (July 17, 2000).

28. Peter Dizikes, "Female focus," *ABC News* (September 19, 2000).

29. Juliet Eilperin and Dan Morgan, "Something borrowed, something blue," *Washington Post* (March 9, 2001).

30. "VIPs asked to remove ties during Bush speech in Indianapolis," *Associated Press* (May 19, 2003).

31. Ibid.

32. James Zogby, "James Zogby: US media helped Bush sell the war," *Palestine Chronicle* (May 9, 2003).

33. Ibid.

34. Ibid.

35. "Bush thanks military contractors," *ABC News*, May 2, 2003.

36. John F. Dickerson, "Home on the range," *Time Magazine* (December 17, 2000).

37. Edwin Chen, "Voters like president, if not performance," *Los Angeles Times* (November 2, 2003).

38. Dickerson, "Home on the Range."

39. "Bush works to make his ranch less 'jungle-y,'" *USA Today* (August 25, 2001).

40. Associated Press, "Working on the Range."

41. Elizabeth McGreevy Seiler, "Untwisting the Cedar," at <www. juniper1.home. texas.net/>.

42. Keen, "Bush escapes life in the 'bubble' at his ranch."

43. Associated Press, "Working on the Range."

44. Patricia Wilson, "Bush plans Texas-sized welcome for Putin at ranch," *Yahoo Daily News,* (August 25,2001).

45. Carney and Dickerson, "The selling of George Bush" and "Bush's life tied to eest [sic] Texas town," *Associated Press* (January 16, 2001).

46. Dickerson, "Home on the Range," and Laurence McQuillan and Judy Keen, "'Texas White House' a refuge from stress," *USA Today*, (April 13, 2001).

47. Ann Rey, "Clean Cities, RRC laud propane's exceptional qualities as a vehicle fuel," *BPN Online Magazine* (December 4, 2001).

48. Jennifer Loven, "Air Force One remains perk of presidency," *Associated Press* (May 11, 2003).

49. Ibid.

50. Deborah Hastings, "Ordinary guy, extraordinary job," *Associated Press* (September 25, 2001).

51. Jimmy Breslin, "Emotions high enough already," Newsday (September 23, 2001).

52. Doug Saunders, "Bushspeak: keep it simple, biblical," *Globe and Mail* (January 28, 2003).

53. Ibid.

54. Dubose, "The making of a president."

55. Ibid.

56. Bumiller, "Keepers of Bush image."

57. Richard Wallace, "Bush: I feel good," *The Daily Mirror* (March 21, 2003).

58. Associated Press, "GOP flexes muscles in Florida," (November 25, 2000).

59. "Key to Florida mob photo," Adam Clymer Fan Club (2000).

60. Stuart Foster, 10-year-old son of former Colorado state legislator Tim Foster, quoted in the *Daily Sentinel*, "Bush photo-op work clothes smelled 'like fresh carpet,'" (August 15, 2001).

61. Jennifer Loven, "Bush touts his environmental progress," *Associated Press* (August 15, 2003).

62. Ibid.

63. Joseph Kellard, "The firefighter seen 'round the world" (March 9, 2002) at <www.theai.net/firefighter.html>.

64. Bumiller, "Keepers of Bush image."

65. Boje, "Bush as top gun," and "Commander in Chief lands on USS Lincoln," CNN (May 2, 2003).

66. Ibid.; "Bush to fly on Navy plane to aircraft carrier," CNN (May 1, 2003); and "President lands safely on Lincoln," NBC (May 1, 2003).

67. Dana Milbank, "Explanation for Bush's carrier landing altered," *Washington Post* (May 7, 2003).

68. Scott Lindlaw, "Bush courts PR opportunity by landing on aircraft carrier," *Associated Press* (May 3, 2003).

69. Milbank, "Explanation for Bush's carrier landing altered."

70. Lindlaw, "Bush courts PR opportunity by landing on aircraft carrier."

71. Ibid. and Reuters, "Bush's carrier landing a costly political stunt, say Democrats," *Guardian Unlimited,* (May 9, 2003).

72. "Bush thanks military contractors," ABC News, and "President lands safely on Lincoln, NBC News.

73. "Bush to fly on Navy plane to aircraft carrier," CNN (May 1, 2003).

74. George W. Bush, "President Bush announces major combat operations in Iraq have ended," *Speech* (May 1, 2003).

75. Bumiller, "Keepers of Bush image."

76. Ken Fireman, Craig Gordon, "Bush: didn't sign off on it," *Newsday* (October 29, 2003)

77. Bumiller, "Keepers of Bush image."

78. Robert Hodierne, "'Lights. Camera. Action.' Military briefers prepare for war." *Army Times* (March 8, 2003) and Andrea Stone, "Lights, cameras, get ready for war," *USA Today* (March 9, 2003).

79. John Doyle, "General Tommy's glam salon of desert-wear chic." *Globe and Mail* (March 26, 2003).

80. Jonathan S. Landlay and Joseph L. Galloway, "Pentagon defends its version of Jessica Lynch rescue," at <www.realcities.com/mld/krwashington/news/columnists/joe_galloway/6032623.htm> (June 6, 2003).

81. At <www.dubyaspeak.com/puredubya.shtml>.

82. Dana Calvo, Rachel Abramowitz, "Hollywood may enlist in unconventional warfare," *Los Angeles Times* (November 10, 2001) and John King, "White House sees Hollywood role in war on terrorism," at <www.edition.cnn.com/2001/US/11/08/rec.bush.hollywood/>. (November 8, 2001).

83. Paul Farhi, "'D.C. 9/11' spins tale of president on tragic day," *Washington Post* (June 19, 2003).

84. Ibid.

85. Brian Lambert, "'9/11' TV movie is little more than Bush campaign film," at <www.twincities.com/mld/twincities/entertainment/columnists/6703544.htm> (September 7, 2003).

86. Farhi, "'D.C. 9/11' spins tale," and R.D. Heldenfels, "'DC 9/11' on Showtime fawning tribute to Bush," *Beacon Journal* (September 7, 2003).

87. Eric Alterman, "9/11/01: where was George?" *The Nation* (September 18, 2003).

88. Lloyd Sachs, "Bottoms/Bush is the man in 'Time of Crisis,'" *Chicago Sun-Times* (September 7, 2003).

89. Elizabeth Bumiller, "Filmmaker leans right, Oval Office swings open," *New York Times* (September 7, 2003).

90. Ibid.

91. At <www.dubyaspeak.com/philosopher.shtml>.

92. Carney and Dickerson, "The selling of George Bush."

93. Carlson, "Suffering for George W."

94. Carney and Dickerson, "The selling of George Bush."

95. Chen, "Voters like president."

96. Ibid.

97. Ibid.

98. David Wastell, "Hesitant Bush draws strength from his 'iron triangle,'" *Telegraph* (September 16, 2001).

99. Paul Krugman, "Man on horseback," *New York Times* (May 6, 2003). Krugman is referring to an attempted coup in 1889 France, by the supporters of heroic-looking General Georges Boulanger (who often appeared on horseback).

100. Eilpern and Morgan, "Something borrowed, something blue."

101. Bumiller, "Keepers of Bush image."

102. Jake Tapper, "I'm not peaking too early," *Salon* (August 4, 1999).

103. Bumiller, "Keepers of Bush image."

104. Ibid.

105. Zogby, "US media helped Bush sell war."

106. Steinman, "Photo op."

107. Dana Milbank, "Mother Earth 1, Bush 0," *Washington Post* (April 23, 2002).

108. Iraq Coalition Casualties, 2004. At <www.lunaville.org/warcasualties/ Summary.aspx>.

109. David Walsh, "Bush documentary: an 'intimate' portrait of an empty vessel," *World Socialist Web Site* (December 9, 2003).

Political Propaganda:
Selling Lies Like Cigarettes

BY ERNEST PARTRIDGE

In this book, and in many others now on the best seller lists, we have encountered an appalling compendium of lies that have been spewed forth by George Bush and his cohorts in defense of his substantively indefensible policies—policies that are clearly contrary to the interests and values of the same general public which has, in large part, been persuaded to accept them.

How is this possible? What black arts of persuasion, and what perversions of language, have been employed to accomplish this astonishing, albeit regrettable, acceptance by the public?

This will be the guiding question of this chapter.

Politics According to the Vince Lombardi Rule

The key insight into the GOP/Bush propaganda machine is a realization that it is completely unscrupulous—literally, without scruple. To these political operatives, Vince Lombardi's rule applies:*"winning isn't everything, it is the only thing."*

Accordingly, if a violation of common decency, or even of the law, is counter-productive to a GOP political campaign, only then might decency and the law might be a constraint. Otherwise, anything goes, so long as it enhances the prospects of political success. Common decency and the law be damned.

The Law? Richard Nixon's willingness to resort to perjury, illegal wiretapping and burglary to further his political ends is well known. The GOP also violated the law in Florida in 2000, as tens of thousands of eligible voters were "purged" from the rolls, as hundreds of military ballots postmarked after the election were counted, and as the official recount of ballots in Miami-Dade County was interrupted and then cancelled, as the offices were besieged in the "yuppy riot" carried out largely by congressional GOP staffers.

Arguably, a Supreme Court decision cannot violate a law, since it validates laws. Even so, the consensus of legal scholars is that the December 12, 2000 decision, *Bush v. Gore*, is an absurd, incoherent and indefensible concoction specifically devised to enact a pre-ordained result: the selection of George W. Bush as President.

With such a history as this, can the public be assured that the "paperless" touch-screen voting machines, all manufactured by companies owned and controlled by Republican partisans, will accurately and fairly record the votes in the upcoming Presidential election?

Common Decency? Consider the distortions and lies that the right wing propaganda mill has fed the voters:

a. Dukakis vs. Bush I and the infamous "Willie Horton" ad. Horton, a Massachusetts prisoner, committed a violent crime while on furlough during Dukakis's term as Governor. The ad does not point out that the furlough program was established during the term of Dukakis' predecessor, a Republican.

b. In the 2002 Georgia senatorial campaign, Max Cleland was characterized as "unpatriotic" by his opponent, Saxby Chamblis. Cleland is a Viet Nam veteran who lost three of his limbs in combat. Chamblis dodged the draft during the Viet Nam war.

c. In the 2000 Presidential campaign, Al Gore was slandered as a "serial liar" and a "self promoter." Examples? He claimed, among other things, to have "invented the internet," and to have "discovered the Love Canal toxic waste site." In fact, the "lies" were made by the GOP campaign. Gore never made such claims, and one is hard-pressed to find any examples of deliberate lying in his public record.[1]

d. The outpouring of grief at the memorial for Paul Wellstone was denounced by the GOP as a "cheap political rally."

e. In the crucial 2000 South Carolina primary campaign, John McCain, an authentic war hero, was smeared by a barrage of false accusations: that he is mentally unstable as a result of his experiences as a prisoner of war, that he fathered a black child, that his wife is an alcoholic, etc.[2]

Politicians who gain their offices through slander, election fraud, and lies, can be expected to continue such behavior once in office—and they do.

None of this behavior would be successful if the media reported and criticized it, and if the public repudiated it at the polls. But they don't. Instead, the GOP campaign propaganda tests the limits, encounters little resistance and is rewarded by success, and so the limits of corrupt political campaigning are stretched ever further.

Accordingly, in the conditions of contemporary politics, Leo Durocher's rule applies: "Nice guys finish last."

Making the Case vs. Selling the Product

Adlai Stevenson conducted his 1952 and 1956 campaigns with the slogan, "let's talk sense to the American people."

How noble! How high-minded! *How naive!*

Because much of the Democratic "brain trust" is drawn from the scholarly and legal professions, Democratic candidates and campaign managers are inclined to treat political campaigns as if they took place in a seminar room or a court room. They assemble their evidence and put it into a logical structure, and then proceed to "make their case." *Ho Hum!*

Republican campaign strategists come from an entirely different place—the marketplace. Their methodology is that of the salesman: the candidate as "product," and the voter as "customer." Their commanding objective is to "make the sale," by whatever means are found to be effective toward that end. They are utterly undeterred by qualms about committing fallacies or even about staying within the bounds factual accuracy and truth. "Salesmanship" has little interest in such concerns. "Facts," as Ronald Reagan once said, "are stupid things." Thus lying is just another weapon in their rhetorical armory, to be utilized whenever it is found to be effective.

In advance of their political campaigns, GOP "salesmen" examine comprehensively the public mind, through polling and focus groups. There they discover the "hot button" words, concepts, images and (less significantly) issues. With this information, they then target the emotions (in "the post-9/11 context," primarily *fear*), motives (security and economic gain), and self-image (hard-working, free, God-fearing) of the public, all this toward the objective of what Noam Chomsky describes as "the manufacturing of consent."

Then the GOP campaign machine strikes early, defining their opponents and framing the contest, whereupon the Democrats find themselves constantly on the defensive. In addition, the Republicans resolve to "stay on the message" which they repeat and repeat and repeat, until the public perceives the repetition as proof—a tactic which has come to be known as "the big lie."

Democrats also use polls and conduct focus groups, but primarily to discover public opinion concerning "the issues"—i.e., the economy, homeland security, health care, foreign policy, etc. Time and again, they discover that a majority of the public is "with the Democrats" on the issues. Time and again, the Republicans prove that the issues are of secondary importance to imagery and the public's perception of the personalities of the candidates.

For example, in 1984, when the pollsters surveyed public opinion regarding the positions of the two parties on public issues, carefully excluding references to the candidates and the parties, on virtually every issue, the preponderance of public opinion was on the side of the Democrats. And yet in that election we were told over and over that it was "morning in America" (whatever that meant) and the smiling Gipper face was omnipresent on the TV screen. Reagan trounced Mondale. In 2000 election, the GOP image-makers successfully, albeit unfairly, portrayed Al Gore as untrustworthy, self-absorbed, aloof and cold. George Bush, on the other hand, was presented as a compassionate "straight-shooting" and "likeable" guy. Again, on the issues, a considerable majority of the public was on the side of the Democrats, as the voters might have noticed had they paid attention to the issues in the debates and the campaign. However, the media spin-meisters redirected public attention to the concocted caricatures of the candidates, which narrowed Gore's margin of popular vote "victory" sufficiently to allow the GOP, with the aid of five Supreme Court justices, to steal the election and the presidency.

With Bush & Co. safely installed in the White House and his party in control of the Congress, the Supreme Court, and the mass media, the sales campaign continues—with manifest success.

How else is one to explain the endorsement by a large portion of the public of policies that clearly work against their interests. Among them:

- policies that are designed to redistribute wealth "upward" from the poor and middle class to the wealthy
- tax reductions for the wealthy that result in massive federal deficits, borrowing from the Social Security funds and threatening to bankrupt this most popular federal program along with other social services such as Medicare, Head Start, Americorps, etc.
- enactment and enforcement of legislation, such as the USA PATRIOT Act, which directly violate Constitutional protection of citizen rights and privacy
- policies that open up the national parks and other public lands to private exploitation, and that relax or abolish environmental regulations designed to protect the air, water, endangered species and ecosystems.
- foreign wars that will gain them nothing while possibly costing the lives of themselves or their loved ones—wars that are ordered by individuals who stand to gain financially, and who them-

selves have managed to avoid military service. ("They had other priorities" as Dick Cheney put it).

Summing up, to the degree that the Democratic strategists approach political campaigns from the traditions of scholarship and the law, they perceive their task as that of "making the case"—i.e., their objective is *to prove*.

In contrast, the Republicans approach political campaigns from the perspective of the marketplace, and perceive their task as that of "selling the product," which is to say the candidate. Their objective is *to persuade*—by any means available, so long as they can "get away with it."

History tells us which approach has been more successful.

GOP-Speak and the Vindication of George Orwell

The fundamental operating principles of right-wing and Bushista propaganda were clearly set forth in 1948 in "The Principles of Newspeak"—an appendix to George Orwell's *1984*.

> The purpose of Newspeak was not only to provide a medium of expression for the [Party's] world-view and mental habits..., but to make all other modes of thought impossible. It was intended that when Newspeak had been adopted once and for all and Oldspeak forgotten, a heretical thought—that is, a thought diverging from the principles of [the Party]—should be literally unthinkable, at least so far as thought is dependent on words. Its vocabulary was so constructed as to give exact and often very subtle expression to every meaning that a Party member could properly wish to express, while excluding all other meanings and also the possibility of arriving at them by indirect methods. This was done partly by the invention of new words, but chiefly by eliminating undesirable words, and by stripping such words as remained of unorthodox meanings. . . Newspeak was designed not to extend but to diminish the range of thought. . .[3]

Orwell wrote this as a warning. The Republicans and the Bush Administration has adopted it as a guidebook.

In Orwell's "Newspeak," words were corrupted by assigning them to their conventional opposites: "War is Peace," "Freedom is Slavery," "Ignorance is Strength." In the government of *1984*, the military command is housed in The Ministry of Peace. The secret police and the torture chambers operate out of The Ministry of Love. And propaganda, including the rewriting of history, issues from The Ministry of Truth. Note in this regard that the organ of Soviet propaganda was named *Pravda*. English translation: "truth."

The torture of the English language in the hands of the Bush Administration is scarcely less bizarre. A Bush Administration policy that will let loose the chain saws of the timber corporations upon our national forests is dubbed "healthy forests." Another policy which allows increased power plant emissions into the atmosphere is called the "Clear Skies Initiative." The military occupation of the once-sovereign nation of Iraq was accomplished under "Operation Iraqi Freedom." And the USA PATRIOT Act abolishes citizen rights and protections of law in defense of which authentic patriots in our history pledged their lives, fortunes, and sacred honor, and often gave their lives.[4]

The right-wing corruption of the word "conservative" deserves special attention. Webster's Unabridged defines "conservatism" as "the practice of preserving what is established; disposition to oppose change in established institutions and methods." This scarcely describes a political movement that attacks our Constitutional rights, extends government surveillance of the private lives of citizens, curtails free expression, stifles free enterprise, rejects the accumulated learning of the sciences, decides national elections by judicial decree, violates treaties, and initiates wars with sovereign nations that pose no threat to us—and this list is incomplete. Better to call such an ideology "regressive" or "radically reactionary."

For this reason, I have refrained in this essay (as I do in most of my writings) from applying the word "conservative" to either the Bush administration or the Republican party.

Yet this right-wing faction insists upon calling itself "conservative," and does so with such persistence, that even its left-wing and centrist opponents have thoughtlessly fallen into line and routinely refer to the radical right as "conservative."

The radical right attack on the word "liberal" exemplifies Orwell's warning that when a powerful political party takes control of a language, "a heretical thought—that is, a thought diverging from the principles of [the Party]—should be literally unthinkable, at least so far as thought is dependent on words."

In the hands of the radical right propagandists, the word "liberal" has come to signify hippies, socialism, moral relativism, political correctness, "tax and spend" big government, welfare cheats, "bleeding heart" giveaways to the unworthy, and so on. According to Ann Coulter, "liberals" (roughly half the population of the United States) are nothing less than "traitors."[5]

Joe Conason counters this caricature in his book *Big Lies*:

The most basic liberal values are political equality and economic opportunity. Liberals uphold democracy as the only form of government that derives legitimacy from the consent of the governed, and they regard the freedoms enumerated in the Bill of Rights as essential to the expression of popular consent. Their commitment to an expanding democracy is what drives liberal advocacy on the behalf of women, minorities, gays, immigrants, and other traditionally disenfranchised groups.[6]

When a public opinion poll asks a sample of American citizens how they would label their political orientation, "liberal" generally comes in a poor third to "conservative" and "moderate." However, when the "liberal" label is set aside and ordinary citizens are asked their opinions about such particular issues as Social Security, Medicaid, public education, the United Nations, voting rights, affirmative action, environmental protection, government regulation of commerce, reproductive freedom, etc., a considerable majority expresses support of these policies and issues which are, in fact, central to the liberal point of view. Thus it seems that although the American public endorses the *content* of traditional liberalism, the radical right has so successfully sullied the label "liberal" that it has become an effective political weapon of the right—like a piece of rotten fruit to hurl at an opposing candidate.

And so, in tune with the principles of Newspeak, the right has so corrupted political discourse that the political faction which advocates "reforms tending toward democracy and personal freedom for the individual" (Webster's), formerly designated as "liberalism," has now been deprived of its traditional name. And thus, lacking a name, it has become far more difficult to articulate and thus even think of and defend the "liberal" principles of such political giants as FDR, LaGuardia, Adlai Stevenson and Jacob Javitts, and Wendell Wilkie.

So now we see the rise of the label "progressive" in place of "liberal"—presumably, until such time that this label too is besmirched by the mighty media propaganda machine of the right.

Language and the Social Order

A well-ordered and well-integrated society rests upon a foundation of shared meanings—a language with a rich vocabulary, capable of expressing novelties, relatively constant, but at the same time evolving through ordinary use, rather than political manipulation. Put simply, language functions best as a *conservative* institution.

However, as Orwell so clearly pointed out, political propaganda is destructive of this "conservative" function of language. Heedless of the cost in social disorder, right wing propaganda deliberately and willfully distorts language to serve the purposes of the party, of the faction, of the sponsor. This is no secret. In his GOPAC memo of 1994, Newt Gingrich candidly identified language as "a key mechanism of control."

Propagandistic manipulation and distortion of political discourse is subversive of democratic government whether or not it is successful. If the "Newspeak" of the controlling party is uncritically accepted by the public, it becomes an instrument of control by that government. If it is rejected, the institutions of government and the rule of law are likewise rejected, and anarchy ensues.

Furthermore, a degraded political language can cause havoc in the society as it undermines clarity of ordinary discourse and with it the capacity of ordinary citizens to communicate. To trust each other, and thus participate in and sustain a democratic government. Civil society then dissolves as individuals retreat into themselves and are reduced from citizens to self-seeking consumers, and society is reduced to a mere marketplace—if that.

It is thus the urgent duty of the opposing party, civic organistions an educational institutions to restore to political discourse the clarity and order of a natural language—what Confucius called a "recitfication of names"—which is pre-requisite for open, intelligent and productive political debate.

Conclusion

From this analysis we may conclude that the lies of the Bush Administration, the Republicans and the radical right are not simply moral lapses added on the routine business of politics (though they are that too). Much more than that, the lies of the right issue from the very foundations of right-wing theory and practice. In an enterprise that prizes winning above all else, moral qualms about fair-play and truth-telling drop far down the list of priorities, and perchance off that list entirely. Right-wing campaign strategists feel no more obliged to tell the truth to the public than tobacco marketers feel obliged to publicize the health risks of their product to the teen-agers they are endeavoring to "hook." Indeed, many of the advertising agencies that hawk cigarettes also work for the Republican National Committee.

Neither the public in general, nor the Democratic party in particular, are helpless in the face of the propaganda barrage from the right. First of all, the founders of our republic set up a system of "checks and balances" in the structure of the government that might serve to curb the abuses of government. Unfortunately, the onslaught from the right has severely crippled these institutions—the Congress, and the courts.

Even so, they are not beyond recapture by an aroused and determined public and opposition party.

The founders also looked to the press as a remedy against the abuses of power, wealth and privilege. The press—or "the media" as we now call it—are likewise also severely compromised as organs of opposition and reform, due to their ownership by fewer and fewer corporate conglomerates. But the public is sensing the dangers of media concentration and is resisting it. Witness the public outcry against the FCC decision to relax ownership rules. Note too the emergence of the Internet as a medium of dissent.

NOTES

1. Eric Boehlert, "Gore's too-willing executioners," Salon (October 27, 2000) at <www.dir.salon.com/politics/feature/2000/10/27/media/index.html>; Molly Dickerson, "Who's lying, Gore or the media?" on TomPaine.com, (October 8, 2000) at <www.tompaine.com/feature.cfm?ID=3729&view=print>; Robert Parry, "He's no Pinnochio," *Washington Monthly* (April, 2000).

2. Jake Tapper, "Getting Ugly," Salon (November 14, 2000) at <www.dir.salon.com/politics/feature/2000/11/14/sc_pols/index.html> and PBS, *Online NewsHour*, "Showdown in South Carolina" (February 17, 2000) at <www.pbs.org/newshour/bb/politics/jan-june00/sc_primary_2-17.html>.

3. George Orwell, *1984* (New York: Signet Classic 1992, pp. 246-7).

4. Elaine Cassel, "The Bush administration and the end of civil liberties," *CounterPunch* (April 27, 2003) at <www.counterpunch.org/cassel 04262003. html>; Jennifer van Bergen, "Repeal the USA PATRIOT Act," *Truthout* (April 1, 2002) at <www.truthout.com/docs_02/04.02A.JVB.Patriot.htm>; and The Crisis Papers, "USA Patriot Act," at <www.crisispapers.org/topics/usa-patriot. htm>.

5. Ann Coulter, *Treason: Liberal Treachery from the Cold War to the War on Terrorism* (New York: Crown Forum, 2003).

6. Joe Conason, *Big Lies: The Right-Wing Propaganda Machine and How It Distorts the Truth* (New York: Thomas Dunne, 2003), pp.2-3.

See also my essays at www.crisispapers.org, including "Don't Give Up on the Media," <www.crisispapers.org/essays/media.htm> (January, 2004), and "The Dragon at the Gate," <www.crisispapers.org/Editorials/dragon-at-gate.htm> (January, 2003)

Part Three
Bush Domestic Lies

An Economic Train Wreck
And Bush's Lies

BY THE BREW[§]

On January 20, 2001, as George Bush was being sworn in as the 43rd president of the United States of America, the official unemployment rate as reported by the US Department of Labor stood at 4.1%; near its all-time low. In the year prior to Bush's inauguration, the Federal Government had reported a surplus in excess of two hundred billion dollars, an all-time high. Over the next ten years, the surplus was projected to be in excess of five trillion dollars, another all-time high. For the first time, the prospect of paying off the enormous debts incurred in previous administrations seemed within reach. As Bush took his oath of office on that rainy Saturday, the Dow Jones industrial average had closed the week at 10,659, and the nation had just completed 31 consecutive quarters of increases in the gross national product; a peacetime record. By any measure, the Bush administration inherited an economy is fantastic shape, arguably the best shape in the history of the United States. All of that would change. The inauguration of George Bush marked the beginning of a free fall in the economic fortunes of the United States.

By February of 2003, things had gotten so bad that Bush had been forced to replace virtually the entire economic team he had brought to Washington. John W. Snow had been brought in to take over as Treasury secretary and Stephen Friedman had taken over as head of the White House National Economic Council. On February 27, Harvard economist N. Gregory Mankiw was nominated to head Bush's Council of Economic Advisors. On the day of Mankiw's nomination, the Dow Jones industrial average had fallen to 7,884 and unemployment had risen to 5.8%. Breaking the streak of 31 straight quarters of growth under the Clinton administration, three of the first nine quarters Bush was in office the nation's GNP declined. The worst of those falls, a decline of 1.6%, came in the

---

[§]The Brew is a psuedonym for a West Coast attorney, author, and former adjunct professor of law and finance at a PAC-10 university who is a political activist and publishes The Daily Brew (www.thedailybrew.com).

second quarter of 2001, after Bush's first set of tax cuts had been signed into law, and before the terrorist attacks of September 11.

As the shakeup in Bush's economic team made plain, the administration had begun to feel the political heat generated by the collapsing economy. While the appointment of Dr. Mankiw to the Council of Economic Advisors wouldn't stem the decline in the nation's economic fortunes; (unemployment would rise to 6.4% in the next four months), it did provide a microcosm of the ideological bent of the Bush administration. It was an ideology that would prove to be completely undeterred by the economic collapse.

If Bush's economic policies had a single constant, it was that tax cuts were a remedy for any economic condition. Campaigning in 1999, Bush had repeated a mantra that the surplus should be "returned to the people." Bush argued that when times were good it was better to lower tax rates than to pay down the massive debts that the United States had incurred when his father had been Vice President and then President. Bush argued that there was enough money to provide significant tax cuts, pay down the debt, and privatize social security. Based on Bush's campaign rhetoric, one might reasonably expect that Bush's fondness for tax cuts might have vanished with the surplus. But a funny thing happened after Bush's first round of tax cuts passed in 2001. The nation was plunged into recession, and the surplus was replaced with a deficit. Even though the economic conditions had essentially reversed themselves, Bush's prescription for sound economic policy did not. Bush continued to push for more tax cuts, arguing now that more tax cuts were needed to stimulate the economy. Bush's nominee to head the Council of Economic Advisors had heard that argument before.

In a chapter in his textbook on economics, *Principles of Economics*, Dr. George Mankiw included a chapter titled "Thinking Like an Economist: Why Economists Disagree." His analysis is highly revealing:

> An example of fad economics occurred in 1980, when a small group of economists advised presidential candidate Ronald Reagan that an across-the-board cut in income tax rates would raise tax revenue. They argued that if people could keep a higher fraction of their income, people would work harder to earn more income. Even though tax rates would be lower, income would raise by so much, they claimed, that tax revenue would rise. Almost all professional economists, including most of those who supported Reagan's proposal to cut taxes, viewed this outcome as too optimistic. Lower tax rates might encourage people to work harder, and this extra effort would offset the direct effects of lower tax rates to some extent. But there was no credible evi-

dence that work effort would rise by enough to cause tax revenues to rise in the face of lower tax rates. George Bush, also a presidential candidate in 1980, agreed with most of the professional economists: He called this idea "voodoo economics." Nonetheless, the argument was appealing to Reagan, and it shaped the 1980 presidential campaign and the economic policies of the 1980s (George Mankiw, *Principles of Economics*, 1st Edition, 1995)

Mankiw went on to note that Congress passed the cut in tax rates, "but the tax cut did not cause tax revenue to rise." Instead, Mankiw observed, "tax revenue fell" and the government "began a long period of deficit spending," the "largest peacetime increase in the government debt in U.S. history." It was perhaps telling that by the time Dr. Mankiw had been asked to join the Bush administration, these passages had been removed from the subsequent editions of Dr. Mankiw's book. While the nation had just come out of a recession, and the surplus had been replaced with a deficit, the Bush administration had apparently forgotten the economic history recited by Dr. Mankiw. Instead, the Bush administration was now arguing that more tax cuts would stimulate the economy, and in 2003, Bush signed into law yet another round of tax cuts.

Right wing ideologues have long argued with economists about the economic effects of tax cuts, but no amount of argument is able to refute a few simple facts. When Bush and Reagan cut taxes, the deficit exploded. When Bill Clinton raised them, the deficit turned into a surplus. Admittedly, this is an oversimplification of the economic history of the past 25 years. At the same time, no current projection of US government spending and tax revenues, including those prepared by the White House itself, projects a return of the federal budget to a surplus assuming the levels of expenditures and taxation currently written into law are made permanent. The Bush economic policy thus calls for the federal government to borrow money this year, next year, and every year thereafter, forever. These economic results provide compelling evidence that in the first edition of his book, Dr. Mankiw was right. There is no such thing as a free lunch.

How could the Bush administration sell such a policy? Simple. They lied. To contain the costs of the 2001 tax cuts, Congressional Republicans and the Bush administration relied on "sunset clauses" that would make all of the tax cuts disappear in ten years. With the sunset provisions in place, the official cost of the 2001 tax cuts were estimated at $350 billion. However, if the sunset clauses are removed, the cost balloons to $800 billion. Not surprisingly, from virtually the moment the 2001 tax cuts were passed, both Congressional Republicans and the Bush administration have argued that the law should be amended to make the tax cuts permanent. Both the 2001 and the 2003 tax cuts were also sold to the public as primarily benefiting the middle class. But the numbers didn't add up.

The heart of the 2001 act was a reduction in the rate paid at the top income bracket and the elimination of the estate tax. Cuts in the top rate were obviously skewed towards the very affluent, and contrary to popular belief, only the richest 2% of all estates have any liability for estate taxes at all. Once fully phased in, forty-two percent of the benefit of the 2001 tax cuts will go to the top 1% of taxpayers.

The foundation of the 2003 tax cut was a reduction in the tax rate for dividend income. The Bush administration told America that "92 million Americans will receive an average tax cut of $1,083." This was sort of like saying that if Bill Gates walked into a homeless shelter, the average person standing in the soup line would be a millionaire. According the Tax Policy Center, families with incomes of over one million dollars a year, less than two tenths of one percent of the population, will receive more of the benefits of the 2003 tax cut than the bottom 70 percent. The minority staff for the Congressional Committee on Government Reform estimated that Dick Cheney—the President's key tax negotiator—would have his tax bill cut $116,002 a year, John Snow, Bush's Secretary of the Treasury, would get over $332,000 a year, and Donald Rumsfeld would get as much as $604,000 a year. For about half of American families, the 2003 tax cut provided less than $100 per year, and for the vast majority, less than $500. And for the very poor? To make room for these tax cuts, the Republicans submitted a final bill denying families making between $10,500 and $26,625 a year an increase in the child credit.

Just before the 2003 act passed, in an editorial for the *Washington Post* entitled "Dividend Voodoo" (June 3, 2003), Warren Buffett, perhaps the most successful investor in history, described the effects of the 2003 tax cuts thusly: "Supporters of making dividends tax-free like to paint critics as promoters of class warfare. The fact is, however, that their proposal promotes class welfare. For my class." It would seem that Mr. Buffett had read the earlier edition of Dr. Mankiw's book.

One might reasonably ask, why does any of this matter? As long as the poor and the middle classes were not asked to pay more in taxes, why should anyone care if the wealthy are given a tax cut? The answer is because Bush's tax cuts are being financed with borrowed money. Increasingly this money is borrowed from foreign countries, and sooner or later that bill is going to come due.

In early November of 2003, the Federal Reserve reported that the total holdings of U.S. debt held by foreign central banks had risen to an all time high of over one trillion dollars. That was equivalent to some 10 percent of U.S. gross domestic product, and was up almost 25% from $807.60 billion just a year earlier. Just as banks will not lend to an individual or a business indefinitely, there will arrive a day when the United States will find that it can no longer find lenders willing to loan the money to the United States. So one has to ask; why has Bush deliberately built an unsustainable structural deficit into the federal budget?

One explanation is that Bush is following a strategy promoted by such luminaries as Republican activist Grover Norquist, who hopes to saddle the nation with so much debt that the federal government will be forced to shrink, merely to service the interest on the debt. Mr. Norquist has opined that in so doing, the government can be shrunk to so small a size that it could be "drowned in a bathtub." But if the Bush administration has any intention of drowning the federal government in a bathtub, it certainly isn't apparent from the spending side of the equation.

The Congressional Budget Office's (CBO) current projections demonstrate that the Bush deficits are not merely a function of the tax cuts. True, the Bush administration policies have cut taxes (and thus revenues) as a share of GDP. But Bush administration policies have also raised spending to a level that should alarm anyone concerned about the size of the Federal Government and anyone who believes that a Federal Government that is massively in debt is less able to afford its citizens everything from basic social services to a healthy national defense. If one merely assumes that that the Bush administration will continue to dictate policy on both the tax side and on the expenditure side, current projections show that the nation will endure deficits of more than $500 billion a year until the baby boom generation retires, at which time the deficits will grow much bigger.

Comparing, for example, fiscal 2001 and fiscal 2004, one finds that as the budget has shifted from surplus to deficit, the magnitude of this shift is an amount equal to 5.3% of the nation's Gross Domestic Product (GDP). While 3.0% of this shift is accounted for by the lower revenues created by the Bush tax cuts, 2.3% comes from higher spending. More importantly, in future projections, the picture gets worse. If Bush is able to secure a second term, in the last year of that term, fiscal 2009, the CBO's projections are for revenues to fall from the level of 19.6% of GDP in 2001 value, to 17.8%. Expenditures are projected to rise from 18.4% of GDP in 2001 to 21.6% in 2009. Stated differently, while the tax share of GDP is projected to fall by 1.8% of GDP, the spending share of GDP is projected to rise by 3.25. Bush's plan is to cut taxes, yes, but also to increase spending, and by an amount greater than the tax cuts!

These projections assume that there will be a Medicare drug benefit, which the congress just passed, that the Republicans will be successful in extending the sunset provisions of the tax code, as the Bush administration currently advocates; that the Alternative Minimum Tax will be reformed along the lines also advocated by the Bush administration, and that discretionary spending will grow at the rate of nominal GDP. Using these assumptions, between fiscal 2001 and fiscal 2009, 64% of the structural deficits will be due to higher spending, and only 36% will be due to lower taxes. A full 8% of the increase in spending will be a result of interest costs created by this new debt, and not higher spending on social services or defense, which rises by only 0.4% of GDP from 2001 to 2009 assuming current Bush administration policies.

The surpluses generated by the Clinton administration were projected to pay down a large portion of the national debt. But the Clinton administration also saw that they had a train coming at the end of the tunnel. Even under Clinton's policies, deficits were still projected to return when the baby boom generation began retiring in large numbers after about 2010, due to their sheer numbers. Even a substantial lowering of the national debt made possible by the Clinton era surpluses were not projected to be sufficient to overcome the financial obligations tied to this demographic bubble.

The Bush administration sees this same train coming. But instead of hitting the brakes, the Bush administration has instead chosen to stomp on the gas as hard as it can. What that means is that we are going to meet that train as hard and as fast as possible. The motives for this are no longer relevant. All that is left to be determined are the consequences.

Part II. Bush's Economic Lies, edited by Jerry "Politex" Barrett

1. "There was only one problem with President Bush's claim Thursday that the nation's top economists forecast substantial economic growth if Congress passed the president's tax cut: The forecast with that conclusion doesn't exist. Bush and White House Press Secretary Ari Fleischer went out of their way Thursday to cite a new survey by "Blue-Chip economists" that the economy would grow 3.3 percent this year if the president's tax cut proposal becomes law. . . "I don't know what he was citing," said Randell E. Moore, editor of the monthly Blue Chip Economic Forecast, a newsletter that surveys 53 of the nation's top economists each month. "I was a little upset," said Moore, who said he complained to the White House. 'It sounded like the Blue Chip Economic Forecast had endorsed the president's plan. That's simply not the case'" (*Newsday* February 24, 2003).

2. "45 percent of all of the dividend income goes to people with $50,000-or-less incomes, family incomes. Nearly three-quarters of it goes to families with $100,000 or less family income" (White House senior adviser Karl Rove, discussing the Bush tax proposal in a meeting with reporters, as reported by Dana Milbank in the *Washington Post,* January 28, 2003).

"Not exactly. It is true that 43.8 percent of tax returns with dividend income are from households with less than $50,000 in income and 73.8 percent of such returns are from households with less than $100,000. But that doesn't mean the little guy earning less than $50,000 gets '45 percent of all the income' or that the Main Street earners below $100,000 get 'three-quarters' of dividend income.

"In fact, those earning less than $50,000 get 14.7 percent of dividend income, and those earning less than $100,000 get 32.7 percent, according to a Brookings Institution/Urban Institute analysis. The former would get 6.8 percent of the benefit of Bush's dividend plan, while the latter would get 20.9 percent" (Dana Milbank, *Washington Post,* January 28, 2003).

3. "The budget differs from those of other recent presidents in two important ways. Nowhere does Mr. Bush make balancing the budget an important goal. And he makes no claim that the era of big government is over, or even nearing an end. 'This is a president of big projects and big ideas,' his budget director, Mitchell E. Daniels Jr., said today....Paying no heed to the notion of a balanced budget, Mr. Bush advocates deep tax cuts on top of the large ones enacted two years ago. By contrast, when big deficits began to appear after President Ronald Reagan drove tax cuts through Congress in 1981, Mr. Reagan approved offsetting tax increases....Mr. Daniels said this morning, 'A balanced federal budget remains a high priority for this president.' But unlike the submissions of recent predecessors, this budget describes no plans to reach that goal" (David E. Rosenbaum, *New York Times,* February 4, 2003).

4. "In his speech unveiling his tax plan, Bush sold his package by noting that a family of four making $40,000 would see its taxes in 2003 fall a whopping 96 percent from $1,178 to $45—mostly due to the expansion of the child credit. . . As the Center on Budget and Policy Priorities notes, Bush's example could come true. But it adds, 'the tax cuts that would benefit this family constitute less than one-quarter of the overall cost of the bill.' In other words, you could dump three-quarters of his package and still assist middle-income families. To suggest this package overall is of direct assistance to middle- and lower-income individuals is dishonest. Only pieces of it—the smaller pieces—do that" (David Corn, *The Nation,* January 14, 2003).

5. "Bush opened his final radio address of the year this way: "In 2002, our economy was still recovering from the attacks of September the 11th, 2001, and it was pulling out of a recession that began before I took office." Bush concluded 2002 with the same dishonesty that defined his economic policy throughout the year—a mendacity that ranged from denying the tax cut had anything to do with the re-emergence of the deficit to arguing that the terrorism insurance bill would create 300,000 construction jobs. In fact, there is no evidence that the economy was in recession when President Bush took the oath of office on January 20, 2001. . .Bush is probably not conversant with NBER's "recession dating procedures." But it's a sure thing his economic and political advisers are. So shame on them for feeding him dishonest lines" (Daniel Gross, *Slate*, December 30, 2002).

6. "The entire public rationale for the tax cut was not merely wrong or reckless, but outright dishonest. When Bush took office, remember, most people wanted to pay off the national debt and spend money on things like education and prescription drugs far more than they wanted tax cuts. Bush was only able to make his tax cuts acceptable by convincing the public that he first planned to take care of popular priorities and only cut taxes with all the leftover money. . . But the truth—which subsequent developments now expose—is that Bush always placed his tax cut ahead of debt reduction or the various government policies he endorsed as a 'compassionate conservative.' It wasn't just some giant miscalculation. It was a lie" (Jonathan Chait, *Slate*, December 4, 2001).

7. "Bush lied. About the cost of his tax cut. About who benefits. About his budget. He lied when he claimed he could throw money at the military, fund a prescription drug benefit, pass his tax cut and still not touch the Social Security surplus. And he's lying now as his budget office cooks the books to mask the fact that he's already dipping into the Social Security surplus—without counting the full cost of his military fantasies, or a decent drug benefit, or the inevitable tax and spending adjustments yet to come....Bush says his tax cuts are needed to help the economy revive; that's right—only he's lying about his tax cut. Most of it doesn't kick in for years and goes to the already rich. . . Now we have a dishonest debate: Bush lies. . ." (Robert L. Borosage, *The Nation*, September 7, 2001)

8. It's a nonsense set of statistics—Treasury Secretary Paul O'Neill, commenting on the Citizens for Tax Justice study showing that 43 percent of the proposed Bush tax cut (since revised upward to 45 percent) would go to the richest 1 percent. . .

"In truth, the number is neither difficult to obtain nor highly disputed. The richest 1 percent of Americans would get between 31.3 percent and 45 percent of Bush's tax cut. Without the estate tax cut—which is about a quarter of Bush's tax package—the haul for the richest 1 percent would be 31.3 percent, according to Citizens for Tax Justice. . . 'It's not a controversial number,' [O'Neill] said" (Dana Milbank, "Tax Cut Statistics Disputed," *Washington Post,* March 2, 2003).

9. Bush "said throughout the campaign [that] the huge surpluses forecast for the next 10 years make a massive tax cut only fair and proper. On the other hand, he warns now, the declining economy requires a massive tax cut to prop it up. Believing that the country faces, at the same time, a declining economy and huge unending surpluses is the trick that the Bushies manage effortlessly. It's a belief that while a recession is about to reduce our tax revenues now—or might already be doing it — we can confidently dispense the ones projected for 2010" (*Oregon Live,* February 8, 2001).

The Five Big Lies Bush Made to Working Families

By Nathan Newman

Lie #1: Bush Said He'd Help Workers Losing Jobs in the Wake of 9/11

Promoting corporate bailouts while ignoring direct help for workers has been Bush's policy from day one of his administration. When a financial package for airlines was passed after the September 11th attacks, none of the $15 billion in money went to help the workers laid off by the airlines.[1] Worse, both before and after the attacks, the administration intervened to block strikes at Northwest, Delta and United Airlines to prevent workers from demanding fair treatment by the airlines.[2]

It was bad enough that Bush's initial bailout of the airlines did nothing to help laid-off workers. But the Bush administration used conditions on those loans to push attacks on union wages of surviving workers in the airline industry. As early as January 2002, it was clear that Bush officials were using the loan guarantees to demand hard-line negotiations against the airline unions. In negotiations with the its maintenance workers and baggage handlers in fall 2002, United demanded a 10% cut in wages, arguing those concessions were a requirement for qualifying for the loan guarantees by the government.[3]

The White House panel entrusted with the power to issue loans to help airlines had rejected any help initially for United because of insufficient "cost savings" (i.e. pay cuts).[4] No deep pay cuts for workers, no loans. Period. This was why United and other airlines careened towards bankruptcy.

And forcing United into bankruptcy was a good model threat used by other airlines looking to put a further squeeze on workers in the airline industry. Rival airline stocks surged on news of United's pending bankruptcy because, as *Reuters* put it, of the "cost savings airlines will be able to achieve by wringing out concessions from employees by wielding the bankruptcy hammer."[5]

Only after the unions at most of the airlines were forced to give wage concessions, either in bankruptcy court or on threat of going there, did the White House then hand over the loan bailouts.[6]

Terrorists hijacked United Flight 175 to destroy the south tower of the World Trade Center and plunge the airline industry into its downward spiral.

But it was the pro-corporate fundamentalists in the White House who decided to make sure the pain would deepen and continue for years for the workers at United and throughout the airline industry.

Lie #2: Bush said Union Rights for Federal Employees were a Threat to Homeland Security

The central lie in the Homeland Security Bill was that the goal was "national security" when the Bush administration extinguished the union rights of 170,000 federal workers transferred into its Department of Homeland Security. Don't believe that this proposal was just a minor rearranging of the deck chairs. It constituted the most fundamental assault on federal employee rights in decades and undermined the independence of judgment that our century-old civil service laws were designed to protect.

Fifty-five% of the 1.8 million-member federal workforce was previously covered by union contracts. Employees in traditional national security duties, including the military, CIA, and FBI, were barred from union membership. But clerical personnel, including 44% of the Defense Department's workers, had all been represented by unions—with no evidence that this had ever undermined national security.[7]

"This proposal appears to be an attempt to punish and blame rank-and-file federal employees for the security lapses that made our nation vulnerable to the September 11 attack," argued Bobby Harnage, president of the American Federation of Government Employees (AFGE) at the time.[8] "In opening the door to hiring and firing on the basis of politics and favoritism, the legislation would impose a modern day 'spoils system,' undermining the nation's long-standing civil service principles that ensure the integrity of our government."[9] And the reality was that undermining such workers rights only further endangered our national security, as the retaliation suffered by whistleblowers trying to expose incompetence in non-union agencies like the FBI has highlighted.

And make no mistake; the proposal was part of a well-planned ideological assault on federal workers. Michael Franc, an analyst at the conservative Heritage Foundation think tank, stated publicly that the Homeland Security proposal was "*the* conservative agenda" for the 2002 legislative year.[10] In his view, using the legislation to undermine unions, eliminate race and gender hiring goals, and end prevailing wage rules was a way to mobilize conservative voters. And since Franc's old boss, Dick Armey, was named chairman of the committee overseeing the process of creating the agency, the conservatives had a strong representative to push through their anti-union agenda.[11]

There was plenty of warning of this anti-union goal by the Bush Administration. On January 7, 2002, Bush signed Executive Order 13252[12] which removed 1000 Justice Department lawyers from union jurisdiction on "national security" grounds, including those in the U.S. Attorney's offices, the Criminal Division, the U.S. Central Bureau of Interpol, the National Drug Intelligence Center and the Office of Intelligence Policy and Review.[13] And the order came the day of a Miami hearing by the Federal Labor Relations Authority to review a petition by DOJ employees requesting union representation. As a letter by lawmakers protesting the executive order noted, "To an outside and objective observer, this timing appears to be more than coincidental."[14]

Similarly, the legislation federalizing airport screeners across the country exempted those employees from automatic union and civil service protections.[15] Under the old private system, the Service Employees International Union (SEIU) had organized 2000 screeners—who lost collective bargaining rights with the new law.[16] "What the administration will have done is take advantage of this law to disenfranchise people who previously had the right to unionize," commented AFGE's Beth Moten.[17]

Ironically, on the same day in June that the administration announced its proposed Homeland Security Department, Bush signed an order that rescinded the designation of air traffic controllers as "inherently governmental" employees.[18] This opened the doors to privatizing air traffic operations and undermining the air traffic controllers union that has painfully reconstituted itself since its predecessor PATCO union was destroyed by Reagan. This order just shows the anti-union cynicism of the administration, since it's hard to imagine in the wake of 911 anything more relevant to national security than air traffic control

Bush lied that undermining workers rights in the Department of Homeland Security was a necessary tradeoff for greater national security—a false and cynical fig leaf by the administration for union busting it has been promoting since the first day of its administration.

To add obscenity on this lie were GOP candidates' accusations that Senators like Max Cleland, who lost two legs and an arm serving in Vietnam, were being "unpatriotic" because they resisted this demagoguery and sought to block these anti-union provisions.[19]

Lie #3: Bush's Photo-ops at Union Events Disguised his All-out Assault on Workers

Bush has appeared repeatedly at photo-op events with union workers— from announcing tariffs on imported steel as a way to supposedly protect steel jobs to promising oil drilling jobs in the Arctic National Wildlife Refuge (ANWR) to the Teamsters union. Doesn't this mean that Bush's "compassionate conservatism" includes some pro-union component?

Hardly.

Despite all the media fuss over the Teamsters and some building trades support for ANWR drilling, the media largely ignored the opposition to Bush's energy policy by major unions ranging from the Service Employees International Union to the Communication Workers of America.[20] As for steel tariffs, Bush's policy ignored a key demand of the Steelworkers union: guaranteeing the health care and pensions of workers threatened by the bankruptcy of their previous employers.[21]

Bush may be trying to clothe his anti-worker actions by cutting a few deals with union leaders, but even most top Teamster officials weren't buying it within Bush's first year. Chuck Mack, the Teamsters Vice President for the Western Region, has called Bush's labor policy "a nightmare for workers."[22] The AFL-CIO Building Trades Department labeled Bush's policies "nothing short of a declaration of war on construction workers."[23] And these were supposedly the unions closest to the administration.

It's not hard to see why the attacks on Bush are so scathing, since beneath his rhetoric, he has mounted an attack on unions and workers rights on a sweeping scale. Following is just a partial review since his taking office.

In his first days in office, Bush issued four executive orders to directly undermine labor organizing:

- Ending Project Labor Agreements: The first order barred what are known as project labor agreements (PLAs) on all federally funded construction projects, agreements that encourage union contracts and labor peace that have been regularly used since the 1940s.
- Ending Rights When Federal Contractors Change: The second order revoked a rule, designed to reduce turnover in low-wage jobs, which had required federal contractors to rehire displaced workers when the government changed contractors.
- Abolishing Labor-Management Systems: The third order abolished employee participation systems in the federal government that had given employees a voice and led to numerous cost-savings measures benefiting all taxpayers.
- Undermining Union Dues: The fourth required government contractors to post notices highlighting ways for workers to object to union dues, while not requiring the posting of any other workers rights to organize or join unions.[24]

Bush followed these orders with a "review" and termination of a number of Clinton-era pro-worker regulations. These included:

- Killing Ergonomics Regulations: Bush signed off on killing regulations to prevent on-the-job injuries from repetitive motion and other ergonomic problems, instead promoting "voluntary" measures by the very businesses that had contributed millions of dollars to the GOP to kill the regulations.[25]
- Reopening Contracts for Corporate Criminals: The Bush administration repealed "responsible contractor" rules that would have denied billions of dollars in government contracts to chronic corporate violators of our environmental, labor and safety laws.[26] And amidst a series of anti-worker policies, Bush pushed through two especially lethal assaults on working families.
- Burying Unions in Regulatory Paperwork: Even as, post-Enron, the administration fought serious regulation of business, it pushed through massively burdensome financial reporting requirements on unions to bury them in paperwork and allow employers greater knowledge of organizing strategies.[27]
- Undermining Overtime Rules: In new regulations, Bush took away overtime pay from as many as eight million white collar workers, including declaring paralegals, emergency medical technicians, licensed practical nurses, and other groups nominal "professionals" thereby denied the law's protection.[28]

And all of these initiatives were complemented by the appointment of the most anti-union cast of appointees in modern American history.

Lie #4: Bush Said His Pension Tax Breaks Were Designed to Help Average Workers Save for Their Retirement

Forget discussing Bush's income tax cuts—even the worst of the media admit that the wealthy received almost all the benefits, while working families gained little.

But even middle class families thought they were gaining something from the expansion of retirement tax breaks to help them save for retirement.

Wrong.

The first inequality is that tax deductions are worth more to wealthy people in higher tax brackets. Here's the math on a $45,000 yearly contribution to a 401(k)— the maximum that will soon be allowed between employee and employer contributions.

For a millionaire with a marginal tax rate of 40% in state and federal income taxes, that 401K contribution is worth $18,000 in extra cash courtesy of the government.

For working families in the 15% tax bracket, none of them can afford to put $45,000 of their income into a 401(k), so even if they save $5,000 each year—a heroic achievement for most families trying to pay for health care and other mounting costs for their family—the government will reward them with only a $750 cut in taxes versus the $18,000 each year that the government pumps into the wealthy person's pocket. And this inequality just expands exponentially as the money in the 401(k) multiplies tax-free until retirement.

Worse yet, given the complicated taxation rules on retirement income, economic studies by researchers at the Federal Reserve and National Bureau of Economic Research have found that all the tax gains for working families are erased when they retire and most even end up paying *more* taxes than they would have if they never participated. But those same studies show that high-income individuals end up with a significantly higher lifetime after-tax income because of the 401(k) tax breaks.[29] So working and middle class families would do better if they had never been lured into a tax break that, in the end, doesn't benefit them at all.

With Enron's failure, 15,000 employees lost $1.3 billion out of their 401(k) savings; the saving grace is that those employees will still qualify for the guaranteed monthly Social Security check when they retire.[30] (Notably, the 1000 or so unionized Enron employees had their retirement savings protected by their union.[31]) The looting of Enron 401(k) pensions to benefit insider investors just highlights the fundamental lie made by Bush that these tax breaks and schemes like privatizing Social Security would be any gain for working families.

Lie #5: Bush Said His Tax Cuts Would Create Job Growth

There was probably no bigger lie by Bush than that his tax cuts would increase jobs.

In 2001, the Bush Administration promised that its first round of tax cuts would expand the economy and deliver millions of new jobs. Instead, between March 2001, when the recession officially started, and October 2003, as I write, the economy had lost 2.4 million jobs.

Now, Bush and his defenders will blame 911 for all economic problems, but after a few more rounds of tax cuts, it's hard to take that excuse seriously at this point.

And the Administration renewed its pie-in-the-sky lies to sell its 2003 tax cuts. Early in the year, Bush's Council of Economic Advisors promised 306,000 new jobs each month, starting in June 2003, from the new round of tax cuts. Instead, while job hemorrhaging stopped, there were still 995,000 fewer jobs in the economy than had been promised early in the year.[32]

And even these harsh job loss numbers only touch on the severity of the job slump. In the period since 1939, when job numbers were first systematically measured, in no other time have job numbers fallen over a two and a half year period. During Bush's tenure, even as jobs were shrinking by 1.8%, the working age population was growing by 3.4%—leaving 6.9 million people without the jobs they would have had if job growth kept up with expansion of the working population.[33] Even if there is an uptick in job growth in 2004, this will still leave the US with far fewer jobs created than during any other Presidential term in modern history.

Bush can keep backpedaling on his promises, but the fact remains that his economic policies have been a miserable failure and a colossal lie about promised jobs made just to sell his tax cuts.

NOTES

1. Ellyn Ferguson, "GOP maverick looks out for airline workers, taxpayers with aid bill 'no' vote," *Gannett News Service* (October 10, 2001).

2. "Bush takes action to block Northwest strike." *CNN.com.* March 9, 2001; "Bush acts to delay United Airlines strike," *BBC News* (December 20, 2001).

3. Marilyn Adams, Barbara De Lollis, "Feds influence airline finances," *USA Today* (January 14, 2002).

4. Edmund L. Andrews, "Airline Shock Waves: The Overview; U.S. Panel Rejects Plea For Loan Aid By United Airlines," *New York Times* (December 5, 2002).

5. Jon Herskovitz, "Gains Seen for Rivals in United's Bust," *Reuters* (December 5, 2002).

6. Edward Wong, "Market Place; Rivals Are Likely to Imitate American's Stance on Labor," *New York Times* (April 2, 2003).

7. Jim Drinkard, "Unions Say Bush Blocking Them," *USA Today* (June 12, 2002).

8. Dave Boyer, "Democrats call terror bill 'ruse' to fire civil workers," *Washington Times* (June 20, 2002).

9. "AFGE Responds To President's Homeland Security Bil," *AFGE News Release,* June 18, 2002.

10. Karen Masterson, "Bush security initiative could doom other bills," *Houston Chronicle* (June 20, 2002).

11. David Firestone, "Department's Employees May Lose Role In Civil Service." *New York Times* (July 17, 2002).

12. 67 FR 1601, January 11, 2002.

13. Naftali Bendavid, "Unions barred at justice agencies;Bush cites security concerns; labor leaders cry foul," *Chicago Tribune* (January 12, 2002).

14. "Labor relations Lawmakers protest exclusion of unions at Justice," *Federal Human Resources Week* (February 19, 2002).

15. "Unions Decry Bush Stance On Screener Whistleblower Rights," *Aviation Daily,* February 26, 2002.

16. David Bacon. "Screened out: how 'fighting terrorism' became a bludgeon in Bush's assault on labor." *The Nation* (May 12, 2003).

17. Mark Murray. "Holding the Union Cards," *The National Journal* (March 23, 2002).

18. Tanya N. Ballard, "FAA says air traffic control not 'inherently governmental,'" *Government Executive Magazine* (December 19, 2002).

19. "Cleland compares election loss to losing limbs," Associated Press (June 14, 2003).

20. Liz Ruskin, "Unions split on ANWR Drilling: Organized labor cannot agree on whether to support it," *Anchorge Daily News* (November 1, 2001).

21. Christian Millman, "Retirees disappointed but not surprised; Bush offers no health care plan to help former steelworkers," *Morning Call* (Allentown, PA) (March 6, 2002).

22. "Bush's aim clear in ignoring working people," Associated Press (July 22, 2002).

23. Pamela M. Prah, "Bush Executive Orders Will Skewer Unions," *Kiplinger Business Forecasts* (February 12, 2001).

24 *Ibid.*

25. "Bush signs repeal of ergonomic rules into law," *CNN.com* (March 20, 2001).

26. Jason Peckenpaugh. "Bush administration scraps contractor responsibility rule," *GovExec.com* (December 28, 2001).

27. Steven Greenhouse, "Unions See Politics in New Disclosure Rules," *New York Times* (October 5, 2003).

28. Ross Eisenbrey and Jared Bernstein, "Eliminating the right to overtime pay: Department of Labor proposal means lower pay, longer hours for millions of workers," *EPI Briefing Paper,* Economic Policy Institute, June 26, 2003.

29. Laurence J. Kotlikoff, Jagadeesh Gokhale, "Who gets paid to save?" *Working Paper* 0114, Federal Reserve Bank of Cleveland, 2001.

30. Elaine S. Povich. "'Victims Of Enron's Lies'; Emotional testimony at Senate hearing." *Newsday* (February 6, 2002).

31. William Greider, "Crime in the Suites," *The Nation* (January 17, 2002).

32. Economic Policy Institute, *Jobs Watch* (October, 2003).

33. Lee Price with Yulia Fungard, "Understanding the severity of the current labor slump," *EPI Briefing Paper* #146, Economic Policy Institute (November 7, 2003).

The Bush Energy Scheme:
Disempowering America

BY CHERYL SEAL

It seems unlikely that even George W. Bush could expect Congress (dominated by rightwingers though it is) to approve the outrageous demands of his energy scheme. His real objective appears to have been a sham "compromise" giving him exactly what he really wants. Meanwhile, the "secret energy task force," along with periodic legal "show downs" with the GAO and Judicial Watch have created diversions that act as a smokescreen, hiding Bush's maneuvers in other directions and deflecting scrutiny of the litany of lies that make up Bush energy policy.

LIE: "We face a shortage of energy. It is real. It is not the imagination of anybody in my administration. It's a real problem" (George W. Bush, May 17, 2001 in speech at the Energy Center in Nevada, Iowa in wake of California blackouts).
TRUTH: There is no true — or should I say "unengineered" — energy crisis. The Deptarment of Energy's (DOE) own Energy Information Administration data show the US produced and imported more natural gas in 2001 than was consumed. However, to add credence to the "crisis" scenario, Bush has allowed the nation's oil stockpiles to drop to the lowest levels since 1976.

Paul MacAvoy, an economist at the Yale School of Management and author of *The Natural Gas Market: Sixty Years of Regulation and Deregulation*, asserted that the 2001 blackouts were "a condition of artificial scarcity that costs consumers billions of dollars a year."[1] In February 2001, most states were reporting sufficient energy levels, with at least 10 states reporting substantial surpluses. In 2003, the coal industry set an all-time record for coal production: 101.5 million tons in a *single month*. In 2001, ExxonMobil reported a first-quarter profit of $5 billion (more than a 50% increase), while BP Amoco reported a first quarter profit of $4.1 billion.

The so-called "electrical power shortage" is in fact a problem of distribution. The current system is aging and not designed to handle the uneven surges placed on it by the exponentially expanding information technology network.[2] To assert that the solution to the power shortage is drilling more oil and building new coal-fired and nuclear power plants is like saying that if your faucet is plugged up, you should go dig a new well. To mitigate the power crunch, the computer networking systems that create many of the surges should be upgraded using new approaches. Such an initiative would provide plenty of work for the thousands of currently un- or underemployed techies in the U.S.

As to fossil fuel supplies, according to the 19th edition of the *Survey of Energy Resources* by the World Energy Institute, reported in 2001, "conventional commercial fossil fuels, encompassing coal, oil and natural gas, remain in adequate supply, with a substantial resource base."[3] By 2002, OPEC reported a world oil surplus that was expected to continue even with increasing global demand.[4]

LIE: "The only way to become less dependent on foreign sources of crude oil is to explore at home" (George W. Bush, October 3, 2000, Presidential debate). SUPPORTING LIE: "The FreedomCAR and Fuel Initiative will "reverse America's growing dependence on foreign oil by developing the technology needed for commercially viable hydrogen-powered fuels" that will generate no greenhouse gases (George W. Bush, Proclamation May 9, 2003).

TRUTH: When Bush stepped into office, there was data available at the White House showing how energy conservation alone could reduce the need for new power plants to a few hundred at most. One study said this number could be shrunk even further, to 170 new plants.[5] Bush, however, chose to ignore these findings and instead promote unmitigated energy consumption. With just 5% of the Earth's population, the US sucks up 25% of the planet's oil, mostly in the form of gasoline. Yet on taking office, Bush killed the $2 billion fuel economy Partnership for a New Generation of Vehicles (PNGV) program developed by the Clinton/ Gore administration. The PNGV had actually produced prototype 70 mpg autos. Where are those autos now? PNGV was replaced with the FreedomCAR (Cooperative Automotive Research) initiative, a $1.7-billion giveaway to Daimler-Chrysler, General Motors, and Ford. Lucky for them, Bush's "initiative" does not require that any of the companies actually MAKE an alternative vehicle.[6]

Another boondoggle, the Freedom Fuel Initiative, touted as a plan for developing hydrogen technology, does not require the development of any technology. The $1.7 billion put into this scheme will go to "research affordability and cost competitiveness of hydrogen fuel." Meanwhile, Bush's tax plan calls for a handsome reward in the form of a tax credit to people who drive gas-guzzling SUVs—up to $75,000.[7] The Freedom Fuel initiative for developing hydrogen technology, does not require the development of any technology. The $1.7 billion will instead go to "research affordability and cost competitiveness of hydrogen fuel."[8]

LIE: "Our energy plan will speed up progress on conservation where it has slowed and restart it where it has failed" (George W. Bush, Speech, May 17, 2001).
TRUTH: In the 2002 budget for the Energy Department, funding for renewable energy R&D was reduced by 37.2%, while energy conservation funding was cut 22.8%.[9] In contrast, the Clean Coal Technology Initiative got an 800% boost to $150 million, with a whopping $2 billion committed over the next decade.[10] In addition, the 1,300-1,900 new power plants planned by the Bush plan (nearly all will burn coal and natural gas). It hardly seems a move toward cutting energy consumption unless he plans on burning fairy dust. In addition, Bush's Energy Bill S.14 does not call for any regulations or improvements in vehicle fuel-efficiency,[11] even though the average fuel economy of the nation's cars and trucks is now at its worst in 22 years.[12]

One of the most outrageous Bush "alternative energy" schemes calls for solar energy development – but only if it is funded by profits from new oil drilling![13]

LIE: "You bet I want to open up a small part of Alaska [ANWR] because when that field is online, it will produce a million barrels a day. Today we import a million barrels from Saddam Hussein. I would rather that a million come from our own hemisphere, our own country, as opposed from Saddam Hussein" (George W. Bush, from the October 3, 2000, Presidential debate).
TRUTH: The million barrel a day figure represents the absolute peak oil volume ANWR could produce under optimal conditions by 2020, a volume achievable if the operation had gotten under way full tilt by 2001. Studies show that the chances of recovering the amount of oil projected by Bush is just 50%.[14] We will still be importing a minimum of 13-14 million barrels of oil per day in 2020.

What Bush has *never* mentioned is that the cost of extracting oil from ANWR will be roughly $17.00 per barrel – while the international price for oil per barrel in 2020 is predicted to be about $13.00.[15] So what is the real motive? Without any oil actually being recovered from ANWR, the oil barons will make a killing. Between 2000-2001, thanks to "government incentives," profits made just for "oil exploration" by the top 7 oil companies rose in a range of 31% to 192%!

The benefits of exploratory drilling are especially attractive in Alaska, home to Bush buddies Frank Murkowski, Ted Stevens and Tom Wagoner. Senate Bill 185, introduced in 2003, not only offers royalty reductions in parts of Alaska to keep existing oil facilities going as production declines, it gives generous tax credits for exploratory drilling – with the wells furthest from existing facilities (25 miles or more) getting the biggest credit.[16] And this is *in addition* to federal tax credits already in place for exploratory activities. In 1999, $2.6 billion in new oil company tax breaks were granted, including greatly expanded tax breaks for exploration.[17] In 2003, the Energy Tax Incentives Act (S.14) calls for at least *$9.6 billion more* in oil/naturally gas tax breaks and subsidies and lavishes *$12 billion* in price supports and loan guarantees on the Alaska Natural Gas pipeline. S.14 also allows oil and gas companies to immediately deduct geological and geophysical expenditures and avoid taxes, costing American taxpayers over $2.1 billion in 10 years.[18]

Furthermore, the bill allows oil companies drilling on public lands to pay for the royalties owed to taxpayers in barrels of oil — which, of course, the taxpayers will end up paying for![19] This is a modification of the original proposal, which called for eliminating all royalties for public land operations. However, the bill still calls for eliminating royalties on off-shore and deep-water drilling operations – those most likely to cause the most environmental damage. What is worse, the Bush plan builds in a scam that guarantees that the industry will be able to collect the incentives without having to really pump much oil. How? The industry will get a bonus of $300 million simply for making an attempt to extract oil from difficult to reach sites like ANWR. So, a company could get millions just to drill in an out of the way spot, then several million more just for bringing a little oil up, then on top of that, never have to pay royalties on the operation.

LIE: "The president's energy plan [referring to ANWR] will create more than 700,000 good paying American jobs" (Interior Secretary Gale Norton, December 6, 2001, also on November 9, 2001 and June 10, 2002).
TRUTH: This statistic, taken from the 1990 report prepared by WEFA Group for the American Petroleum Institute, has been most often repeated by Gale Norton. Bush has failed to contradict the assertion even once. Even WEFA now says the 700,000 figure is no longer accurate. A study by the Congressional Research Service found that under the most likely scenario, full development of ANWR could cost $6.5 billion and possibly generate 60,000 jobs. Independent economist Dean Baker says other studies indicate the number of jobs would be 50,000 at best — over a 10-year period! Even a 1992 study commissioned by the Bush I Energy Department and performed by a corporate-friendly consulting firm (DRI-McGraw Hill) could only come up with a maximum of

222,480 jobs from ANWR drilling.[20]

In any case, if Bush II really wanted to make the US less dependent on foreign oil *and* create new jobs, he would immediately increase fuel economy standards. A Union of Concerned Scientists study concludes that by increasing fuel economy to 55 miles per gallon, the US would save $28 billion per year in fuel costs, while creating 100,000 new auto industry jobs by 2020.

LIE: To meet the nation's power needs, "1,300-1,900 new power generation plants must be built in the next 20 years" (Statement made by Dick Cheney at the annual meeting of the Associated Press in Toronto on April 30, 2001).[21]

TRUTH: There is no need for 1,300 (let alone 1,900) new plants — not now, not in the foreseeable future. Even Bush's own Energy Department thinks the figure is inflated. The 2000 DOE study *Scenarios for a Clean Energy Future* shows that energy efficiency measures could avoid the need for building approximately 610 of the new power plants Cheney calls for, and that renewable power capacity (wind, geothermal, biomass and others) could expand by the equivalent of about 180 plants.[22] Cheney simply ignored the study.[23] Another study says that with relatively moderate conservation and energy efficiency measures put into place over the next several years, only 170 new plants would need to be constructued.[24]

LIE: "The Administration supports the expansion of nuclear energy in the United States as a major component of our national energy policy. Nuclear energy emits virtually no air pollutants or greenhouse gases, and advanced nuclear technologies offer the potential of efficient, safe, and proliferation-resistant reactor designs" (Bush energy czar Spencer Abraham, September 11, 2003).

TRUTH: Nuclear Plants have never been less safe than they are right now, and are likely to become more vulnerable to "proliferation" in the future:

> 1. A high percentage of existing nuclear plants in the US, build three decades ago, are now deteriorating. But because the plants are now almost paid for, the nuke barons see a huge profit in keeping old plants on line by relicensing. Relicensing is supposed to be a rigorous process that often requires a complete plant overhaul. But under Bush, relicensing is a rush-job sham. Proof is not even required that the repairs prescribed by inspectors have first been made. Yet, according to the Federal Register notice, when the process is honest, relicensing is expected to be responsible for the release of 14,800 person-rem of radiation and the deaths of 12 people during its 20-year life extension.[25]

2. High-level nuclear wastes are, under Bush, becoming a national security risk. The only safe way to store these extraordinarily dangerous materials is in special "dry casks" of steel, lead and cement, which must then be buried in a geologically stable area. Yet in September 2003, the DOE proposed reclassifying high-level wastes as "incidental to processing," so they could be handled more cheaply, and even reprocessed.[26] Japan and France stopped reprocessing any nuclear wastes because of the extreme hazard it posed. Former British nuclear weapons specialist Dr Frank Barnaby of the Oxford Research Group stated in May 2000, that nuclear reprocessing operations would "make it virtually inevitable that terrorists will acquire the plutonium they want from the fuel, and make nuclear weapons with it." In fact, says Barnaby, once the material was obtained, it would not be difficult for a clever terrorist to make a dirty bomb: "A second-year graduate" could do it.[27]

3. Since 9/11, most nuclear plants remain unguarded. It was not until the second week of February 2002, that the White House issued a press release stating it would "soon" order the nation's 103 nuclear power plants to improve security. The Nuclear Energy Information Service revealed in October, 2001 that, under Bush, the Nuclear Regulatory Commission (NRC) "has been experimenting" with a plan to allow the nuclear industry to police itself on reactor security from terrorist assaults. This plan comes after a decade-long series of tests of security at U.S. reactors revealed that over 50% of those reactors "could not resist a determined land-based intruder." Under Clinton, the DOE asked to move TA-18, a facility at Los Alamos containing several burst reactors and tons of weapons-grade uranium and plutonium to a safer location. In September 2001, Bush denied the request.[28]

The Bush energy plan calls for the industry to generate 50,000 more megawatts of power by 2020. To achieve this will require $1.3 billion for research, development and deployment. The plan also calls for the use of federal lands for new plants and for taxpayers to pay for 50% of the cost of establishing new reactors during all the initial stages of development. It will also require the taxpayer to eat $590 billion of the predicted cost of a nuclear accident, while the industry's own liability is capped at $10 billion. And of course, none of this figures in the cost of storing nuclear wastes—a cost, both economically and in risk, that will be born largely by "recipient states" such as Nevada.[29]

LIE: "We will promote renewable energy production and clean coal technology" (George W. Bush, Clear Skies Initiative speech, February 14, 2002).[30]

TRUTH: There is no such thing as clean coal. Not now, not ever, and especially not under G. W. Bush! His Clear Skies Initiative allows the nation's filthiest, oldest coal-fired power plants to remain up and running indefinitely.

These killer plants release more toxic chemical air pollution than the chemical, paper, plastics, and refining industries combined. Each year coal- and oil-fired power plants release nearly nine million pounds of toxic metals and metal compounds — many of them known or suspected carcinogens or neurotoxins. These plants release 27 to 54 times more acid gases than the chemical plants that manufacture acid gases commercially! There are at least 300 of these plants, detrimentally affecting several million people and millions of square miles of the American landscape. A high percentage are sited in nonwhite and/or poor neighborhoods, where asthma and respiratory syndrome deaths are up to three times higher than other areas beyond the plant's sphere of influence.

In general, coal-fired power plants are the largest source of SO_2 (66%), second only to automobiles in nitrogen oxides pollutions, the nation's single largest source of mercury contamination, and the single largest source of CO_2 emissions. They emit 80% of all the acid-raining causing pollutants. The fine particulate matter emitted by coal-fired plants has been conclusively linked a list of health problems, including rising childhood asthma rates.

On top of that, coal plants run — and pollute — between 90-95% of the time compared to gas-fired combined-cycle plants that run 50-60% of the time. Coal plants aredifficult t o get sited, are far more capital intensive and take about twice as long to site as those fired by natural gas.[31]

GAO audits (7 of them, in fact) have found that Bush's pet project, the Clean Coal Technology Program, is most mismanaged of all energy subsidy programs, showing the least results for the millions spent in federal cash. "CCTP may not be the most effective use of federal funds," one GAO report warned, while another stated, "Emerging clean coal technologies will probably not contribute significantly to the reduction of acid rain causing emissions during the next 15 years." The DOE's own evaluations have shown that new "clean coal" technologies were 40% less effective in removing sulfur dioxide emissions than conventional smokestack "scrubbers." Yet Bush plans to lavish $2 billion on the CCTP over the next 10 years, and to site a record number of coal-burning power plants — all while cutting funding from conservation and renewables programs. [32]

The entire amount Bush is spending on R&D in conservation and renewable development is roughly equal to what the Progress Coal company made just in tax breaks for spraying coal with pine resin or diesel and calling it "synthetic fuel" (synfuel) in the past 7 years, and less than what Progress will make from its synfuel scam in the next five thanks to the Bush IRS's October 29,2003 ruling in favor of the scam.[33]

Outrageously, coal barons routinely make more money off the synfuel credit than the coal itself. Credits are $26 a ton while the cost of a ton of Central Appalachian coal is just $21.50 and $24 a ton. The coal barons have more tax credit dollars than they can use, in fact and have created a new sub-scam: trading in credits. About half of all synfuel credits and for sale. All this high-return wheeling and dealing financed, of course, by the taxpayer.[34]

So did the Bush administration follow through with the investigation and pull the plug? Hardly. In March 2001, just a few weeks before announcing his fossil fuel-bloated energy plan, Bush ordered the Treasury to allow the scam to proceed with just one token alteration: the coal has to be crunched down to 3/8" pieces before being sprayed with crap. On October 29, 2003, the Bush IRS announced its final ruling: That spraying coal down with whatever comes to hand is "scientifically valid." So, instead of rescuing taxpayers from an inconscionable rip-off, Bush has endorsed and accelerated the scam. PR&C/RDI projects that production of coal-based synfuel will more than double between 2001 and 2004.[35]

LIE: Bush promised to reduce CO_2 emissions through "mandatory reduction targets" (Statements made George W. Bush on September 29, 2000, in a Saginaw Michigan speech).
TRUTH: Coal burning accounts for most CO_2 put into the atmosphere. Yet Bush ditched any plan to reduce CO_2 — the greenhouse gas that drives global warming. In his final energy report, released on May 16, 2001, he called for increased coal production and for hundreds of new coal-fired power plants. Irl Engelhardt, chairman of Peabody Coal, the world's largest coal producer, served as an energy advisor on the Bush transition team. On May 21, 2001, in the midst of rolling blackouts (which were used by the Bush administration as a hard sell for the construction of the new coal-fired power plants), Peabody issued a public stock offering, raising $60 million more than expected.[36] The same day, Peabody execs threw a $25,000 party for Bush.[37] Shortly thereafter, existing clean air standards for power plant emissions, notably for CO_2,

were rolled back. Bush also sought to loosen the standards for arsenic in drinking water because Engelhardt had lobbied for the changes (arsenic is a byproduct of coal mining operations).

LIE: Government regulations are costly, unnecessary and slow innovation. Allowing industries to self-regulate will save money and speed pollution reduction. Summary of statements made in dozens of speeches and statements including the Clear Skies Initiative speech, during which Bush made this statement: "The Clean Air Act " led to confusing, ineffective maze of regulations for power plants."
TRUTH: Several studies clearly demonstrate that without regulations, corporations cost taxpayers more money, while doing do less to curb pollution. The White House Office of Management and Budget study found that air pollution regulations saved between $120 billion and $193 billion from October 1992 to September 2002 in sick days, health care costs and premature deaths.[38]

A University of California at Berkeley study shows that regulations spur change far more efficiently than any other incentives.[39] Even when the technology is available, corporations won't use it unless forced to. A prime example: Today, 30 years after the dangers of SO_2 and acid rain were made widely known, still, only one in three US power plants is fitted with a scrubber system that extracts SO_2 from flue gases.

An exhaustive study of the US electrical utility industry released in June 2002 by Inovest found a strong correlation between profits and environmental performance. Contrary to the Bush model, companies that invested most in anti-pollution technologies and strategies performed financially, on average, 30% better. The reason? Inovest says the correlation is mindset, not money: the more conscientious plant owners are environmentally, the more conscientious they are across the board. The less conscientious they are environmentally, the less conscientious they are in everything else.[40] Meanwhile, the "freemarket solutions" Bush is basing most of his fossil fuel pollution reductions on have proven time after time *not* to work, despite corporate reports to the contrary.[41]

NOTES

1. Charles Levendosky, "National Energy Report: A Fossil Farce Based on a Hoax." *Casper Star Tribune* (May 20, 2001) at <www.equalitystate.org/ESPC %20Website-%20Generic%20Pages/Opinion%20articles/o20may-2001cst.html>.

2. Editorial, "Roundtable: Future of Electricity," *CIO Insight* (July 1, 2001) at <www.cioinsight.com/article2/0,3959,48965,00.asp>.

3. Keiichi Yokobori, "Survey of Energy Resources," World Energy Council (2001) at <www.worldenergy.org/wec-geis/publications/reports/ser/over-view.asp>.

4. Editors, "Increasing World Demand for Oil." ArabicNews.com (May 6, 2002) at <www.arabicnews.com/ansub/Daily/Day/020506/2002050623.html>.

5. Editors, "How Energy Efficiency Can Turn 1,300 Power Plants into 170," Alliance to Save Energy (May 2, 2001) at <www.ase.org/media/factsheets/facts1300.htm>.

6. Jerry Taylor and Dan Becker, "Stop that Energy Bill!" Cato Institute (November 3, 2003) at <www.cato.org/dailys/11-03-03-2.html>.

7. Jeff Plungis, "SUV tax break may reach $75,000, Environmentalists bash Bush plan" Detroit News, January 20, 2003.

8. Editors, "New House Energy Bill Represents GOP Corporate Welfare." *The Left Coaster* (April 12, 2003) at <www.theleftcoaster.com/archives/000155.html>.

9. Bette Hileman, "Bush Addresses Climate Change," *Chemical & Engineering News* Vol. 79, Number 25 (June 18, 2001) at <www.pubs.acs.org/cen/topstory/7925/print/7925notw1.html>. See also *Chemical & Engineering News* (April 23, 2001), p. 39.

10. Editors, "Sustainable Energy Coalition's Energy Task Force Scorecard." Sustainable Energy Coalition (2003) at <www.sustainableenergy.org/bush_report/scorecard.PDF>.

11. Unattributed, "Fact Sheet on S.-14: The Energy Policy Act of 2003." Nuclear Energy Information Service (2003) at <www.neis.org/alerts/S_14.pdf>.

12. Unattributed, "US Auto Fuel Efficiency at 22-Year Low." *New York Times* (May 5, 2003) at <www.ecology.com/ecology-news-links/2003/articles/5-2003/5-5-03/fuel-efficiency.htm>.

13. Marc Sandalow and Zachary Coile, "Bush Ties Solar Power to Drilling." *San Francisco Chronicle* (March 1, 2001) at <www.mindfully.org/Energy/Solar-Power-Drilling-Tied.htm>.

14. Columbia University had a website devoted to ANWR that was stuffed with facts, figures, charts, statistics, and every possible piece of information — geological, economic, and ecological — you might need to refute the Bush position on ANWR. I used the site often, and in late 2003, cited it as a source in an article on Bush's disastrous energy scheme that ran in *News Insider* and was reposted widely. Sometime between January 2004 and March 2004, the website was expunged from the Internet, not just from Columbia University, but from Google.

James J. MacKenzie, "Potential oil production in the Arctic National Wildlife Refuge." Press release, World Resource Institute (February 15, 2001) at <www.pubs.wri.org/pubs_content_text.cfm?ContentID=1219>.

15. Marcus K. Garner, "Governor signs exploration tax credit, royalty reduction bills," *Alaska Oil & Gas Reporter* (June 24, 2003) at <www.oilandgas reporter.com/stories/062403/ind_20030624007.shtml>.

16. Tim Bradner, "Governor Proposes Exploration Tax Credit." *Alaska Oil & Gas Reporter: IndustryNews"(May 20, 2003) at <www.oilandgasreporter.com/stories/052003/ind_20030520002.shtml>.

17. Unattributed, "Fact Sheet on S.-14: The Energy Policy Act of 2003 at <www.neis.org/alerts/S_14.pdf>.

18. J. D. Wallace, "New Drilling Incentives for Marginal Fields." Alaska State Legislature's Majority [GOP] Organization (May 22, 2003) at www. akrepublicans.org/kohring/23/news/kohr20030522o1p.php>.

19. See Alaska State Legislature GOP website at <www.ak republicans.org/kohring/23/news/kohr20030522o1p.php>.

20. H. Josef Hebert, "ANWR: How many jobs will it produce?" JuneauEmpire.com (March 12, 2002) at <www.juneauempire.com/stories/031202/sta_anwr.shtml<; M. W. Guzy, "The Great Alaskan Snow Job." TomPaine.com (March 13, 2002) at <www.tompaine.com/feature.cfm/ID/5250>; and Steve Sutherlin, "New jobs from ANWR Drilling: a 700,000 Bonanza or Less than One-tenth that Many?"*Petroleum News* (March 24, 2002) at <www. petroleumnews.com/pnarch/020324-14.html>.

21. Carter M. Yang, "VP Warns of Energy Crisis, Previews Changes." ABC News (April 30, 2001) at <www.abcnews.go.com/sections/us/DailyNews/Energy_Cheneyo>.

22. Interlaboratory Working Group on Energy-Efficient and Clean-Energy Technologies, "Scenarios for a Clean Energy Future." Office of Energy Efficiency and Renewable Energy U. S. Department of Energy (2001) at <www.ornl.gov/sci/eere/cef/>.

23. Natural Resource Defense Council, "The Myth of 1,300 Power Plants." *Environmental Media Services* (May 8, 2001) at <www.ems.org/energy_policy/new_power_plants.html>.

24. Editors, "How Energy Efficiency Can Turn 1,300 Power Plants into 170." Alliance to Save Energy (May 2, 2001) at <www.ase.org/media/factsheets/facts1300.htm>.

25. Nuclear Information and Resource Service, "1,200 Could Die Under Bush Relicensing Plan" (July 31, 2001) at <www.mothersalert.org/relicensing.html>.

26. Frank Barnaby, "Response to the Terrorist Attack on the USA, September 11th, 2001." *Scientists for Global Responsibility* (September 22, 2001) at <www.socialismtoday.org/61/nuclear.html> and Editors, "Nuclear Sites a Disgrace." e4engineering.com (June 2, 2003) at <www.e4engineering.com/item.asp?id=48916&pub=&type=Analysis>.

27. Ibid.

28. Editors, "Here Today, There Tomorrow: Commercial Nuclear Reactor Sites are Terrorist Targets." Nuclear Energy Information Services Report (Oct 22, 2001) at <www.neis.org/literature/Reports&Testimonies/full_terrorist_ report_10-22-01.htm>; Jeffrey T. Richelson, "Defusing nuclear terror," *Bulletin of the Atomic Scientists* (March/April 2002) at <www.thebulletin.org/issues/2002/ ma02/ma02richelson.html>; Daniel Hirsch, "What, me worry?" *Bulletin of the Atomic Scientists* (Jan/Feb 2002) at <www.thebulletin.org/issues/2002/jf02/ jf02hirsch.html>; Robert Alvarez, "What About the Spent Fuel Rods?" *Bulletin of the Atomic Scientists* (Jan/Feb 2002) at <www.thebulletin.org/issues/2002/jf02/ jf02alvarez.html>; Danielle Brian, Lynn Eisenman & Peter D. H. Stockton, "The Weapons Complex: Who's Guarding the Store?" *Bulletin of the Atomic Scientists* (Jan/Feb 2002) at <www.thebulletin.org/issues/2002/jf02/jf02brian.html>, (AUTHOR) "Stop the Energy Bill! Section: Nuclear Power and Waste" at <www.energyjustice.net/energybill/>.

29. Danielle Brian, Lynn Eisenman & Peter D. H. Stockton, "The Weapons Complex: Who's Guarding the Store?" *Bulletin of the Atomic Scientists* (January/ February 2002) at <www.thebulletin.org/issues/2002/jf02/jf02brian.html" http:// www.thebulletin.org/issues/2002/jf02/jf02brian.html>.

30. George W. Bush, "Clear Skies Speech" at <www.whitehouse.gov/news/ releases/2002/02/20020214-5.html>; Curtis Moore, "Dying Needlessly: sickness and death due to energy-related air pollution" (SOURCE, DATE) at <www.solstice.crest. org/repp_pubs/articles/issuebr6.html>; Dave Aftandilian, "Dirty coal in Illinois," *Conscious Choice* (February 2001) at <www.consciouschoice.com/note/note1402.html>; David Morgan, "Bush vs the Clean Air Act," *Environmental Defense* (April 3, 2003) at <www.environmentaldefense.org/ article.cfm? ContentID=2727>; Conrad Schneider, *Death, Disease and Dirty Power: Clean Air Task Force Report* (October 2000) at <www.catf.us/publications/ reports/death_disease_ dirty_power.php>; C. Arden Pope III; Richard T. Burnett; Michael J. Thun; Eugenia E. Calle; Daniel Krewski; Kazuhiko Ito; and George D. Thurston, "Lung Cancer, Cardiopulmonary Mortality, and Long-term Exposure to Fine Particulate Air Pollution," *Journal of the American Medical Association* (March 6, 2002) at <www.jama.ama-assn.org/cgi/content/abstract/287/9/ 1132>; Committee on Estimating the Health-Risk-Reduction Benefits of Proposed Air Pollution Regulations Board on Environmental Studies and Toxicology, *Estimating the Public Health Benefits of Proposed Air Pollution Regulations* (Washington, DC: National Academies Press, 2002) at<www.nap.edu/books/ 0309086094/html; and Black Leadership Forum, *Air of Injustice: African Americans and Power Plant Pollution*, at <www.blackleadershipforum.org/articles/ air_injustice.html>.

32. Katherine Abend, "Testimony of PIRG Representative before House Subcommittee of the House Science Committee on Clean Coal Technology Initiative" (June 12, 2001) at <www.house.gov/science/energy/jun12/abend.htm>.

33. Ibid.

34. Donald L. Barlett and James B. Steele, "The Great Energy Scam: How a plan to cut oil imports turned into a corporate giveaway" *TIME* (October 4, 2003).

35. Associated Press, "IRS Plans Resumption of Coal Tax [Synfuel] Credit (October 29, 2003).

36. Judy Pasternak, "Bush's Energy Plan Bares Industry Clout," *Los Angeles Times* (August 26, 2001).

37. Michael Weisskopf and Adam Zagorin, "Getting the Ear Of Dick Cheney," *TIME OnLine* (February 3, 2002) at <www.time.com/time/nation/article/0,8599,198862,00.html>.

38. Eric Pianin, "White House study says environmental rules well worth their cost,"*Washington Post* (September 27, 2003); Reece Rushing, "When Facts Don't Matter" Tom Paine.commonsense (October 21, 2003) at <www.tompaine.com/feature.cfm/ID/9193>; Lisa Heinzerling, "Too Little, Too Late: The Bush Administration Discovers the Importance of Clean Air" at <www.progressive regulation.org/articles/OMB_CB_Report.pdf>.

39. Phillip Ball, "Scientific solutions are spurred by government regulation." *Nature Magazine* (September 17, 2003) at <www.nature.com/nsu/030915/030915-4.html.

40. Innovest Strategic Value Advisors, *The US Electric Utility Industry: Uncovering Hidden Value Potential for Strategic Investors* (New York: Innovest Group, June 2002) at <www.ahcgroup.com/pdfs/US%20Elec%20Util%20Report%206-02%20Excerpt.PDF>.

41. Curtis A. Moore, "Marketing Failure: The Experience with Air Pollution Trading in the United States," Clean Air Trust.org (2002; updated 2003) at <www.cleanairtrust.org/pdf/introandfindings.pdf>.

The Environmental Fire Sale

By Ernest Partridge

If there is a unifying theme to Bush's environmental policy, it is this: "What my corporate sponsors want, my corporate sponsors get." And in fact, it is difficult to find a single environmental proposal, executive order, or draft legislation from Bush's White House that deviates from the wish list of his corporate contributors. "Every administration rewards its friends," wrote *Vanity Fair*, "but never has there been a wholesale giveaway of government agencies to the very industries they're meant to oversee."

This sellout is painfully apparent as we enumerate the array of foxes that the Bush Administration has appointed to guard the environmental henhouse:

- Gale Norton, Secretary of the Interior. (Lobbyist, mining industry).
- James Connaughton, Chairman of the President's Council on Environmental Quality. (Lawyer representing asbestos and toxic polluters).
- Stephen Griles, Deputy Administrator of the EPA. (Lobbyist for mining and energy industry).
- Jeffrey Holmstead, Director of the Air Division of the EPA. (Lawyer for utility industry).
- Mark Rey, Undersecretary for Natural Resources and Environment, Dept. of Agriculture (Twenty years employment with various timber trade associations).
- Mike Leavitt, Bush's EPA Administrator, is noteworthy for his struggles, as Governor of Utah, with the very agency he is now leading. Leavitt has championed deregulation and has resisted enforcement of clean air standards against Utah industries.

And presumably in appreciation of his government "service" to industry, in September, John Pemberton, formerly the chief of staff of the EPA's air and radiation office, joined Southern Co., a power utility with the second worst pollution record in the nation.

Because of this allegiance to the interests of his sponsors, Bush's environmental policies diverge radically from the interests and preferences of the general public. This immediately raises a huge problem for the Bush Administration; namely, how to sugar-coat this bitter pill of environmental sell-out so that the public will swallow it.

From the Bush Administration's encounter with this problem follows its deceptions, evasions and lies regarding the environment.

The most formidable roadblock in the Bushevik sell-out of the environment is, *science.* for it is the scientists who first brought the environmental crisis to public attention and continue to validate its urgency today. Evading the challenge of scientifically confirmed facts requires all the virtuoso skills in sophistry and public relations in use by the Bushista apologists.

"Epistemology" is the philosopher's high-fallutin' word for "theory of knowledge." While scientists and philosophers delve deeply into this issue, in fact everybody has an epistemology, albeit the theory of knowledge of the vast majority of human beings is unconscious, implicit and primitive.

Ask anybody, "why do you believe such-and-such to be true," and you will discover their epistemology—most often, some kind of conventionalism or authoritarianism: e.g., "why?—because everybody believes that!," or "I heard it on FOX," or "'cause the Bible tells me so," and so on.

Similarly, George Bush, who evidently hasn't entertained a philosophical thought since his student days at Yale (if then), betrays his epistemology and his metaphysics in his policies and public pronouncements in general, and in particular in his attitude toward science.

With regard to the natural environment, Bush displays a kind of "subjectivism gone mad."—an unwavering faith in the "feeling" of his fabled "gut." According to the Bushevik subjective metaphysic, the physical world is also just what he (or his corporate sponsors) want it to be: scientific expertise and proof be damned. Bush's thought-world is uncomplicated and free of unintended consequences. This world need not be studied in order to be understood—the opinions of "experts" are of no interest to Bush. Rather, the state of the world is best apprehended by "gut feeling."

In short: "If I don't want to believe what the scientists tell me, then it ain't so."

Of course, this confounds and enrages the scientists. But because relatively few voters are aware of or concerned with what the scientists think, and because scientists tend to be apolitical, this attitude is of little political consequence to the Bushistas.

Even so, the general public is concerned with the condition of their natural environment—the climate, the air, the water, fellow species, natural ecosystems, wild places, etc. So Bush's essential task remains that of appearing "environmentally friendly" to the public, all the while he is giving the environmental store away to his corporate friends.

To accomplish this, of course, he must lie. And so he does.

LIE #1: Global Warming Has Not Been Proven and Needs Further Study.

When Al Gore brought up the issue of global warming in the 2000 presidential debates, Bush's immediate response was that there is still a great deal of scientific dispute about the causes of and appropriate responses to climate change. As further scientific evidence has accumulated, it has been met with an unvarying litany of "not proven" and "more study needed," reminiscent of the decades of denial from the tobacco industry.

Eventually, the tobacco industry caved in under the weight of scientific evidence. The Bushista response to the challenge of climate science has been to ignore it and to hope that no one will notice.

Not proven? Consider the evidence.

In January, 2001, the Intergovernmental Panel on Climate Change, a United Nations consortium of more than two thousand scientists, published its third report. The IPCC report concluded, with 90% confidence, that by 2100, average global temperatures will rise between 2.3 and 9 degrees Fahrenheit. Commenting on this report, seventeen of the world's scientific academies stated:

The work of the IGCC represents the consensus of the international scientific community on climate change science. We recognize the IPCC as the world's most reliable source of information on climate change and its causes, and we endorse its method of achieving this consensus... The balance of the scientific evidence demands effective steps now to avert damaging changes to Earth's climate. (*Science,* May 18, 2001)

Responding to the IPCC report, Donald Kennedy, editor of *Science* (the journal of the American Association for the Advancement of Science) wrote: "[Scientific] consensus as strong as the one that has developed around this topic [of global warming] is rare in science... [T]here is little room for doubt about the seriousness of the problem the world faces. . ." (*Science,* March 30, 2001). Not content with the findings of the IPCC, Bush asked the National Academy of Sciences to prepare a report which "summed up science's current understanding of global climate change." That report confirmed that "the conclusion of the IPCC that the global warming that has occurred in the last 50 years is likely the result of increases in greenhouse gases accurately reflects the current thinking of the scientific community" (National Academy of Sciences, June 6, 2001).

Bush's response was to "shoot the messenger." Specifically, the Bush Administration proceeded, at the behest of his Exxon-Mobil sponsors, to orchestrate the ouster of the IPCC Chair, Robert Watson, and replacing this eminent atmospheric scientists with an Indian economist, Rejandra Pachauri.

More denial was to follow.

For the annual EPA report of 2003, the EPA staff prepared an accurate account of scientific consensus on global warming. The White House returned a demand that key sections of the account be deleted, and other parts be revised to convey a sense of uncertainty not shared by the scientists. In an internal memo, the EPA warned that the White House revision "no longer accurately represents scientific consensus on climate change." The end result was that the entire section on global warming was cut from the report.

The IPCC chair ousted, the EPA report on global warming deleted, perpetual calls for "further study"—all this has had no effect whatever on the physical and chemical laws that apply to the earth's climate.

And so, the atmosphere continues to heat up.

As the industrial nations struggle to deal cooperatively with the urgent global problem of climate change, the government of George Bush has opted out—to the exasperation and consternation of scientists throughout the world. And yet, in June, 2001, Bush declared "My administration is committed to a leadership role in the issue of climate change."

In light of the events and pronouncements that were to follow, this was a bald-face lie.

LIE #2: The "Clear Skies Initiative" Will Reduce Air Pollution.

Bush's "Clear Skies Initiative" display's the Administration's flair for doublespeak. (See "Healthy Forests," below.) And how will this "initiative" improve our air quality? Through the kindness of industrial polluters—i.e., through "voluntary compliance," the same sort of "honor system" that gave Texas the worst air quality in the nation.

In fact, "Clear Skies" is a transparent hoax. When the Bush administration took office, the so-called "New Source Review" (NSR) was in place, requiring that plants that install new equipment or significantly increase their emissions must, install modern pollution control devices. Bush's "improvements" significantly weaken NSRs, allowing old "grandfathered" plants to continue to pollute, unabated. Of this decision, John Walke of the Natural Resources Defense Council said, "the Bush administration decided to allow corporate polluters to spew even more toxic chemicals into our air, regardless of the fact that it will harm millions of Americans . . . Under this administration, the cop is not only off the beat, the EPA is proposing to legalize harmful pollution that today is illegal" (NRDC, November 22, 2002).

In a September 15, 2003 visit to the Detroit Edison power plant in Monroe, Michigan, Bush praised the operators of the facility as "good stewards of the quality of the air." In fact, the plant is the eighth largest emitter of sulfur dioxide in the United States (over 100,000 tons). With the relaxation of the "new source reviews," the Monroe plant will be permitted to continue to dump out its nasties into the common air, in increasing amounts, far into the future.

The man has no shame.

Lie #3: The Air was Safe in Downtown Manhattan Immediately after 9/11.

Soon after the 9/11 attacks on the World Trade Center, the EPA professionals dutifully prepared a report warning the New Yorkers of the health dangers posed by the dust and airborne particles generated by the collapse of the buildings.

A not-so-funny thing happened to the report on its way to New York: it was intercepted by Bush's White House and "sanitized," as cautionary statements fell out and were replaced by unfounded reassurances. Consequently, as the EPA Inspector General belatedly revealed to the consternation of the Busheviks, the New Yorkers were not fairly warned of the hazards they faced.

For example, a week after the attacks, EPA Administrator, Christy Whitman, announced that the air in lower Manhattan was "safe" to breathe. In fact, there was no scientific basis for this reassurance since, at the time, the labs were still at work testing for toxics and had not released its findings.

In the original, pre-White-House draft, the EPA stated that "even at low levels, EPA considers asbestos hazardous in this situation."

The "improvement" by Bush's Council on Environmental Quality (headed by an ex-asbestos industry attorney) stated: "Short-term, low-level exposure [to asbestos] of the type that might have been produced by the collapse of the World Trade Center buildings is unlikely to cause significant health effects" (*New York Daily News*, August 26, 2003).

As a result of these false reassurances, the Wall Street securities industry was up and running again at the earliest opportunity.

First things first.

Lie #4: "Significant Progress in Protecting Water Resources."

Shortly before she left the EPA, Christy Whitman issued a report that stated: "pristine waterways [and] safe drinking waters are treasured re-sources... The nation has made significant progress in protecting these resources in the last 30 years" (Osha Gray DavidsonDavidson, "Dirty Se-crets," *Mother Jones*, September/October 2003).

This is an example of what I call a "grey lie:" a literal truth intended to convey a falsehood. (Example: "I did not have sex with that woman." Clinton meant intercourse, and thus was plausibly telling the truth. But that's not at all he wanted us to believe by the remark).

Whitman's report was quite true: "...in the last 30 years." And that is a great tribute to Bush's predecessors. She did not elaborate on what has happened to the nation's water supply and wetlands in the last two years, or what we are to expect in the future. In fact, the Bush administration is proposing to remove 20% of the nation's wetlands from federal protec-tion. And the aforementioned easing of air pollution standards, with the resulting increase in sulfur dioxide emissions, can only reverse the recent reductions in acid deposition in the northeastern states and the eastern Canadian provinces.

Lie: #5: Oil Development Will Not Harm the Arctic National Wildlife Refuge.

In the Spring of 2002, the US Geological Survey submitted the results of a twelve year study which concluded that oil exploration in ANWR would adversely affect the habitat of the wildlife of the region. True to the Bushistic spirit of "don't come to me unless you have the 'facts' I want," Interior Secretary Gail Norton ordered a reassessment and, sure enough, in just a week got the desired result: arctic wildlife just will love oil rigs (*Seattle Post Intelligencer*, March 30, 2002).

Lie #6: Bush will protect our forests with his "Healthy Forests" Initiative."

When given the chance this year to match words with deeds, Bush failed miserably and spectacularly.

On April 16, 2003, Gov. Gray Davis of California sent a letter to George Bush requesting $430 million to remove dead and diseased trees from 415,000 acres of southern California forests. Forestry experts and the California congressional delegation, recognizing a potential catas-trophe, begged prompt action from the White House. On October 24, they received their reply: the request was denied (*San Francisco Chronicle*, October 30, 2003).

The very next day, the "Old Fire" north of San Bernardino broke out—then a dozen more, claiming twenty lives, 3,500 homes, 750,000 acres, and costing more than $2 billion dollars.

As the Southern California forests burned, some Bush defenders were heard to say "we told you so. Those fires only serve to validate the need to adopt the President's 'safe forest' policy."

However, professional foresters insist that "Healthy Forests" is little more than an invitation to the logging industry to plunder the national forests. Paraphrasing the infamous remark by an officer in Viet-Nam, "we must destroy the forest in order to save it."

As renowned biologist Edward O. Wilson observes:

> The best way to avoid these catastrophic fires is by trimming undergrowth and clearing debris, combined with natural burns of the kind that have sustained healthy forests in past millennia. Those procedures, guided by science and surgically precise forestry, can return forests to near their equilibrium condition, in which only minimal further intervention would be needed.
>
> On the other hand, the worst way to create healthy forests is to thin trees via increased logging, as proposed by the Bush administration (Edward O. Wilson, "Bush's Forest Plan Worse than Fire," *Newsday*, August 29, 2003).

Lie: #7: Environmental Regulations Damage the Economy and Cost Jobs.

We've all heard it, time and again: "Environmental quality is a luxury that the nation's economy can ill-afford. The costs of pollution control, toxic cleanups and the preservation of wild areas are more than the public can or should bear."

However, Bush's own Office of Management and Budget came to a radically different conclusion. As the *Washington Post's* Eric Pianin reports, the OMB concluded "that the health and social benefits of enforcing tough new clean-air regulations during the past decade were five to seven times greater in economic terms than were the costs of complying with the rules" (Eric Pianin, "Study Finds Net Gain From Pollution Rules," *Washington Post*, September 27, 2003).

Will these compelling facts overturn cherished Bushista/corporate dogma? Previous outcomes of the encounter of Bushistic doctrine with hard facts offer little cause for hope.

Etcetera, ad nauseum.

We could go on and on with Bush's lies and deceptions regarding the environment, but we have come to the end of our allowable space. Let the following summaries suffice:

- Bush's plan to protect endangered species? Lift international bans against killing, capturing and importing endangered animals. Allegedly, the fees collected by the host countries for these activities can then be used to protect the remaining rare animals. How do we know that the impoverished governments will do their part? We trust them. Yea, sure!
- In the meantime, the Bush administration has not added a single species to the list of endangered species.
- Bush has opened up millions of acres of previously protected wilderness areas to mining, logging, and oil and gas development.

Small wonder that the League of Conservation Voters gave Bush an "F" on their presidential environmental report card. LCV President Deb Callahan sums it up: "Bush is well on his way to compiling the worst environmental record of any president in the history of our nation" (League of Conservation Voters, "Bush Receives 'F' for Environmental Issues on LCF 2003 Presidential Report Card," Press Release, June 24, 2003).

But Bush tells us: "[our] way of life depends, and always will depend, on the wise protection of the natural environment. It's been a part of your past; it's going to be an important part of the future" (White House, August 22, 2003).

Does he really believe it? Do his policies confirm this pious pronouncement?

We report, you decide.

REFERENCES

MarieCocco, "White House Deceit Covered Up 9/11 Truths," *Newsday* (August 28, 2003).

Osha Gray Davidson, "Dirty Secrets," *Mother Jones* (September/October 2003).

Juan Gonzales, "It's public be damned at the EPA," *New York Daily News* (August 26, 2003).

Paul Harris, "Bush Covers Up Climate Research," *The Observer* (UK) (September 21, 2003).

David Helvarg, "Unwise Use: Gale Norton's New Environmentalism," *The Progressive* (June, 2003).

League of Conservation Voters, "Bush Receives 'F' for Environmental Issues on LCF 2003 Presidential Report Card," Press Release (June 24, 2003).

Christopher Lee, "Effort to ease air rules decried," *Washington Post* (October 19, 2002).

National Academy of Sciences: "Leading Climate Scientists Advise White

House on Global Warming," Press Release (June 6, 2001).

Natural Resources Defense Council, "Bush Weakening of Clean Air Act Threatens Public Health, Says NRDC, Press Release (November 22, 2002).

Robert Perks, "How Bush Spent his Summer Vacation – Undermining Environmental Protections," Natural Resources Defense Council (September 6, 2003).

Eric Pianin, "Study Finds Net Gain From Pollution Rules," *Washington Post* (September 27, 2003).

Robert Salladay and Zachary Coile, "Bush ignored pleas for funds that could have prevented Clifornia fires, *San Francisco Chronicle* (October 31,2003).

Editorial, "US Rejects Study by its Own Arctic Scientists, *Seattle Post-Intelligencer* (March 20, 2002).

Kevin E. Trenberth, (National Center of Atmospheric Research), "The IPCC Assessment of Global Warming 2001, *Failsafe* (Spring, 2001).

U.S. Geological Survey Biological Science Report, "Arctic Refuge Coastal Plain Terrestrial Wildlife Research Summaries" at <www.alaska.usgs.gov/BSR-2002/usgs-brd-bsr-2002-001.html>.

White House Press Release, "President's Remarks on Salmon Restoration" (August 22, 2003).

White House Press Release, "President Visits Detroit Edison Monroe Power Plant in Monroe, Michigan" (September 15, 2003).

Ted Williams, "Down Upon the Suwannee River," *Mother Jones* (September, October 2003)

Edward O. Wilson, "Bush's Forest Plan Worse than Fire," *Newsday* (August 29, 2003).

"Sound Science"
That Only Sounds Like Science

BY CHERYL SEAL

Beginning his presidential election campaign, Bush pledged he would base all his environmental, energy, technical and health care policy decisions on "sound science." Instead, what Bush has given America is a sham, stitched together with lies, that, at best, only *sounds* like science. Here are some of the primary Bush science policies which are, in themselves, lies.

BUSH CORNERSTONE LIE: "When we make decisions, we want to make sure we do so on sound science; not what sounds good, but what is real" (George W. Bush, Clear Skies Initiative Speech, February 14, 2002, also reiterated in dozens of speeches and statements.[1]
REALITY: Bush systematically ignores sound science in favor of the junk science claims that serve corporate interests. For example, in January 2001 when Bush took office, he had immediate access to a recently completed, extensive report by Department of Energy researchers that showed that energy efficiency and renewable power could cover 60% of the national need for new electric power plants over the next 20 years, while dramatically reducing air pollution.[2] This report, based on sound science, was discarded in favor of a scheme to build to build at 1,300-1,900 new electric power plants—"More than one new plant per week," as Cheney stated on April 30, 2001.[3]

Bush also had access to 20 years of research by hundreds of the planet's most respected scientists in the report that shaped the Kyoto Protocol. As many as 2,000 different researchers cumulatively contributed peer-reviewed work to the Intergovernmental Panel on Climate Change (IPCC) reports that concluded that global warming is not only real but a serious problem for the planet. Yet Bush rejected this work in favor of the voodoo 'science' of a handful of 'experts,' many with dubious credentials, all with industry and/or political ties. The number of paid experts in this corporate stable is small. Fred Seitz, who spearheaded a major anti-Kyoto protocol movement, is a materials scientist, a field totally unrelated to climate/atmospheric science. Other "climate experts" have no science background at all! All, however, are well paid.[4] Patrick Michaels of the University of Virginia and Robert C. Balling of Arizona State University together collected $315,000 in fees in just a couple of years as experts debunking global warming for the fossil fuel industry. The work of less than two dozen "experts" accounts for an outrageous percentage of material pushed at the public by the media and the Bush administration. Some the material is laughable: *CO$_2$: A Satanic Gas?* is an hysterical diatribe by Michaels that has been carried by the FOX network's Junkscience.com, the Greening Earth Society's website, and the Cato Institute and other corporate-funded "fronts" dedicated to bashing global warming and any other environmental issue that might lead to tighter regulations.[5]

As to rejecting "what sounds good," the Bush folks are in fact the primary fabricators of "sounds good" pseudoscience. One of their favorite tactics is "redefinition"—a variation on the "same office, different name" corporate ploy. This ploy has been used to bend and break regulations and rules that were created using very sound science—rules that are neither confusing nor unnecessary. Here are some classic examples from the past few years:

- October 2003: The DOE announces its plan to reclassify high-level nuclear wastes as "byproducts incidental to processing" so these deadly materials (including spent fuel rods) can be handled as easily and cheaply as low-level wastes.[6]

- Spring 2002: To open up millions of acres of land to development, the EPA redefined all remote or isolated small water bodies or wetlands as *not* wetlands, and thus not protected. This opened one-fifth of all remaining wetlands in America to development.

- 2001: A bill attached to the Farm Bill redefines "irradiation" of food as "cold pasteurization."

- Ongoing: To promote his anti-abortion agenda, Bush has been seeking to redefine "fetus." If he succeeds, even a fertilized egg could be defined as an independent human being with all the same rights.

- Since January 2001: Bush has pressed for a "retooling" of guidelines for everything from arsenic levels in drinking water to how air pollutants are measured. Even which pollutants are even tested is being shuffled around. Of course all of the changes are in the favor of the polluters, not the citizens who must breathe the polluted air and drink the contaminated water.

- In 2003: Bush redefined thinning brush for wildfire control: Fire control thinning now refers also to logging of old growth forest miles from any high-fire-danger zone.

• In some cases, Bush simply eliminates the "definition problem" by removing the definition. For example, the National Science Foundation's agenda for a sustainable future was eliminated, thereby removing the concept of "future" and "sustainability" from the Bush policy vocabulary.

Bush has actively sought to expunge the idea of "human activity" (a euphemism for the pollution, contamination and degradation of the environment by people) from environmental policies. In an email dated 3 June 2002, Myron Ebell, a director of the Competitive Enterprise Institute (CEI) wrote instructions to Phil Cooney, chief of staff at the White House Council on Environmental Quality on how Cooney could downplay the EPA report that admitted human activity is driving global warming. The CEI is a corporate front group funded in large part by the oil industry. In this same note, Ebell suggests ways to get rid of inconvenient EPA officials, including Christie Whitman.[7]

Many of Bush's top scientific advisors are chosen not because of their "sound science" backgrounds, but because of their connection to the Bush family. A key example is John Mendelsohn. In August of 2001, John Mendelsohn was flown to DC to meet with Bush as a key science advisor on stem cells. Mendelsohn was a former Enron executive, a friend of both Ken Lay and George Bush, Sr. Mendelsohn also worked at the Anderson Cancer Clinic in Houston, where G.H. and Barbara Bush are on the board and was the chief scientist for the much-investigated company, Imclone (of Martha Stewart fame). Mendelsohn himself was investigated but never charged for failing to inform patients participating in the Imclone colon cancer trials of his conflict of interest. Typical of Bush circle ethics, while Mendelsohn insisted on strict adherence to disclosure rules for everyone else at the Cancer Center, he did not feel the rules applied to himself.[8]

Even scientific media appear to be colluding with the Bush NeoCons. Shortly after Bush was enthroned, the staffs of many scientific journals (which rely on corporate and/or federal funding, one way or the other) were shaken up, including those at *Power Engineering, Pollution Engineering,* and *Sea Technology.* Suddenly, editorials were parroting Bush science—there is insufficient science to prove global warming exists, alternative fuel systems are not practical, etc.—while "letters to the editor" from corporate front group "experts" began to show up more often (as a science abstractor, I read an average of 80-100 articles from a wide variety of scientific publications every month so am in a position to notice trends). In *Science* magazine, the highly respected American-based general science journal, research articles of dubious scientific merit that lend support to Bush policy began to appear. For example, the March 7, 2003 issue ran a highly subjective study of mothers pushed off welfare that "proved" that children of these women "thrived" left to babysitters and daycare.

Within just four days of its publication, this study was being cited by Tommy Thompson in testimony to Senate Finance Committee and run in assorted rightwing publications, including Townhall.com.[9]

LIE: "Global climate change presents a different set of challenges and requires a different strategy. The science is more complex, the answers are less certain, and the technology is less developed" (George W. Bush, Clear Skies Initiative Speech, February 14, 2002).
REALITY: Climate science is one of the most exhaustively studied fields of science at present, and draws on some of the most well-developed technology ever created, including some of NASA's best efforts (various satellites, laser probes of the atmosphere, etc). The vast majority of studies conducted of climate change, from every possible angle, from ice core analysis to infrared satellite studies have produced evidence supporting not just the reality of the current global warming trend, but the reality of the contribution of human activity to this trend.

Yet the Bush administration continues to invoke the results of a handful of researchers, including old studies by John Christy of NASA, because they favor corporate interests. Christy's supposedly irrefutable satellite and radiosonde data showed that not only was the lower atmosphere (troposphere) *not* warming, as it should if the Earth were indeed getting warmer, but it was in fact cooling. These findings have been used by the fossil fuel industry to throw all of global warming science into "uncertainty." The media has aided and abetted this effort: Christy's results have been plastered across every website, magazine, newspaper, radio and television program possible, while almost no play at all has been given to the dozens of peer-reviewed papers that questioned Christy's results. Most recently, in the October 10, 2003 issue of *Science*, researchers at the University of Maryland and the National Oceanic and Atmospheric Administration (NOAA) show that not only is the troposphere warming, but Christy's results were based on extremely biased, gap-filled measurements: "We found nothing that would even remotely suggest the existence of a cooling trend in the troposphere temperature for the 1978-2002 period." Christy's data failed to account for "details" like weather-induced instrument noise and natural daily and seasonal temperature variations.[10]

LIE: Federal agencies where scientific research occurs are being "streamlined" and made more cost-effective (Assorted statements by Bush, NASA's Sean O'Keefe, and Bush appointees with the National Institutes of Health and other agencies).

REALITY: These agencies are being purged of all liberal and/or outspoken and/or conscience-bearing people to facilitate the subversion of federally funded research to the Bush/corporate agenda. Collectively hundreds of competent, dedicated researchers have been terminated or harassed out of their positions and replaced with corporate yes men/women. Researchers applying for positions report being subjected to grilling as to their philosophical and religious leanings. In the EPA, in early 2003, 1,200 researchers were asked to take a "survey" that asked probing questions about their sexual lives—a weird attempt, apparently, at weeding out liberals.

Panels of scientists overseeing the ethics and quality of federal research have been either dismantled or stuffed with former corporate employees. Just a few examples:

Michael Wetzman, pediatrician in chief at Rochester General Hospital and author of numerous publications on lead poisoning, was on the Center for Disease Control's panel on childhood lead poisoning. He was dropped from the committee, along with two other highly credentialed doctors with lead poisoning expertise. All were replaced by nominees with close ties to the lead industry.[11]

• Bush's key 'stem cell expert' was John Mendelsohn, a former Enron executive who was investigated for failing to inform patients participating in a colon cancer drug trial (ImClone) that he had a major financial stake in the outcome.

• Bush's choice to head the Food and Drug Administration (FDA) advisory panel that review's women's reproductive health drugs is David Hager, an obstetrician/gynecologist who has recommended Scripture readings and prayers for a variety of women's health problems, from headache to premenstrual syndrome. Hager was chosen over Donald R. Mattison, former Dean of the University of Pittsburgh School of Public Health and Michael F. Greene, director of maternal-fetal medicine at Mass General.[12]

• David Kay, Bush's chief Weapons of Mass Destruction advisor, has no scientific credentials at all. Until 2002, he was vice president of SAIC, which has been showered with hundreds of millions of dollars in Pentagon contracts. Kay worked under Hans Blix back in the early 1990s after Iraq War I—at least until he was terminated for questionable behavior related to his close connection with the Bush Administration.[13]

• In November 2003, a team of biologists who had been studying three endangered Missouri River fish species for ten years were removed after their report conflicted with the Bush agenda. They were replaced by biologists unfamiliar with both the fish species in question AND the Missouri River.[14]

Both *Science* and *Nature* magazines (the two top science journals) have, over the past three years, featured a steady stream of letters to the editor, editorials, news shorts and detailing the assault on sound science by the Bush administration.

LIE: Privatization of research will save the government millions, while making research faster and more efficient and creating thousands of higher-paying private sector jobs.
REALITY: Privatization of federal jobs amounts to the biggest giveaway of tax dollars—and jobs—yet perpetrated on America. Federal jobs have long-term security, while private sector corporate jobs have none. Worse, most privatized federal jobs are being shipped overseas. Since Bush took office, thousands of government jobs have been "outsourced" to India and other countries where labor is cheap and benefits often nonexistent.[15]

Once federal research is privatized, there will little or no oversight of the research. Corporations will be free to fudge results unhindered. As it is, tweaking results to push through a new lucrative drug had become such a common practice that in September, 2001, 13 medical journal editors joined forces to protest and demand greater accountability.[16] Now, under the Bush privatization scheme, corporations use bogus "study results" to legitimize anything they wish, from promoting smoking as "safer than overeating" to advocating strip mining in National Parks as "environmentally friendly."

LIE: Purging tens of thousands of scientific documents from sources accessible to the public, including other scientists is "protecting national security" (Tom Ridge, Donald Rumsfeld, and other White House officials have used this line to defend this practice).
REALITY: Only a tiny fraction of the purged information has anything directly to do with weaponry or other high-risk subjects. Documents on everything from farming to pharmaceuticals were purged. Why? The purged articles either contained information critical of the Bush administration or contained research that was potentially useful to corporate interests. Once made "secret," there's no oversight. And once there's no oversight, what would stop Team Bush from handing out, say, a potential blockbuster drug formula, to a drug baron who made a big donation to campaign 2004? This "free" research can then be used to make a research-overhead-free bundle—all under cover of "national security."

At the same time, the Bush Administration is starting to classify more research—even research that by definition should *not* be classified. For example, DARPA, with a huge science research budget and a monopoly on computer worm research, recently made all of its anti-worm research top secret. One anonymous researcher stated in the British science magazine *Nature* (September 18, 2003) that "Once you start classifying, it shuts down that field of inquiry." But it leaves the "top secret" results up for grabs to corporations like Microsoft, which has been treated extremely well by the Bush Administration. Once research is classified, how could anyone ever know the fruits of taxpayer-funded research had been given away to the highest Bush campaign donor?

LIE: Bush medical research priorities are motivated by concerns for national security. This had been endlessly reiterated by Bush and Co.
REALITY: Bush is funneling billions of dollars in the name of "Homeland Security" into the pockets of the pharmaceutical companies. In exchange for developing vaccines for anthrax or smallpox, the companies get a huge pool of captive consumers: the US military, whose injections are paid for by tax dollars. Meanwhile, even though 20% of all hospital infections are now highly antibiotic resistant and kill tens of thousands of Americans each year, the same pharmaceutical companies are abandoning antibiotic research. Why? Because doctors tend to use new antibiotics sparingly to insure they remain effective, so there's just no profit in it. Better to peddle needless exotic vaccines to the federal government than address the *real* number one security risk in terms of disease: antibiotic resistant infections.[17]

LIE: Bush is committed to improving science education in American schools. The oft-repeated promise of the "education president."
REALTIY: Corporations have been circling schools since the late 1980s, trying to dump pseudoscience materials—free of course—on unsuspecting and/or needy teachers. As Bush starves state budgets, the temptation to fall back on corporate "educational materials" will become greater. These materials aggressively target environmental education, with a special emphasis on debunking global warming. An example of a suggested exercise for elementary school teachers in one free "classroom package" provided by the Western Fuel Association: take students to a greenhouse and show them how lush and rich life in a greenhouse Earth could be! By 2008, we could expect schools in which students sat at desks with corporate logos under corporate poster-covered walls learning about the joys of industrial pollution from corporate-provided "science books."[18]

Here are some other signs that "improving" science education is as far from the real Bush goal as Earth is to the nearest quasar:

- Bush's Math and Science Partnership Initiative is getting $90 million to promote the corporate approach to science. At the same time, Bush is trying to suck $110 million away from the National Science Foundation's noncorporate math/science education funding, thereby eliminating any competition to his new "initiative."
- The Hoover Institute (of which Condi Rice and Donald Rumsfeld are fellows) has called for an educational agenda in which much less time will be spent on teaching critical thinking. Instead of promoting creative, critical thinking and what might be achieved for the good of mankind through science, Bush is pushing "freemarket" science, as in how it can be used for the good of corporations.

NOTES

1. George W. Bush, "President Announces Clear Skies & Global Climate Change Initiatives," Press Release (February, 2002) at <www.whitehouse.gov/news/releases/2002/02/20020214-5.html>.

2. . Interlaboratory Working Group on Energy-Efficient and Clean-Energy Technologies, *Scenarios for a Clean Energy Future*, Office of Energy Efficiency and Renewable Energy, U. S. Department of Energy (2001) at <www.ornl.gov/sci/eere/cef/>.

3. Carter M. Yang, "VP Warns of Energy Crisis, Previews Changes," ABC News (April 30, 2001) at <www.abcnews.go.com/sections/us/DailyNews/Energy_Cheney010430.html>

4. Editors, "Hall of Shame: Journalists and Academics who Promote their Careers by Denying Climate Change." *Rising Tide: Taking Action on the Root Causes of Climate Change* (2003) at <www.risingtide.org.uk/pages/voices/hall_shame.htm>.

5. *Ibid.*

6. Alex Fryer, "Washington Lawmakers Stop Bush from Reclassifying Nuclear Wastes," *Seattle Times* (October 10, 2003) at <www.nuclearpolicy.org/NewsArticlePrint.cfm?NewsID=732>.

7. Greenpeace Press Release, "Smoking Gun Memo: White House/Exxon Link" at <www.highcountrypeace.org/article.php?sid=1244>.

8. Bill Aishman, "Imclone Debacle: What Does It Mean?" PSA Rising (2003) at <www.psa-rising.com/upfront/aishman/imclone.php>

9. Tommy Thompson, "Welfare Reform; Building on Success," Testimony to Senate Finance Committee (March 12, 2003) at <www.hhs.gov/asl/testify/t030312.html>. See also Rich Lowry, "Welfare Mothers are People Too,"

TownHall.com (March 11, 2003) at <www.Townhall.com/columnists/richlowry/rl20030311.shtml>.

10. Konstantin Y. Vinnikov and Norman C. Grody, "Global Warming Trend of Mean Tropospsheric Temperature Observed by Satellites," *Science* (October 10, 2003.

11. Jeff Nesbith, "Scientists' Research Backs Global Warming Trend," Cox News Service (September 12, 2003) at <www.bayarea.com/mld/cctimes/news/6753452.htm>.

12. Editors, "Administration Stacks Scientific Advisory Panels," *OMB Watch* (March 19, 2003) at <www.ombwatch.org/article/articleview/1384/1/4/>.

13. James Gordon Prather, "In Defense of Hans Blix," World Net Daily (June 28, 2003) at <http://wnd.com/news/article.asp?ARTICLE_ID=33307>.

14. Press Release. "Bush Administration Sidelines Seasoned Missouri River Scientists," US Newswire (November 4, 2003) at <www.releases. us-newswire.com/GetRelease.asp?id=144-11052003>.

15. Merrill Goozner, "NIH Privatization Under Fire," *The Scientist* (October 22, 2003) at <www.biomedcentral.com/news/20031022/07>.

16. Editors, "Medical Journals Take Stand against Conflict of Interest," Acnem.org (October 2001) at <www.acnem.org/news_archives/2001/october_2001_news.htm>. See also editorial by Arnold Relman (former editor of the New England Journal of Medicine) in *New Scientist* (September 22, 2001).

17. Thomas May, Ross Silverman, "Bioterrorism Defense Priorities," *Science Magazine* (July 4, 2003).

18. Cheryl Seal, "Scared Green: How John Stossel, ABC, Rightwing Think Tanks and the Chemical Industry Are Colluding to Trash Environmental Education." Democrats.com (April, 2001) at <www.democrats.com/view2.-cfm?id=2648>.

Substituting Deception For Sound Public Health Policy

By Sara S. DeHart

The first purpose of responsible government is to provide for public health and safety. Institutions responsible for safety range from local police departments to the Department of Defense. Public health responsibility is also found in a broad array of institutions including the Public Health Service and Centers for Disease Control. Policy related to these two foremost functions of government originates from local, state and federal authorities.

Public Health refers to those institutions that provide protection and promotion of good health through organized community and governmental action. Beginning with the first administration of Franklin Roosevelt in 1933, extensive federal money and resources were allocated to strengthen state Public Health Departments. The subsequent enactment of the Public Health Service Act in 1941 served as the national bulwark against epidemics and other health related threats to the US.[1]

During the Al Gore and George Bush 2000 election campaign, the media did not ask any questions pertaining to public health policy nor were they asked about privatizing the Public Health System. No one asked Mr. Bush, a political conservative dedicated to the privatization of Social Security, how he would manage public health policy for the nation. That was a critical oversight.

Following the attacks of September 2001 against the US and the anthrax letters episode two months later, public fear was whipped to unprecedented heights. The corporate media sustained a constant barrage about the threat of anthrax-laden letters often quoting statements about bioterrorism issued by members of the Bush Administration. Exploiting public fear of bioterrorism is discussed by Laurie Garrett in *The Coming Plague* in which she points out that "Fear [of disease] without potential mitigating solutions, can be very volatile."[2] But, rather than calming public fears by providing viable solutions to a perceived threat, the Bush Administration exploited fear with lies, distortions and disinformation. Based upon "facts" that began emerging in late summer 2003, this was interpreted as a means of justifying preemptive war against Iraq. One obvious example occurred when Secretary of State Colin Powell dramatically held aloft before the UN Security Council a vial of faux anthrax bacillus proclaiming "if this were filled with anthrax such as Saddam Hussein has hidden, it could kill millions."[3]

As Commander-in-Chief, with ultimate responsibility for public health policy, George Bush's statements and actions carry special weight and significance. There are myriad rulings, decrees and executive orders that have emerged from the White House that demand careful scrutiny. Four areas are considered Bioterrorism, AIDS Prevention and Stem Cell Research, Medicare/Medicaid and Health Insurance.

Bioterrorism and Bioshields: The Case for the Iraqi War

In November 2001, anthrax-laden letters were delivered to certain Democratic Senators' offices and news agencies. These events portrayed the US Postal Service as an unwitting conduit for deadly bioweapons distribution to the general public. The letters, coming on the heels of the September 11 attacks, had a shattering effect on the security assumption that Americans held as their birthright. Initially, efforts were made to link the letters to Middle East terrorists, as had been done with the September 11 attacks. But, no link was found. When it was scientifically proven that the letters contained the Ames strain of anthrax that had been weaponized according to American bioweapons techniques, the FBI was compelled to admit that the perpetrator was not an Arab terrorist but more likely an American scientist.[4] The questions that subsequently emerged included who among the small field of scientists had access to weaponized anthrax bacilli and was vaccinated against the disease? Who wrote crude letters designed to implicate an Arab terrorist? And why would the FBI float the story that the probable intent of the letters was not to harm anyone but, rather, alert the government to the vulnerabilities of biowarfare?

As the number of putative experts appeared on talk radio and television programs, the fear level among Americans was palpable. Bioterrorism was served on a daily basis to the American public and the Bush administration did nothing to mitigate the resulting fear. Once the anthrax scare quieted down, these same experts began to talk about weaponized smallpox. Questions were raised in ominous tones about the evil Saddam Hussein who was purported to have vast stores of anthrax, botulinum, bubonic plague and possibly smallpox. Judith Miller, columnist for the *New York Times,* speculated that Russian scientists might have been hired by Saddam Hussein.[5] She often noted that Russia was suspected of developing weaponized smallpox but rarely, if ever mentioned that a number of Russian scientists had immigrated to the United States, Great Britain and Israel.

By August 2002 the American public was inundated with reports of a possible biowarfare terrorist attack stemming from Saddam Hussein and during that time the bioweapon of choice became smallpox.

In 2002 the US experienced an epidemic of West Nile virus infection that attacked wildlife, domestic animals and humans. More than 14,000 horses died that summer, eagles, crows and other birds fell from the sky and at least 241 human deaths were attributed to the disease. In response to this genuine health threat, George Bush declared war on smallpox, the only disease the World Health Organization has successfully eradicated. The last recorded case occurred in 1977.[6]

In light of the Iraqi-anthrax hoax one might conclude that smallpox was deliberately chosen to reinforce the propaganda designed to justify preemptive war against Iraq. Consistent with Garrett's findings, fear levels approached an almost crisis level. When this occurred the American people fell into line behind the plans for war against terrorism to support the invasion of Iraq. The Bush Administration's pre-emptive war campaign proved successful, smallpox became an official Weapon of Mass Destruction (WMD); the Bush Administration went to war to protect the well being and health of the American public.

Smallpox fits all the requirements of a tool to incite fear. First, people know something about smallpox, the scourge that in the twentieth century killed more people than all the wars combined. Second, a vaccine was potentially available and since children had not been vaccinated since 1971, a large percentage of the population was vulnerable.[7] Third, although the only vials of smallpox virus known to exist were secured in Russia and the United States, it was easy to insinuate without proof that Saddam may have purchased the virus from Russian scientists. That story ran in multiple newspapers even though the scenario was highly unlikely because other, equally deadly microorganisms were more easily available as bioweapons.

Every major player in the Bush administration from Colin Powell, who held aloft a vial of faux anthrax before the United Nations Security Council to Dick Cheney's September 14, 2003 continued contention that two trailers discovered in Iraq could have been used to make smallpox has contributed to the public-fear campaign. Cheney continues the charade even though "team pox," the six-member crew sent to Iraq with the specific assignment to search for any sign of smallpox, officially stated in its report, "we found no physical or new anecdotal evidence to suggest that Iraq was producing smallpox or had stocks of it in [its] possession."[8] Further, the Kay Bioweapons Interim Report to Congress documented that there were no stores of anthrax or other deadly microorganisms in Iraq.[9] A single ten-year-old vial of botulinum is all that was found there. Although George Bush has tried to use this as evidence of Saddam's intent of biowarfare, biological weapons experts report that there is no evidence that Iraqi scientists or anyone else has ever succeeded in using botulinum B for biowarfare.[10]

With the smallpox bioweapons scare in motion, George Bush and the Republican Congress negotiated a deal with selected pharmaceutical companies for 250 million doses of smallpox vaccine for $509 million. The vaccine stockpile was to be used for mandated vaccinations of the entire U.S. population should the Secretary of Homeland Defense declare a bioterror alert. Also, in other legislation and hidden within the Homeland Security Bill, Dick Armey (R, TX) inserted a "midnight rider" to protect Eli Lilly from existing and future vaccine legal rulings that could be equivalent to the asbestos class action lawsuits.[11]

The Bush White House substituted sound public health policy with fear mongering and deception. *Bioshields,* the Bush White House program whose purported goal is "to protect against attack by biological and chemical weapons or other dangerous pathogens"[12] is a superficial program whose stated goal is not possible to achieve. The *Bioshield Program* is dangerous and serves only to reward the pharmaceutical industry for political contributions to members of the Republican Party.

While West Nile virus rampaged and AIDS continued to devastate its victims, and SARS emerged as a new biological threat, George Bush's response was to stockpile sufficient smallpox vaccine to inoculate the entire American population. This heralded bioshield is, of course, not an option for a significant portion of the population including those who are immune deficient, very young, very old, or suffering from heart disease or eczema. There is no vaccine that can protect Americans from all infectious diseases and there is no vaccine to protect Americans from poor public health policy decisions.

AIDS Prevention and Stem Cell Research:
When Politics and Science Collide

Both AIDS prevention and stem cell research policy are governed primarily by what is acceptable to Bush's Conservative Christian core supporters and corporate interests. This is a classic case of what happens when politics, science and religion collide.

Stem Cell Research:

According to the National Institutes of Health, research on human embryonic stem cells offers great promise for those suffering from

Parkinson's, Alzheimer's, and heart disease, as well as spinal cord injury and diabetes. Conservative Christians vehemently oppose this research because fertility clinic embryos are used to extract the cell lines. This group does not appear to object to the destruction of the embryos, only to their use for stem cell research. Although the embryos are frozen for specified contractual periods of time, they are eventually discarded because long term storage is not a feasible or cost effective option. Religious conservatives consider the use of stem cells from fertility clinic embryos morally and ethically unacceptable.

During the 2000 presidential campaign, Bush said he opposed federal funding of embryonic stem cell research. This generally was viewed as a vow to conservative Christians to solidify his political base. Upon entering the White House one of his first acts was to freeze all federal funding for stem cell research. Bush announced his long-awaited decision about permitting limited stem-cell research in August 2001. He maintained that the 60 existing stem cell lines were sufficient to conduct all needed research. Further, Bush stipulated that no new cell lines could be developed through federal funding. There are now grave concerns about that decision for two major reasons. First there are not 60 stem cell lines and second those lines that are available may be contaminated with viruses.

NIH Director Dr. Elias Zerhouni informed congress in May 2003 that rather than 60 stem cell lines, only 11 lines are available to researchers. All of these lines are potentially contaminated as a result of being developed with mouse feeder cells and might not be appropriate for human use because of the potential for infection. Addressing this problem, scientists at Johns Hopkins University recently announced the discovery of a method for developing uninfected stem cell lines on feeder cells from adult humans. Scientists cannot work with new cell lines developed with this method, however, because George Bush's policy prohibits the use of any cell lines developed after April 2001.[13, 14]

This is the ultimate dilemma for Bush and the American people. If Bush changes his position to allow further stem cell lines to be developed he will alienate his Conservative Christian political base. If he does not change his position the potential for grave human harm is present. Meanwhile, scientists worldwide are moving forward with this research making it highly unlikely that American scientists will develop cures for Alzheimer's, Parkinson's or other debilitating diseases unless they leave the United States.

AIDS Prevention

In his January 2003 State of the Union address, George Bush announced the Emergency Plan for AIDS Relief, a five-year, $15 billion initiative to turn the tide in the global effort to combat the HIV/AIDS epidemic.[15] In July, he asked Congress for only $2 billion with specific stipulations requiring that one-third of the AIDS prevention funds be spent on the Sexual Abstinence until Marriage Program. This was interpreted by public health workers in the field as an end to dispensing condoms to prevent sexually transmitted diseases. In addition, George Bush has tried to cut urgently needed U.S. contributions to the Global Fund, a nonprofit multinational partnership dedicated to fighting AIDS with public and private funds.

Nicholas Kristol reported in the *New York Times* that "prudery kills." He quoted Jeffrey Sachs, an economist and expert in Public Health on the Bush Administration's AIDS Prevention Policy.

> It is utterly inexcusable that 7.5 million people in Africa have died on their watch, and they've not even reached 500 Africans for treatment in US AID supported programs. They've talked and procrastinated and dissembled while millions of impoverished people have died. Ultimately history will judge them very severely.[16]

In countries such as South Africa and Zimbabwe, where 20 to 25% of the population is infected, AIDS will claim the lives of about half of all 15 year-olds. Pharmaceutical firms took the South African government to court to fight their initiative to purchase less expensive generic drugs to treat AIDS/HIV. The suit was dropped only after rising international pressure and accusations of genocide harmed drug firms' reputations.

In both stem cell research and the AIDS initiative, George Bush has basked in the glow of the moment for his grand pronouncements. Unfortunately, his words are not consistent with his actions. To this day stem cell research has barely inched forward following his August 2001 announcement, while promised funds to fight AIDS in Africa remain unallocated.

Medicare and Medicaid

> Our goal is a system in which all Americans have got (sic) a good insurance policy, in which all Americans can choose their own doctors, in which seniors and low-income citizens receive the help they need...[O]ur Medicare system is a binding commitment of a caring society, we must renew that commitment by providing the seniors of today and tomorrow with preventive care and the new medicines that are transforming health care in our country (George W. Bush, Medicare Address, March 4, 2003).[17]

George Bush's words imply choice, but the Prescription Drug and Medicare Improvement Act of 2003 recently passed by a Republican controlled Senate and Congress emphasizes pushing seniors into managed care plans that provide only partial drug benefits while limiting the choice of treatments and physicians. The much touted Medicare sponsored private PPO/HMO model relies on Primary Health Care Physicians serving as gatekeepers. Preferred Provider (PPO) and Health Maintenance Organization (HMO) physicians are paid to guard the gate well to reduce expenses and increase shareholder profits. Hence, practices like an aspiration biopsy rather than an excision biopsy for cancer detection will be mandated to minimize costs. This is a questionable medical practice and one more likely to result in a false negative (report is negative, but cancer is present) if the needle happens to land in a spot without cancer cells. This practice may delay treatment during the earliest and most treatable stages of disease. The traditional Medicare program that offered a free choice of doctor and hospital is now endangered.

Bush repeatedly uses the Federal Employees Health Benefit Program as a model but that is not what he supports for senior citizens. He recommended reduced funding of $400 billion for Medicare through 2013. This level of projected funding is 40 percent less than that allocated for the tax supported health care benefits approved for members of Congress. In fact, Bush's Medicare plan requires Congress to cut $169 billion from the program over 10 years. This plan will result in Medicare cuts that will be used to pay for partial prescription-drug benefits.[18] The beneficiaries of this plan are drug and private insurance companies, not senior citizens the program is supposed to serve.

Further concern about the Medicare Improvement and Modernization Act of 2003 came from Public Citizen in a report about conflict of interest for at least one of Bush's advisors, Gail R. Wilensky, who is credited with drafting the revised program. Dr. Wilensky holds shares and stock options valued at $10.5 million (September 2001 prices) in health care insurance companies. Many of these companies will benefit from the Bush plan for Medicare and Medicaid.[19]

Public Citizen (Congress Watch Report) identified key problems with the disappointing history of private insurance plans and Medicare. For example, between 1999 and 2003 there were a total of 2.4 million occasions where Medicare beneficiaries were forced to search for new providers after their HMOs ceased providing service as part of a state contract. Texas, Florida, California lead in states dropped by HMOs.[20]

George Bush does not just have his eyes on Medicare; he has taken on the Medicaid program as well. Medicaid is a medical assistance program jointly financed by state and federal governments for low income persons and administered by the Health Care Financing Administration. As the law now stands states may not impose citizenship or residency requirements other than requiring that an applicant be a resident of the state. Patients are restricted to pre-approved physicians and providers. Recipients are further restricted because many physicians limit the number of Medicaid patients in their practices.

States are required to offer some services while others are considered "optional." Optional services are not frills and may, in fact, provide life-saving treatments. The Bush administration is promoting block grants to states for Medicaid, while allowing them carte blanche authority to deal with optional benefits. This provision is a prime opportunity for cash starved states to allow benefits to dwindle and for the medically indigent to be cut from the rolls. States receiving block grants will be able to trim their Medicaid rolls with impunity. Expect states like Texas with the highest number of uninsured in the nation (24.7%) to further compromise Medicaid recipients. For example, the Texas Workforce Commission has a proposal to redefine *work* in a way that could end Medicaid benefits for thousands of Texans who do not follow a list of state behavioral rules. These rules are already in effect for Texas Welfare assistance and Republican Texas legislators are pushing for the rules to expand to Medicaid.[21]

Through a campaign of slick advertising, the Bush Administration uses one model, Federal Employees Health Benefit Program, to promote something entirely different for senior citizens. The issues are complex and for the American public that does not like to ferret out information, deception and partial information are often accepted at face value.

The complexity with which the bill is written precludes most citizens from fully understanding what the Republican majority in the Congress and Senate hurriedly passed before their Thanksgiving recess. Politicians used the term *choice* to sell the bill to the public. The bill, as written, is not about choice; it is about destroying Medicare. The Medicare system needed modest revision for prescription drug coverage. In addition, a growing number of doctors currently refuse new Medicare patients because the insurance plan paid them too little to cover the costs of caring for the elderly.[22]

The Medicare revision passed by Congress and Senate will not do what George Bush promised senior citizens. It is, in fact, nothing more than an entitlement program for the drug and insurance industries. *Boondoggle* is an apt term to describe what elected representatives awarded them.

The bill specifically mandates that Medicare can not negotiate collective drug prices as do PPOs/HMOs. Republican law makers mandated "competition" by constricting Medicare's bargaining power to make it less competitive. Insurance companies' subsidies and increasing drug prices can, and will, bleed Medicare to death.

In his Medicare speech, George Bush said: "Our Medicare system is a binding commitment of a caring society; we must renew that commitment by providing the seniors of today and tomorrow with preventive care and the new medicines that are transforming health care in our country."[23] Americans can legitimately ask, *how will rewarding insurance and drug industries assist older adults obtain health care?*

We, the people, need to carefully reflect on Bush's words from his January 2001 inaugural address ". . .when we see that wounded traveller on the road to Jericho; we will not pass to the other side."[24]

Dare we ask what road and with whom George Bush travels?

To be heard and seen by the present administration, older adults apparently need a $1 billion political fund to match monies spent by the drug and insurance industries; monies that clearly tailored revision of Medicare to support their interests. The rewards given to these special interests in the Medicare Improvement and Modernization Act of 2003 give a whole new dimension to the term perfidy. The Teapot Dome Scandal pales in comparison.[25]

Health Insurance and the Unemployed

The "middle class" is now feeling the pinch of both unemployment and loss of health insurance. For the first time many are experiencing the uncertainty and vulnerability that loss of health insurance brings. Mr. Bush stated, "Our goal is a system in which all Americans have got (sic) a good insurance policy."[26] The American people must ask, *what does he mean by that?*

American Health Insurance coverage is a patchwork system tied to one's job. Reinhardt noted there is no reasonable explanation for the US, a nation that spends close to 70% more on health care per capita than does the next most expensive health system in the world (Germany), to leave more than 15% of its population without health insurance. He posits that unless the nation slides into a serious recession so that the middle class is affected with loss of health care benefits, there will be no real change in how lack of health insurance is managed.[27]

The Bush solution of income tax credits does not address the serious issue of job loss among a growing number of American workers. The Bush solution essentially adds more patches for the insurance industry quilt and leaves the unemployed uncovered.

Dr. Reinhardt summarized information about why there are so many uninsured Americans and asks whether the problem is permanent. He presents data that while politically incorrect is accurate. The uninsured represent a politically and economically marginal socio-economic group without much leverage in the commercial or political market place. However, the dynamic of this situation is rapidly changing as the number of uninsured and underinsured escalates in the middle class.

He further notes that unless the nation slides into a serious recession little will actually be accomplished to alleviate the situation. Short of a major recession, we shall be lucky if, by the year 2010, the current number stands only at today's (2001) level: 40 million or so.[28] In 2003 those numbers increased to 43.6 million (2.4 million more than 2002) with little relief in sight as the number of jobs continues to be exported to cheaper labor markets.[29]

An unforeseen problem is that a growing number of those serving in the military reserve have lost employee health insurance benefits and cannot afford COBRA insurance that can run in excess of $700 per month. The federally mandated COBRA health insurance program was designed to ensure that health insurance could be continued in the event of a job loss.[30] Since an employer is not picking up any part of the premium, it is a prohibitive bill for many who have lost jobs. For young married reservists who need to support families and make mortgage payments, COBRA insurance is not an option. He or she may decide to pay the mortgage and hope that no one gets ill.

To cover their own fiscal policies that place the nation's economy and health at risk, Bush and Cheney repeatedly state "We inherited a recession." While they did not inherit a recession, they did inherit the medically uninsured, whose numbers are growing at an alarming rate as jobs continue to be lost. The current numbers of the medically uninsured exceeds the aggregate population of 24 states.[31] It is reasonable to expect that this problem will continue to expand as more people in the middle class are affected.

It is unlikely that the large deficit generated by Bush policies will allow for a solution to problems of the uninsured and underinsured. When the next president is sworn into office in 2005 this issue must be dealt with and rhetoric will not be the answer. Some hard choices that will disadvantage the upper 2% of the population must come into play or the problem will grow to geometric proportions.

Summary
More than half of those surveyed in the U.S. for an October 2003 *Time/CNN* poll responded that George Bush is trustworthy. It is remarkable that a majority of Americans trust George Bush whose Administration

trademark is secrecy, lies and disinformation.

First, George Bush and his Administration generated fear of bioterrorism as a propaganda tool to drive the public into supporting an illegal preemptive war against Iraq.[32]

Second, the grand promises of George Bush about stem cell research are false. The prohibition against research using new stem cell lines eliminates the opportunity for American scientists to use cutting edge technology in their search for a cure for Alzheimer's, Parkinson's or other debilitating diseases.

Third, promises were made to fight the AIDS epidemic that has killed 7.5 million Africans since 2001 yet the Bush Administration underfunded its own loudly touted program by $1 billion the first year.

Fourth, the Medicare Prescription Drug Improvement and Modernization Act of 2003 supported by George Bush does not permit medical service choices but, instead, enforces limited-option medical dictates for senior and indigent citizens. The revised bill is not about choice, it is about destroying Medicare and Medicaid—a long held goal of some conservative legislators.

Fifth, the steady stream of job losses occurring during George Bush's Administration has further increased the number of medically uninsured. That number now stands at 43.6 million Americans without health insurance, an increase of 2.4 million over 2002. With health insurance tied to jobs and the steady increase in unemployment the problem is ominous. Mr. Bush's tax credit solution meets the needs of the insurance industry, not the uninsured.

If recent opinion polls accurately reflect the US public's assessment of George Bush it is profoundly clear that the American people are unable to transcend the expediency of political rhetoric and propaganda. This inability to comprehend what George Bush and his Administration are doing to damage the immediate and long-term well being of American citizens may be the real terror facing the United States.

NOTES

1. Laurie Garrett, *Betrayal of Trust: The Collapse of Global Public Health*, (New York: Hyperion Press), 2000.

2. Laurie Garrett, *The Coming Plague,* (New York: Penguin Books), 1994.

3. Secretary Colin Powell, Presentation before U.N. Security Council (February 5, 2003).

4. B. H. Rosenberg, "All American Anthrax Scare: Made in the USA," *BWC News* (November 12, 2001).

5. *PBS*, "Nova Presents Bioterror" (November 13, 2001).

6. Laurie Garrett, *Betrayal of trust: The collapse of global public health*, (New York: Hyperion Press), 2000.

7. "Vaccinia (Smallpox) Vaccine Recommendations of the Advisory Committee on Immunization Practices," 2001. www.cdc.gov

8. D. Linzer, "Team Pox" finds no smallpox in Iraq," *Associated Press*, Cleveland Plain Dealer (September 19, 2003).

9. David Kay, "Report to Congress on the Activities of the Iraq Survey Group (October 2, 2003).

10. B. Drogin, "Experts Downplay Bioagent," *Los Angeles Times* (October 17, 2003).

11. "The Man Behind the Vaccine Mystery," *CBS News* (December 12, 2002).

12. "Bioshields Program,"<www.whitehouse.gov>.

13. H. Waxman, <www.house.gov/reform/min/politicsandscience>.

14. Elias Zerhouni, "Testimony before the Senate Committee on Appropriations, Subcommittee on Labor, Health and Human Services, and Education, Federal Funding for stem cell research," 108th Congress (May 22, 2003).

15. AIDS/HIV Prevention Program, <www.whitehouse.gov>.

16. Nicholas D. Kristof, "When Prudery Kills," *New York Times* (October 8, 2003).

17. George W. Bush, "Medicare Address"(March 4, 2003).

18. Drake Bennett, Heidi Pauken, "All the President's Lies," *American Prospect* (May 1, 2003).

19. Drake Bennett, Heidi Pauken, "All the President's Lies," *American Prospect* (May 1, 2003).

20. "Private Insurance Plans & Medicare: The Disappointing History," Private Citizen Congress Watch (June 2003).

21. Dave Harmon, "Texas Workforce Commission,"*American Statesman* (October 12 2003).

22. Robert Pear, "More doctors say they are refusing Medicare patients," *New York Times* (March 17, 2002).

23. George W. Bush, "Medicare Address"(March 4, 2003).

24. George W. Bush, "Inauguration Speech" (January 21, 2001).

25. *Encyclopedia Americana*, "Teapot Dome Scandal," (1924).

26. George W. Bush, "Medicare Address"(March 4, 2003).

27. Uwe E. Reinhardt, "Why are there so many uninsured Americans? Is the problem permanent?" *Harvard Health Policy Review* (Spring 2001).

28. Ibid..

29. R. Pear, "Big leap in ranks of the uninsured," *New York Times* (September 29, 2003).

30. Consolidated Omnibus Budget Reconciliation Act (COBRA), 1986

31. R. Pear, "Big leap in ranks of the uninsured," *New York Times* (September 29, 2003).

32. Mike Hersh, "Colin Powell is Lying" (February 6, 2003) at <www.mikehersh.com/Colin_Powell_is_Lying.shtml>.

President Bush:
The False Prophet of the Christian Right

BY BENNET G. KELLEY

> Beware of false prophets which come to you in sheep's clothing,
> but inwardly they are ravening wolves.
> (Matthew 7:15)

Religion has played an important role throughout American history and today may be a defining issue in American politics.[1] The prominence of religion in current debate is largely attributable to President Bush's infusion of religion into his words and policies like no other president in modern times. Yet even in his role as "Pastor-in-Chief", Bush has engaged in the same pattern of deceit and deception as he had in non-pastoral matters.

The "Wall of Separation"
Although the early settlers fled the religious battles raging in Europe for the New World to freely practice their faith, they were no more tolerant of non-majority denominations whose followers were imprisoned, exiled or even killed.[2] Among those persecuted was Roger Williams who opposed the use of civil power "to judge the convictions of men's souls" and believed that forced religion constituted "spiritual rape" which "stinks in God's nostrils."[3]

Williams ultimately founded the colony of Rhode Island based on his vision that there should be a "hedge or wall of Separation between the Garden of the Church and the Wilderness of the world," and that religious freedom must extend to all and not just Christians.[4] Rhode Island became "the safest refuge of conscience" and home to New World's first Baptist church and synagogue.[5] Other states began to follow the Rhode Island model and by the late seventeenth century "an American pattern of religious liberty displaced the European pattern of a single national church."[6]

The seed sown by Williams ultimately blossomed into the First Amendment prohibiting Congress from establishing a religion or interfering with the free exercise of religion. The Founding Fathers were clearly committed to the principles of religious liberty and the separation of church and state. In 1790, President Washington assured the congregation of Rhode Island's Touro Synagogue that under the new nation "all possess alike liberty of conscience and immunities of citizenship."[7] Thomas Jefferson believed that religious freedom was necessary to preserve other freedoms and was the first President to articulate the concept of "a wall of separation between church and state."[8] This wall was invoked by James Madison, who drafted the First Amendment, in vetoing a bill to incorporate an Episcopal church within the capitol city and another to provide federal land for a Baptist church.[9]

The Supreme Court has tried to follow the Founders' conviction that "a union of government and religion tends to destroy government and degrade religion."[10] The Court has drawn the line between church and state to *prohibit* the government from speaking in a religious voice (e.g., school prayer) or discriminating against religious speech in a public forum that welcomes secular speech; but permitting the provision of indirect (e.g., vouchers) and direct assistance to religious organizations so long as recipients are selected in a religious-neutral way and the aid is given for a secular purpose.[11]

Salvation in Jesus or Karl Rove?

From the moment during an Iowa caucus debate when Governor Bush identified his favorite political philosopher as, "Christ, because he changed my heart", critics questioned whether he simply was pandering to the religious right or lacked the intellectual capacity to identify any philosophers.[12] Al Franken raised the point in his recent book, noting that as a candidate Bush deflected discussion of the Bible passage he read in the morning by stating, "I think you're trying to catch me as to whether or not I can remember where I was in the Bible."[13]

Given Bush's mendacity in almost all other areas and his father's swift conversion from Yankee moderate to Reagan conservative, such questioning is not surprising. In 1988, the younger Bush learned the importance of the Christian Right within his party both by witnessing Pat Robertson's "victory" in Iowa and as the campaign's liaison to the Christian Right.[14] Bush used a former evangelist to write *Man of Integrity* "a campaign biography [of his father] wrapped in religious garb" and followed this same model in 2000 with his autobiography, *A Charge to Keep,* whose title is taken from an old hymn.[15]

Bush clearly understood the importance of the Christian Right as he entered the race in 2000, particularly since one of their leaders (Gary Bauer) was a candidate. Bush began his campaign with a meeting with televangelist and spiritual advisor James Robison, who, although surprised to find Karl Rove was present for what he thought was a "spiritual meeting," ultimately became Bush's liaison to the Christian Right and helped secure endorsements from Pat Robertson and others.[16]

While some of Bush's critics, such as Michael Kinsley, have openly questioned the sincerity of Bush's faith,[17] what most concerns his critics is not the sincerity of his beliefs but instead "the content and meaning of that faith and how it impacts his administration's domestic and foreign policies."[18]

The Bush Theocracy

At the start of this administration, Bush stressed that "I strongly respect the separation of church and state," but no President has made such a concerted effort to breach this wall.[19] Bush has assumed the role of Pastor-in-Chief, repeatedly using speech writers from the evangelical community to evoke religious texts in political contexts.[20]

God's Man in the White House. What is most disturbing is Bush's belief that he has been "chosen by the grace of God to lead" at this time in history and is reported to have said that "God told him to strike at al Qaeda [and] at Saddam".[21] We know all too well that the pages of history are filled with the tragedies and sorrows inflicted by past and current leaders, such as Osama bin Laden, who shared Bush's messianic visions.

A religious scholar found that "Bush is very much into the apocalyptic and messianic thinking of militant Christian evangelicals [which includes a] worldview that there is a giant struggle between good and evil culminating in a final confrontation."[22] This is evident in Bush's language of a "crusade" or "a monumental struggle of good versus evil."[23] This approach, however, creates a culture of stubbornness and arrogance within the White House in which "[n]o one's allowed to second-guess, even when [they] should."[24]

Religious Tests. While the Constitution provides that "no religious Test shall ever be required as a Qualification to any Office or public Trust under the United States", President Bush has ensured that the people in his administration share his evangelical world view.[25] For example, when Dr. William R. Miller was vetted for a position on the National Advisory Council on Drug Abuse he was asked whether he was (i) sympathetic to faith-based initiatives; (ii) supported abortion rights; (iii) supported the death penalty for drug kingpins; and (iv) voted for Bush.[26] When it comes to judicial nominees, Bush seeks judges who "understand that our rights are derived by God."[27]

The application of this Christian Right litmus test has yielded appointees such as:

- Attorney General John Ashcroft who declared at the infamous

Bob Jones University ("BJU") that America's greatness stems from the triumph of "eternal authority over civic authority";[28]

- Jerry Thacker, a BJU alumnus, to the Presidential Advisory Council on HIV and AIDS even though Thacker denounced the "sin of homosexuality" before a BJU audience, referred to AIDS as the "gay plague" and advocated "reparative" therapy to "cure" homosexuals of their "aberrant" behavior;[29] and

- W. David Hager, M.D. to the FDA Reproductive Drugs Health Advisory Committee, even though Hager refuses to allow his patients to use contraceptives and prescribed prayer and Bible readings to combat ailments like PMS and headaches.[30]

The Bush administration also has included representatives of the Christian Right and the Vatican in U.S. delegations in international forums on reproductive issues; and Jerry Falwell and others from Christian Right are reported to be in the White House "all the time".[31]

Bush's evangelical army has had a broad influence on administration policy on issues ranging from stem-cell research to Israel and are participants in the administration's strategy of deception. This is most evident in their assault on documented facts that do not fit their religious views, such as:

- Bush's decision to cancel $34 million in funding to the U.N. Population Fund on the basis that the money was being used to force abortions, when U.N. and State Department investigations reached an opposite conclusion;[32]

- Forcing the National Cancer Institute to remove "well established" information on the absence of a link between abortions and increased risk of breast cancer and replacing it with a characterization suggesting that the link remained an open issue;[33]

- Removing evidence of the effectiveness of condoms or sex education programs from websites for the Center for Disease Control and the Agency for International Development;[34] and

- Launching an investigation into a Texas Tech professor who gave medical school recommendations only to students who could "truthfully and forthrightly affirm a scientific answer" to the origins of the human species.[35]

Bush's Faith-Based Initiative: Myths v. Facts

The centerpiece of the Bush administration's assault on the wall between church and state is its Faith-Based Initiatives ("F-B-I") to provide funding to religious groups for certain social services. The White House admits that the program has a clear political purpose: energize the party's base of evangelical Christian voters and convince heavily Democratic African-American voters that "his outreach to inner city churches proves he is a compassionate conservative".[36] The White House, however, has promoted F-B-I based on a series of myths, raising questions about the administration's true intent.

Widespread Bias against FBO's. Promptly after coming into office, the administration released a report claiming that there "exists a widespread bias against faith-based organizations ("FBO's") in Federal social service programs."[37] Long before the F-B-I, FBO's had qualified for millions in federal grants and experienced FBO's stated "quite unequivocally . . . that we have not encountered restrictive conditions as a result of our religious orientation and our religious affiliation."[38] Two recent independent studies confirmed the absence of barriers to FBO's participation in government programs."[39]

The White House claims that the requirement that government contractors comply with federal civil rights laws in hiring is a major obstacle, despite the fact that "there's no hard evidence that hiring requirements are keeping [FBO's] from applying for government contracts."[40] Nonetheless, the Bush administration fulfilled "a firm commitment" given to the Salvation Army by granting an exemption from civil rights laws to permit FBO's to discriminate in hiring based on religion, sexual preference and other grounds if it is "important to its religious identity" despite repeated Supreme Court pronouncements that "the Constitution does not permit the state to aid discrimination ."[41]

FBO's Are More Effective. While the President repeatedly asserts that FBO's are as good as or better than their secular counterparts in providing social services, his staff concedes there is no evidence to support this claim.[42] The findings of recent empirical studies in this area, however, are that at best FBO's performed as well as secular organizations and, in several cases, performed worse.[43]

The most relevant study, however, may be an analysis of the first five years of Bush's Texas faith-based program which detailed "a system that is unregulated, prone to favoritism and commingling of funds, and even dangerous to the very people it is supposed to serve."[44]

The Faith-Based Initiative Is Constitutional. Despite the President's claims that he "strongly respects" the separation of church and state and that his "job is not to try to convert people," with respect to the F-B-I the evidence suggests otherwise.[45] Bush's statements on the program, such as:

- "America can be saved . . . one soul . . . at a time";[46]

- "People need to know a higher power";[47] and
- "[hope and a sense of purpose can be restored when] some good souls puts an arm around a neighbor and says 'God loves you.'"[48]

are overtly religious and emphasize the religious and not the social services provided by FBO's. This also is evident in his praise of programs such as the Set Free Indeed addiction program which believes "recovery begins at the Cross" and relies "solely on the foundation of the Word of God to break the bands of addiction."[49]

The Bush administration also has assumed the role of determining which faiths are acceptable under F-B-I. For example, Bush indicated that he would not allow the Nation of Islam to receive funding because they promote "spite and hate,"[50] while James Towey, the Director of the White House Office of Faith-Based and Community Initiatives stated that pagan groups would not receive funding since they have "no interest in caring for the poor."[51] This type of discrimination and government involvement in religion is precisely what the Founders sought to prevent.

Finally, the regulations implementing F-B-I ignore established legal precedent and permit funding for religious facility construction and misstate Constitutional limitations to only prohibit use of program funds for worship, religious instruction and proselytizing when the courts *also* prohibit use of funds for institutions or activities that are pervasively or inherently religious.[52] The regulations also provide little guidance on the distinction between an FBO maintaining its religious character (permissible) and engaging in religious activity (impermissible).[53]

What is most troubling is that oversight of FBO's will mostly be limited to "self audits."[54] This lack of meaningful oversight combined with a lack of clear direction is a invitation for abuse; particularly when studies have found that most FBO's *do not* know that government funds cannot be used for religious activities and the Bush administration has awarded grants to several FBO's who openly dismiss the separation of church and state as a mere "fiction."[55] When Bush permitted similar lax regulation and oversight in Texas the end result was government money being used for religious purposes.[56]

Bush's Commitment to the Faith-Based Initiative

Bush's commitment to the F-B-I is summed up by the fact that in 2001 he promised to create a $700 million "Federal Compassion Fund" but failed to allocate a dime for it in his budget.[57] FBO's are now dismissing the program as an "empty reality" that is "just . . . a financial watering hole for the right-wing white evangelists."[58]

Bush's initial Director for F-B-I programs, John DiIulio, exposed the true nature of the Bush White House, explaining that:

> [t]here is no precedent in any White House for what is going on in this one: a complete lack of policy apparatus. What you've got is everything – and I mean everything – being run by the political arm. [A]fter 9/11 . . . [t]here has been no domestic policy, really. Not even a pretense of it.[59]

DiIulio's comments and the administration's neglect of the F-B-I program make it evident that the Bush administration is using the program to cloak the administration's absence of a domestic policy or even compassion while at the same time pandering to the Christian Right. In the process, Bush has systematically undermined the Constitutional separation between church and state.

It is true that "America can be saved," as Bush claims, but only by following, not abandoning, the path set by its Founders 200 years ago which enable all Americans to embrace the religion of their choice without government interference or favoritism.

NOTES

1. Kathy Li, "Kristol Identifies Religion as Primary Issue in U.S. Politics," Daily Princeton News (March 12, 2003).

2. Edwin S. Gaustad, *Proclaim Liberty Throughout the Land: A History of Church and State in America* (Oxford University Press 2003), pp. 2-10 .

3. *Ibid* at 7; Rob Boston, "The Forgotten Founder," Americans United for Separation of Church and State (April 2003) at <www.au.org/churchstate/03-04-feature2.htm>.

4. *Ibid.*

5. Rob Boston, "The Forgotten Founder."

6. Edwin S. Gaustad, *Proclaim Liberty Throughout the Land*, p. 13.

7. Letter from George Washington to the Hebrew Congregation in Newport, Rhode Island (1790) at <www.au.org/resources/foundingdocs/Washingtons_Letter_To_Touro_Synagogue.htm>.

8. Edwin S. Gaustad, *Proclaim Liberty Throughout the Land*, p. 32; Joel Lancetta, "Illinois Senator Durbin Elaborates on Religious Freedom," The Chicago Maroon (September 25, 2003); Rob Boston, "The Forgotten Founder."

9. Edwin S. Gaustad, *Proclaim Liberty Throughout the Land*, p. 36.

10. Ibid, p. 80 (quoting *Engel v. Vitale*, 370 U.S. 421, 431 (1962)).

11. Ira C. Lupu and Robert W. Tuttle, *Government Partnerships with Faith-Based Service Providers: The State of the Law* 22 (The Roundtable on Religion and Social Welfare Policy 2002).

12. Joaquin Cabrejas, "Bush: The New Face of the Religious Right" 5 (American Humanist Association 2002).

13. Al Franken, *Lies and the Lying Liars Who Tell Them* (New York: Dutton 2003), pp. 213-15, 282. Franken also noted that Bush's long-time Bible-study companion (and current Commerce Secretary) Don Evans was unfamiliar with the very book of the New Testament that *Newsweek* reported he and Bush read daily.

14. Stephen Mansfield, *The Faith of George W. Bush* (New York: Tarcher/Penguin 2003), pp. 83-84. While Senator Dole won the 1988 Iowa caucus, it was Robertson's surprisingly strong second place finish ahead of Vice President Bush that made him the media winner.

15. Ibid., pp. 11-12, 83-84. The 2004 campaign season will feature another donning of the religious garb with *George W. Bush on God and Country* and friendly third-party books such as Stephen Mansfield's *The Faith of George W. Bush* and David Aikman's *A Man of Faith: The Spiritual Journey of George W. Bush*.

16. Stephen Mansfield, *The Faith of George W. Bush* at 109, 112.

17. Michael Kinsley, *Taking Bush Personally*, Slate (October 23, 2003) at <slate.msn.com/id/2090244/>. Kinsley reacted to Bush's decision to limit stem cell research based on false premises (and thereby delay breakthroughs against afflictions such as Parkinson's disease) by charging that Bush is "a hardened cynic, staging moral anguish he does not feel, pandering to people he cannot possibly agree with, and sacrificing the future of many American citizens for short-term political advantage." Ibid; *see* David Corn, "Stem Cells and Star Wars" in *The Lies of George W. Bush*(New York: Crown Publishers 2003), pp. 117-123.

18. Jim Wallis, "Dangerous Religion," *Sojourners Magazine* (September-October 2003).

19. Press Conference by the President, February 22, 2003.

20. See Jim Wallis, "Dangerous Religion." For example, in a ceremony commemorating the first anniversary of September 11, Bush described America as "the hope of mankind" that "lights our way. And the light shines in the darkness and the darkness has not overcome it." The last two sentences come straight from the Gospel of John except the light is the Word of God not the United States. "To confuse the role of God with that of the American nation, as George Bush seems to do, is a serious theological error that some might say borders on idolatry or blasphemy," comments Wallis. Other examples of Bush's use of religious text in political contexts can be found at Juan Stam, "Bush's Religious Language," *The Nation* (December 2003), and Chris Mooney, "W's Christian Nation," *The American Prospect* 34 (June 1, 2003).

21. Jim Wallis, "Dangerous Religion" ; also Ira Chernus, "Did Bush Say God Told Him to Go To War?" CommonDreams.org website (June 30, 2003) at <www.commondreams.org/view03/0630-04.htm>. This Messianic view is not limited to the President himself, as the White House Office of Public Liaison declared that "President Bush is God's man at this hour." Bill Berkowitz, "Bush's Faith-Filled Life," WorkingForChange.com website (November 5, 2003) at <www.workingforchange.com/article.cfm?itemid=15937>.

22. "Bush's Messiah Complex," *The Progressive* (February 2003).

23. Juan Stam, "Bush's Religious Language." Jim Wallis notes that Bush ig-

nores the fact that the gospel "teaches that the line separating good and evil runs not between nations, but inside every human heart" (Wallis, "Dangerous Religion,"). In doing so, says Stam, Bush follows the "false prophets of the Old Testament [who instead of proclaiming] sovereignty of Yahweh, the god of justice and love who judges nations and persons, the false prophets served Baal, who could be manipulated by the powerful." (Stam, "Bush's Religious Language").

24. Howard Fineman, "Bush and God," *Newsweek* (March 10, 2003). The White House's messianic view also creates an atmosphere that encourages statements such as General Boykin's characterizing the current struggle in the Middle East as the battle between "a Christian nation" and "Satan" (which the administration has tacitly embraced by its failure to both repudiate the statement and discipline General Boykin). Johanna Neuman, "Bush's Inaction over General's Islam Remarks Riles Two Faiths," *Los Angeles Times* (Nov. 23, 2003).

25. U.S. Constitution, art VI.

26. House Committee On Government Reform – Minority Staff, *Politics and Science in the Bush Administration* 28-29 (November 13, 2003).

27. Joaquin Cabrejas, "Bush, The New Face of the Religious Right," pp. 8-19. Bush was thrilled when he reviewed a memo on the vetting of Judge Robert Brack that indicated his judicial philosophy was "best defined through the words of the Old Testament prophet Micah: 'What does the Lord require of you, but to act justly, love mercy and walk humbly with your God.'" Also, Stephen Mansfield, *The Faith of George W. Bush*, pp. 164-65.

28. John Ashcroft, Address at Bob Jones University ((May 8, 1999) at <www.abcnews.go.com/sections/politics/DailyNews/ashcroft_bjutranscript010112.html.>. Ashcroft also told the BJU audience that he "thanked God for this institution."

29. Joaquin Cabrejas, "Bush, The New Face of the Religious Right," pp. 21-22.

30. Ibid, pp 23-34.

31. Ibid, pp 13-15; Ron Suskind, "Why Are These Men Laughing," *Esquire* (January 2003).

32. Joaquin Cabrejas, "Bush, The New Face of the Religious Right," p. 14.

33. *Politics and Science in the Bush Administration*, p. 22. The *New York Times* called this an "egregious distortion of the evidence." Editorial, "Abortion and Breast Cancer," *New York Times* (January 6, 2003).

34 *Politics and Science in the Bush Administration*, pp. 6, 11-13.

35. Chris Mooney, "W's Christian Nation," p. 36.

36. Mary Leonard, "Bush Presses Funding for Faith Groups," *Boston Globe* (November 30, 2003). This was evident in 2002 when the administration promoted F-B-I through meetings with faith-based organizations which were "overwhelmingly held in congressional districts pivotal [to] the Republican[s]." *The Faith-Based Initiative Two Years Later: Examining its Potential Progress and Problems* 11 (Pew Forum on Religion in Public Life 2003).

37. Centers for Faith-Based & Community Initiatives, *Unlevel Playing Field: Barriers to Participation by Faith-Based and Community Organizations in Federal Social*

Service Programs (January 29, 2001).

38. The Pew Forum on Religion in Public Life, *Lift Every Voice: A Report on Religion in American Public Life* 16 (2001), at <www.pewforum.org/publications/reports/lifteveryvoice.pdf>.

39. John C. Green & Amy L. Sherman, *Fruitful Collaborations: A Survey of Government-Funded Faith-Based Programs in 15 States* — Executive Summary 7 (Hudson Institute 2002); also Ira C. Lupu and Robert W. Tuttle, *Government Partnerships with Faith-Based Service Providers*, p. 55.

40. Jane Eisner, "Far from Promised Land, Faith Initiatives Are Starving," *Philadelphia Inquirer* (July 6, 2003). The White House masks its discriminatory animus under the guise that they are protecting FBO's "fundamental civil rights." *Protecting the Civil Rights and Religious Liberty of Faith-Based Organization: Why Religious Hiring Rights Must Be Preserved* 3 (White House Office of Faith-Based and Community Initiatives 2003). In doing so, the administration relies on the Religious Freedom Restoration Act even though the law has been interpreted to permit imposing conditions on discretionary government benefits to religious institutions. See *Developments in the Faith-Based and Community Initiatives*, pp. 15-16.

41. Dana Milbank, "Bush Legislative Approach Failed in Faith Bill Battle," *Washington Post* (April 23, 2003); Marci Hamilton, "The Salvation Army, Church and State: A Closer Look At The Charity's Proposed Deal With The White House," FindLaw.com website (August 2, 2001) at <www.writ.corporate.findlaw.com/hamilton/20010802.html>; Ira C. Lupu and Robert W. Tuttle, *Developments in the Faith-Based and Community Initiatives*; *Norwood v. Harrison*, 413 U.S. 455, 465-66 (1973); see also *Dodge v. Salvation Army*, 1989 U.S. Dist. LEXIS 4797, 48 Empl. Prac. Dec (CCH) ¶ 38,619 (S.D. Miss. 1989) (Salvation Army's firing employee because of her religious beliefs from government funded position violates First Amendment Establishment Clause).

The Constitutionality of this exemption may be resolved in the near future as there are two cases pending on this point, both involving an FBO firing of a gay employee for religious reasons. See *Charitable Choice: First Results from Three States* 88-89 (Center for Urban Policy and the Environment, 2003); Eyal Press, "Faith-Based Discrimination: The Case of Alicia Pedreira," *New York Times* (April 1, 2001).

42. Editorial, "The Bush 'Faith-Based' Initiative: Why It's Wrong," Americans United for Separation of Church and State (February 20, 2001) at <www.au.org/press/pr22001.htm >.

43. Mark A. R. Kleiman, "Charitable Choice: First Results from Three States at iv; , Faith-Based Fudging," Slate (August 5, 2003) at <www.slate.msn.com/id/2086617/>; OMB Watch, "New Studies Examine Faith-Based Initiative," (Dec. 2, 2003) at <www.ombwatch.org/article/articleview/1947/1/47/>; Alan Cooperman, "Faith-Based Charities May Not Be Better, Study Indicates," *Washington Post* (May 25, 2003).

44. Texas Freedom Network, "The Texas Faith-Based Initiative at Five Years," (2002) at <www.tfn.org/issues/charitablechoice/report02.html>.

45. Press Conference by the President (February 22, 2001); "Interview with

Presidential Candidate George W. Bush," Beliefnet.com website (Fall 2000) at <www.beliefnet.com/story/47/story_4703_1.html>.

46. Americans United for Separation of Church and State, "Bush's Adjustments Fail to Address Faith-Based Initiatives' Fatal Flaws," (June 27, 2001).

47. President George W. Bush, "Remarks at the Dedication of the Oak Cliff Bible Fellowship Youth Education Center in Dallas, Texas," (October 29, 2003).

48. President George W. Bush, "Remarks at Downtown Marriott Hotel, Philadelphia, Pennsylvania" (December 2, 2002).

49. Americans United for Separation of Church and State, "Bush-Backed Addiction Programs Promote Religion, Shouldn't Get Public Funds, Says AU" (January 29, 2003) at <www.au.org/press/pr030129.htm>.

50. Wendy Kaminer, "Faith-Based Favoritism," *The American Prospect*, (April 9, 2001). Of course, this also would appear to exclude Pat Robertson and Jerry Falwell who blamed 9-11 on pagans, feminists, gays, lesbians and civil libertarians, yet Pat Robertson's "Operation Blessing" received a $500,000 grant in 2002. See Chris Mooney, "W's Christian Nation," p. 35.

51. Alan Cooperman, "White House Aide Angers Pagans," *Washington Post* (December 8, 2003); "Ask the White House: Online Forum with Jim Towey" (November 26, 2003) at <www.whitehouse.gov/ask/20031126.html_>. Towey's comments had no basis in fact since pagan groups have collected food and donated money to shelters for the homeless and battered women, food banks, the American Red Cross and other charities.

52. *Developments in the Faith-Based and Community Initiatives: Comments on Notices of Proposed Rulemaking and Guidance Document*, pp. 7, 11-12.

53 Ibid, p. 10;

54. "Guidance to Faith-Based and Community Organizations on Partnering with the Federal Government 5" (White House Office of Community and Faith-Based Initiatives 2003).

55. "Charitable Choice: First Results from Three States" p. v; *Bush's Christian Nation*, p. 35. Grantees include Pat Robertson who often stated that the phrase "separation of church and state" is not in the Constitution but was part of the Soviet constitution. Americans United for Separation of Church and State, "They Said It!: Religious Right Leaders in Their Own Words" at <www.au.org/relrightresearch/They_Said_It.pdf>. It is worth noting that Robertson's claim is repeated by Bush advisor Marvin Olasky, the alleged brain behind compassionate conservatism. Joaquin Cabrejas, "Bush, The New Face of the Religious Right," p. 13.

56. *The Texas Faith-Based Initiative at Five Years*, p. 10.

57. Joshua Green, "Bad Faith," *The American Prospect* (July 30, 2001).

58. Ibid; also Mary Leonard, "Bush Presses Funding for Faith Groups," *Boston Globe* (November 30, 2003).

59. Ron Suskind, "Why Are These Men Laughing".

Bush Isn't an "Education President," He Just Plays One

BY MADELEINE BEGUN KANE

A man as English-language challenged as George W. Bush might seem an unlikely candidate for "education president:"[1]

> "You teach a child to read and he or her will be able to pass a literacy test."[2]

> "What's not fine is, rarely is the question asked, are, is our children learning?"[3]

But despite his frequent battles with the English language, then Governor Bush portrayed himself as an education reform warrior throughout his first Presidential campaign. Routinely describing education as his "number one priority,"[4] he touted his Texas education accomplishments, including "exemplorary" schools[5] and a statewide testing system designed to end the "soft bigotry of low expectations."[6] He vowed to accomplish for the nation what he'd done for Texas with education reforms featuring accountability and local control, and to "renew parents' faith in the schools their children attend."[7]

As it turns out, George Bush isn't an "education president" after all, although he does play one in the White House. For while President Bush did reform our nation's education system, he based his plan on a Texas system that's a far cry from the "miracle" he claims to have accomplished there. Moreover, his federal reforms amount to unfunded mandates which impose massive new burdens on our nation's schools without coming close to footing the bill.

But I'm getting ahead of myself. Back during the 2000 Presidential campaign, Bush's Democratic opponent, Vice-President Al Gore, highlighted many defects in Bush's education plan and observed that Bush's "major proposal in this campaign is a giant, $2.1 trillion tax giveaway—which would be certain to force cuts in public education."[8]

Al Gore's words were prophetic.

We now know that Bush's "Texas miracle" was at best, as *USA Today* columnist DeWayne Wickham put it, a "mirage."[9] Wickham was relying on a report by the Rand Corporation, a non-partisan think tank, which challenged the "Texas miracle" claims. The Rand report found that 1998 Texas test score improvements weren't reflected when students took a national test (the NAEP).[10]

The Rand results were echoed in a study reported in the *New York Times* on December 3, 2003:[11]

> In recent years, Texas has trumpeted ... academic gains ... largely on the basis of a state test, the Texas Assessment of Academic Skills, or TAAS. As a presidential candidate, Texas's former governor, George W. Bush, contended that Texas's methods of holding schools responsible for student performance had brought huge improvements in passing rates and remarkable strides in eliminating the gap between white and minority children. . . .
>
> But an examination of the performance of students in Houston by The New York Times raises serious doubts about the magnitude of those gains. Scores on a national exam that Houston students took alongside the Texas exam from 1999 to 2002 showed much smaller gains and falling scores in high school reading.
>
> Compared with the rest of the country, Houston's gains on the national exam, the Stanford Achievement Test, were modest. The improvements in middle and elementary school were a fraction of those depicted by the Texas test. . .

But the Texas system went well beyond "mirage" into fraud territory, with cooked books worthy of Enron and Arthur Andersen. In *Bushwhacked*, Molly Ivins quoted education expert Linda McNeil, who spearheaded a study of the Texas system:

> We disappear our kids,' McNeil said . . . If test scores are low, schools are rated low-performing. In low-performing schools, principals lose their jobs. Tests as a single criterion to evaluate schools provide an incentive for principals to disappear weak students to keep their campus test scores high. . . .
>
> The low-performing students encouraged to go quietly are mostly Latino, African-American, and students with limited English proficiency (LEP). After they leave, the Texas Education Agency cooks the books. In 2001 the agency released dropout figures-all under 4 percent. But the conservative Manhattan Institute came up with a dropout rate of 52%. . .[12]

And so the "Texas miracle" might more accurately be described (if I might borrow from U.S. Congressman and 2004 Presidential contender Richard Gephardt) as "a miserable failure."[13]

Nevertheless, that "miracle" helped parlay Bush into the presidency. And his reforms based on that "miracle" are a centerpiece of his administration.

In his Inaugural Address, Bush pledged to "reclaim America's schools, before ignorance and apathy claim more young lives."[14] Days later he introduced his education package, which David Corn summarizes here:

> A cornerstone of the plan was more testing for students. In order to ensure 'accountability and high standards,' Bush called for annual reading and math 'assessments' (read: tests) for every child in grades 3 to 8. Using these tests as the key measurements, states and districts would monitor schools. Schools that did not make 'adequate yearly progress for one academic year' would be identified as needing improvement. A school that did not meet 'adequate yearly progress after two years' would be designated a 'failing school,' and it would have to implement 'corrective action' and offer a choice of another public school to its students. If a school screwed up for three years, low-income students could use federal funds to transfer to a better public school or a private school. A voucher system of sorts would kick in.[15]

When Bush sent his education bill to Congress, he said:

> Both parties have been talking about education reform for quite a while. It's time to come together to get it done, so that we can truthfully say in America: No child will be left behind, not one single child.

He also promised local independence, adding:

> The agents of reform must be schools and school districts, not bureaucracy. One size does not fit all. Educational entrepreneurs should not be hindered by excessive rules and red tape and regulation.[16]

Senator Edward Kennedy became Bush's unlikely education reform ally[17] and proudly participated in the January 8, 2002 ceremony when the No Child Left Behind Act ("NCLB") was signed into law. But Kennedy's pride was short-lived: Several weeks later Bush announced his 2003 budget which, in addition to diverting $4 billion to private school tuitions and eliminating 40 education programs, fell $90 million short of the federal education dollars mandated by the NCLB.[18] Responding in an April 6, 2002 radio address, Senator Kennedy said:

We cannot remain silent when the President now fails to fund his own education bill. It was a wonderful promise—but it has become a hollow promise.

In fact, his budget proposal actually cuts funds for public school reform, while providing 4 billion dollars to private schools—and 600 billion dollars in new tax breaks for the wealthy.[19]

U.S. Senator Dodd (Democrat, Connecticut) objected also, voicing his 2003 budget protest in a Hartford Courant column:

. . . When he signed the No Child Left Behind Act, President Bush promised that the federal government would make sure schools would have the resources necessary to meet the three key requirements of the new law: closing the achievement gap for low-income students, minority students and students with disabilities; having a highly qualified teacher in every classroom; and holding schools accountable for all students performing at a high level.

In February, with the ink on the new law not yet dry, the president submitted his new education budget to Congress, and the resources were not there.

In fact, the president took an enormous step backward by proposing to cut federal support for the No Child Left Behind Act.

For example, more than 10 million low-income children attend schools in areas that are eligible for federal assistance to hire and train teachers and buy textbooks, computers and other necessities. The president's education budget for next year would provide only 40 percent of the assistance that these schools need, leaving more than 6 million children behind. . . .

The president also wants to cut federal support for critical after-school and bilingual education programs. This shortfall in resources would force roughly 25,000 children nationwide out of bilingual education and more than 30,000 children out of after-school programs.

. . . In this year's State of the Union address, the president called for hiring and training more quality teachers to address a national shortage. Yet the president's new budget would eliminate high-quality training programs for nearly 20,000 teachers.[20]

To add insult to educational injury, Bush's 2004 budget compounded the problem, cutting funding "drastically" for the new programs, as Senator Kennedy put it. The "hypocrisy is breathtaking," he added. [21]

Numerous educators and local officials have spoken out against Bush's funding failures and the Act's rigid standards, even as they try to comply. *This Economist* article explains the funding issue:

> The biggest 'unfunded mandate' is the No Child Left Behind Act of 2001. This requires all public schools to test students, in order to improve their education. In theory, the act fully finances the new tests. In practice, say local officials, implementing the act requires changes in the whole education system, not just adding a few extra tests. The cost, they say, is $35 billion a year more than the act provides for.[22]

The National Education Association ("NEA") condemned the Bush administration for turning the NCLB into an unfunded mandate in violation of the law itself. Indeed, the NCLB does contain this clause: "Nothing in this Act shall be construed to authorize an officer or employee of the Federal Government to...mandate a State or any subdivision thereof to spend any funds or incur any costs not paid for under this Act."[23]

The NEA also cited a "General Accounting Office study that estimates that states will be required to expend between $1.9 and $5.3 billion of their own money to implement the testing provisions of the No Child Left Behind Act between 2002 and 2008."

Bush's failure to fund isn't the only problem. According to NEA President Reg Weaver, "there is a problem with the rigid and unrealistic rules of the so-called 'No Child Left Behind' law when 87 percent of schools in Florida and 51 percent in Pennsylvania failed to meet federal standards this year."[24]

Okay, so our states are now (1) required to comply with education reforms modeled on a failed and (some say) fraudulent system; (2) threatened with sanctions if they don't comply; and (3) denied the very money that was promised them and that's necessary to achieve compliance. So how does Bush respond? He (1) downplays the need for money; (2) lies about his budgets; and (3) portrays NCLB as a success.

Let's start with Bush's minimizing the need for money. Here's how the White House responded to Senator Kennedy's radio address: [25]

> "We've seen in the past [that] money is not the answer," said spokeswoman Anne Womack. "Most importantly, meaningful reform is being enacted to ensure that every child has the access to a top-rate education."

The Bush White House even denied imposing unfunded mandates, asserting that the states have the (obviously unrealistic) option of not taking the money at all.[26]

As for Bush education budget lies, they started even before NCLB was enacted. An April 2001 analysis by the independent Center on Budget and Policy Priorities concluded that under the President's 2002 budget, "education funding would grow 5.3 Percent" and that "the claimed 11.5 percent increase is a distortion.[27]

More recently, David Corn deconstructed a Bush whopper made in a prepared speech in a Tennessee Elementary School on September 8, 2003:

> September is back-to-school time, and Bush hit the road to promote his education policies. During a speech at a Nashville elementary school, he hailed his education record by noting that "the budget for next year boosts funding for elementary and secondary education to $53.1 billion. That's a 26-percent increase since I took office. In other words, we understand that resources need to flow to help solve the problems." A few things were untrue in these remarks. Bush's proposed elementary and secondary education budget for next year is $34.9 billion, not $53.1 billion, according to his own Department of Education. It's his total proposed education budget that is $53.1 billion. More importantly, there is no next-year "boost" in this budget. Elementary and secondary education received $35.8 billion in 2003. Bush's 2004 budget cuts that back nearly a billion dollars, and the overall education spending in his budget is the same as the 2003 level.[28]

Bush lied in Jacksonville, Florida too:

> We've got a brand new reading initiative where we will have spent, since the No Child Left Behind Act was passed, $1.2 billion for reading instruction. By the way, we're trying to promote curriculum which actually works. We want to make sure if we spend money on reading that children learn to read. We want to make sure as we spend money on reading, teachers know how to teach that which works...[29]

That statement runs counter to the teacher training and other cuts pointed out in Senator Dodd's column,[30] Bush's Even Start literacy program cuts,[31] his proposal to de-federalize Head Start,[32] and the fact that states have been lowering their education standards in order to avoid NCLB sanctions.[33]

In his Jacksonville speech,[34] Bush also touted low-income tutoring and parental options to transfer their children away from failing schools. But there is a "lack of resources for students eligible to transfer out of a failing school."[35] Moreover, Bush shortchanged Title I funding, the primary program for economically disadvantaged students, with a budget request that "falls 33% short of what Congress considers full funding under the law." This means that "more than half of all poor children eligible for additional instruction and intensive services will be left out."[36]

In Jacksonville Bush defined a "hopeful America" as a place "where children say, you know, I'm going to get an education early and I'm going to go to college."[37] But as Senator Dodd observed:

> ...the president's budget cuts would cause hundreds of thousands of potential college students to lose financial assistance. And the president even proposed putting college out of the reach of even more middle-class and low-income students by increasing the interest on their student loans by thousands of dollars.[38]

An October 21, 2003 *New York Times* editorial entitled "Bait-and-Switch on Public Education" condemned "the Bush administration's mishandling of education policy generally, and especially its decision to withhold more than $6 billion from the landmark No Child Left Behind Act, the supposed centerpiece of the administration's domestic policy." The editorial concluded with these words:

> The Bush administration wanted to trumpet No Child Left Behind, then fail to pay for it—without the voters taking notice. But Americans, who value education, can tell a bait-and-switch when they see one. If this issue comes back to bite the G.O.P. in the next election, the party will have only itself to blame.[39]

Notes

1. See Bush prepares education package for Congress, CNN.com, January 22, 2001, <www.cnn.com/2001/ALLPOLITICS/stories/01/22/bush.wrap/>, which describes Bush as "The man who ran for the White House through the 2000 campaign season promising to be "'the education president.'"

2. George W. Bush, Tennessee, February 21, 2001, quoted in Molly Ivins and Lou Dubose, *Bushwhacked* (New York: Random House, 2003, p. 72) and in *Thanks For the Memories, Mister President*, by Helen Thomas, (New York: Scribner, 2002, p. 208).

3. George W. Bush, January 2000, as quoted in *The Bush Dyslexicon*, by Mark Crispin Miller, page 138 (New York: W. W. Norton & Company Inc., 2001, p. 138), citing the *Los Angeles Times*, January 14, 2000 as its source.

4. George W. Bush, St. Louis Debate, the Oct 17, 2000, as quoted in <www.issues2000.org/Celeb/George_W__Bush_Education.htm:> "I have been the governor of a big state; I've made education my number one priority. That's what governors ought to do. They ought to say this is the most important thing we do as a state."

5. For the "exemplorary" schools quote, see Dubyaspeak.com, www.-dubyaspeak.com/education.shtml, which attributes the quote to Manhattan Institute for Policy Research (New York), Oct. 5, 1999.

6. For one of many references to ending the "soft bigotry of low expectations," see George W. Bush, Hyde Park Elementary, Jacksonville, Florida, September 9, 2003, at <www.georgewbush.com/Education/Read.aspx?ID=2014>, where Bush also mischaracterizes the arguments against his education accountability system, saying "You know, I've heard all the debates about accountability systems. I mean, you hear it's discriminatory to measure."

7. According to an AP Story, *New York Times* (September 25, 2000), Bush said: "My plan will renew parents' faith in the schools their children attend. I will insist on accountability, local control and the importance of teaching every child to read."

8. Al Gore, Lansing, Michigan (May 5, 2000) at <www.mea.org/Design.cfm?p=2836>.

9. "Questions Raised About Education Gains," DeWayne Wickham, *USA Today* (November 27, 2000).

10. Issue Paper, Rand Education, "What Do Test Scores in Texas Tell Us?', see <www.rand.org/publications/IP/IP202>.

11. Diana Jean Schemo and Ford Fessenden, "A Miracle Revisited: Gains in Houston Schools: How Real Are They?" *New York Times* (December 3, 2003).

12. Molly Ivins and Lou Dubose, *Bushwhacked*, pp. 72-96.

13. See Dick Gephardt for President: "George W. Bush: A Miserable Failure," at <www.amiserablefailure.com>.

14. George W. Bush, Inaugural Address (January 20, 2001).

15. David Corn, *The Lies Of George W. Bush* (New York: Crown Publishers, 2003), pp. 70-71.

16. George W. Bush, Announcement of Education Bill, 1st bill sent to Congress (January 23, 2001).

17. Kathy Kiely, "Kennedy, Bush team up for nation's schools," *USA Today* (June 13, 2001).

18. Noy Thrupkaew, "A Dollar Short: Bush's budget defunds Bush's education plan," Prospect.org (June 3, 2002) at <www.prospect.org/print/V13/10/thrupkaew-n.html>. See also "Bush's Broken Promises: Education Reform," <www.democrats.org/specialreports/brokenpromises/education.html>.

19. "Senator Ted Kennedy Delivers Weekly Radio Response on Bush's Broken Promise to America's Schools," at <www.democrats.org/news/200204050001. html>.

20. Senator Christopher J. Dodd, "Bush Has Left Education Reform Behind," *Hartford Courant* as reprinted in *The Smirking Chimp* (May 13, 2002).

21. Editorial, "Next on Bush domestic agenda: education," *USA Today* (September 6, 2003). For more information, see also <www.house.gov/appropriations_democrats/caughtonfilm.htm>; <www.house.gov/apps/list/press/ri01_kennedy/pr030214bcrae.html>; and <www.edworkforce.house.gov/democrats/statement 61003.html>.

22. Editorial, "The Head Ignores The Feet," *Economist* (May 22, 2003).

23. "National Education Association To Challenge Provisions of No Child Left Behind Act," News Release (July 2, 2003). See also transcript of U.S. House of Representatives Committee on Rules, Hearing On 1996 Unfunded Mandates Reform Act (July 16, 2003) at <www.house.gov/rules/rules_tran_ unfunded.htm>.

24. NEA News Release, "NEA Supports Proposals to Improve 'No Child Left Behind'" (September 10, 2003). For information on the problems facing West Virginia schools, see this October 13, 2003 MSNBC article: <www.stacks.-msnbc.com/news/979595.asp?osl=-12>. For Oregon Gov. Ted Kulongoski's characterization of the NCLB as a "hoax," see <www.oregonlive. com/news/oregonian/index.ssf?/base/news/106890151550090.xml>. And for a ten state projected costs study, see <www.pdkintl.org/kappan/k0305mat.htm>.

25. "Senator Ted Kennedy Delivers Weekly Radio Response on Bush's Broken Promise to America's Schools," at <www.democrats.org/news/200204050001.html>.

26. Kenneth Cooper, "$5B reading program; mixing phonics & literature," *Washington Post* (April 2, 2000).

27. Richard Kogan, "Under President's Budget, Education Funding Would Grow 5.3 Percent, The Claimed 11.5 Percent Increase is a Distortion," Center on Budget and Policy Priorities (April 25, 2001).

28. See David Corn, "Capital Games," *The Nation* (September 15, 2003). The transcript of the Bush speech Mr. Corn is commenting on is here: <www. whitehouse.gov/news/releases/2003/09/20030908-2.html>.

29. George W. Bush, Hyde Park Elementary, Jacksonville, Florida (September 9, 2003).

30. Senator Christopher J. Dodd, "Bush Has Left Education Reform Behind," *Hartford Courant*.

31. "Bush Budget and Education," <www.aflcio.org/issuespolitics/education/ns0205b2002.cfm.>

32. Diana Jean Schemo, "Head Start Plan Worries Supporters," *New York Times* (February 12, 2003).

33. Sam Dillon, "States are Relaxing Education Standards to Avoid Sanctions from Federal Law," *New York Times* (May 5, 2003).

34. George W. Bush, Hyde Park Elementary, Jacksonville, Florida (September 9, 2003).

35. Amy F. Isaacs, "Replace Act with Laws That are Effective," *Miami Herald* (November 15, 2003).

36. Daily Mislead (Oct. 7, 2003) at <www.misleader.org/daily_mislead/Read.asp?fn=df10072003.html>.

37. George W. Bush, Hyde Park Elementary, Jacksonville, Florida (September 9, 2003).

38. Senator Christopher J. Dodd, "Bush Has Left Education Reform Behind," *Hartford Courant*. Regarding Pell college aid grant cuts, see Greg Winter, "Tens of Thousands Will Lose College Aid Report Says," *New York Times* (July 18, 2003). See also Mary Leonard, "Kennedy Rips Bush Plan to Let College Loan Rates Float," *Boston Globe* (April 29, 2002). Additional information is here: Bob Batchelor, "Go to Pell: The Bush administration's dumb anti-student initiative,"

May 2, 2002, at <www.prospect.org/webfeatures/2002/05/batchelor-b-05-02.html and here: www.house.gov/appropriations_democrats caughtonfilm.-htm>.

39. New York Times Editorial, "Bait-and-Switch on Public Education" (October 21, 2003).

Additional Notes

Space did not permit me to detail numerous other Bush "education president" failures and deceptions. Here are some I couldn't include in the body of my essay:

a. Distorted scientific evidence about what works in sex education in order to push an abstinence only agenda. See <www.house.gov/reform/min/politicsandscience/example_abstinence.htm>.

b. Suppressed and censored The U.S. Department of Education website's information in order to further the Bush administration's political priorities. See: <www.house.gov/reform/min/politicsandscience/example_education.htm>.

c. Slashed after-school funding. See: Kwame Kilpatrick, "Kids will be left behind: Bush prepares for war, sacrificing after-school programs along the way," *Detroit Free Press*, February 28, 2003,

d. Budget proposed to stop compensating schools for teaching children of military personnel who are not living on bases. See: "School officials slam Bush plan for military kids," CNN.com, February 7, 2003, <www.cnn.com/2003/EDUCATION/02/07/military.schools.ap/>.

e. Cut school lunch programs and food banks for the poor to finance special livestock drought-relief program. See, Thomas Edsall, "Money for School Lunches Diverted to Livestock, Report Contends," *Washington Post*, November 2, 2002.

Bush Lies on
Women and Minorities Policy

by Kevin J. Shay

When it comes to Bush's attitudes toward women and minorities, actions speak louder than words, and more than a few of Bush's words are lies. It's hard to find any outwardly racist remarks by Bush, such as conservative talk show host Rush Limbaugh telling a black caller to "take that bone out of your nose."[1] Likewise, sexist statements by Bush are difficult to unearth. Bush is no Arnold Schwarzenegger or Bob Packwood with numerous such skeletons rattling out of the closet.

Bush's bias against women and minorities is more subtle. You have to look at how he touts certain programs and advances and does not follow through on such promises, such as his 2000 campaign vow to not use abortion as a litmus test in appointing judges. You have to review how he campaigns for politicians who have made overtly insensitive racial remarks like Sen. Jeff Sessions of Alabama. Sessions once called a black assistant U.S. attorney "boy" and a white civil rights attorney a "disgrace to his race," according to The New Republic.[3] You have to look at how Bush supported the Willie Horton ad—which many said employed a racial stereotype for political advantage—during the 1988 presidential campaign of his father.

"He is very tricky," said Roy Williams, a Dallas civil rights activist who ran for U.S. Senate in Texas as a Green Party candidate in 2002. "His falsehoods are more subtle than some politicians, but they are there. He claims to be for minority inclusion, but the African Americans he appoints to offices are mostly conservatives who have worked against minority inclusion. Even Secretary of State Colin Powell has distanced himself from the African American community since he left New York."

Bush's Lies Against Women

When it comes to women, Bush has made a practice out of talking like he is a moderate regarding abortion and other issues, then acting much more conservative. Bush's lies against women included the 2000 campaign, when he steered clear of specifics about abortion and made voters believe that he would not work to reverse *Roe v. Wade*. He tried to reach moderate voters by speaking only in generalities about the issue. For instance, in his first 2000 debate with Al Gore, Bush said he would be conservative but fair-minded in his selection of nominees to the federal courts, especially on their views on abortion. "The voters should assume I have no litmus test on that issue or any other issue," Bush said.[4] That statement turned out to be false.

According to an analysis by NARAL Pro-Choice America, six of 14 nominees to U.S. Circuit Courts of Appeals that the White House announced in January 2003 had "clear anti-choice records while none has any hint of a pro-choice outlook."[5] "President Bush has repeatedly shown that when it comes to judicial nominations, he values anti-choice ideology first and all other considerations not at all," said Kate Michelman, president of NARAL Pro-Choice America.[6]

As Texas governor, Bush signed no less than 18 anti-abortion laws, according to Patricia Ireland, former president of the National Organization for Women.[7] Once he took over the White House, his anti-choice executive orders like the 2001 gag order prohibiting funding to overseas family planning groups that provide abortion services and cabinet appointments showed more of his true colors. Many of Bush's federal judicial nominations, such as Priscilla Owen, Charles Pickering, Michael McConnell, Dennis Shedd, Lavenski Smith, Carolyn Kuhl, William Pryor, D. Brooks Smith, and Claude Allen, stridently opposed abortion.

The *New York Times* even editorialized in January 2003 that "undermining the reproductive freedom essential to women's health, privacy and equality is a major preoccupation of his administration—second only, perhaps, to the war on terrorism."[8]

Another lie during the 2000 campaign came when Bush said that he would not try to overturn the Food and Drug Administration's approval of mifepristone, or RU-486, the controversial abortion pill. "I don't think a president can even overturn it. The FDA has made its decision," Bush said.[9]

But Bush found ways to undermine the FDA's decision. In 2001, Bush's Secretary of Health and Human Services, Tommy Thompson, said he would seek FDA re-evaluation of mifepristone. The Bush administration went on to restrict Medicaid funding for mifepristone to cases of rape, incest or saving a pregnant woman's life.[10] Bush also appointed a strident RU-486 opponent, W. David Hager, to an FDA panel on women's health policy in 2002. The 11-member Reproductive Health Drugs Advisory Committee made the key recommendation in 1996 that led to the approval of the abortion pill. Hager, an obstetrician-gynecologist who assisted the Christian Medical Association in 2001 with a petition against RU-486, is no stranger to telling falsehoods, himself. His resume listed himself as a University of Kentucky professor, but *Time* reported that the position was voluntary and involved working with interns at Lexington's Central Baptist Hospital, not the university itself.[11]

Bush has said he doesn't discriminate against women. But former White House spokesperson Ari Fleischer said during a 2002 press conference that Bush does not consider discrimination against women to be as serious as racial or ethnic discrimination. Fleischer said that membership in a group that excludes women is not "a disqualifying factor" for candidates to Cabinet posts. He added that racial discrimination is a "very different category for the president."[12]

It's true that with his first Cabinet, Bush did better than most recent presidents. His four female appointments bested the three each during the entire terms of his father, Reagan, and Carter.[13] But Bush had a ways to go to catch Clinton, who appointed 11 women to his Cabinet. And at least one of Bush's appointees, Interior Secretary Gale Norton, has been singled out by an influential minority organization for statements she made that were less than inclusive. The National Association for the Advancement of Colored People opposed Norton's nomination, citing comments she made in 1996 in which she stated that the cause of states' rights suffered a grievous blow with the defeat of the Confederacy in the Civil War.[14]

Another of Bush's female appointees to a lower board has a record that suggests she is not really open to advancing women's rights. Diana Furchgott-Roth, whom Bush named director of the Federal Housing Finance Board, was a fellow for the far-right American Enterprise Institute and co-authored a book that denied the existence of a glass ceiling and argued that women were no longer affected by discrimination in the workplace.[15]

Bush has also been caught telling some falsehoods concerning family issues that affect women. In 2000 and 2001, Bush often spoke of a mythical single-mom waitress, making $22,000 or so, who would suddenly become middle class via his tax cuts. But the accounting firm of Deloitte & Touche found in 2000 that his waitress would receive no reduction in her taxes under his plan. In 2001, the Center on Budget and Policy Priorities found that this waitress might gain $200 from Bush's tax cuts if she managed to earn $25,000 a year. But such a sum would not place her on the highway to the middle class.[16]

Bush also said he supported programs that helped single mothers such as Even Start, an Albuquerque, N.M., program that offers tutoring to preschoolers and literacy and job training for their parents. During a

2002 visit to New Mexico, he touted Lucy Salazar, a volunteer with Even Start. But Bush's support for the program turned out to be another falsehood. A few months earlier, he proposed a 20 percent funding cut from the previous year for Even Start, according to the U.S. House Appropriations Committee and an Associated Press article.[17]

Bush also cut funding for children's hospitals, the Boys and Girls Clubs, and other family-friendly programs that he claimed to support. Health insurance was another issue about which Bush lied. During the 2000 debates, Bush said he "spent a lot of money to make sure people get healthcare in the state of Texas."[18]

That was another falsehood, when comparing Texas to other states. In 2000, Texas ranked 49th out of the 50 states for children and women with health insurance, and 50th for families with insurance. A falsehood reiterated by more people than Bush, including First Lady Laura Bush and National Security Adviser Condoleezza Rice, was the one justifying the invasion of Afghanistan partly on improving rights and conditions for women in that country. For example, Laura Bush had this to say in a November 2001 radio address: "Because of our recent military gains in much of Afghanistan, women are no longer imprisoned in their homes. They can listen to music and teach their daughters without fear of punishment."[19]

But several sources, including Amnesty International, released reports that condemned conditions for women two years later.

"Two years after the ending of the Taliban regime, the international community and the Afghan Transitional Administration, led by President Hamid Karzai, have proved unable to protect women," the Amnesty report said. "Amnesty International is gravely concerned by the extent of violence faced by women and girls in Afghanistan. The risk of rape and sexual violence by members of armed factions and former combatants is still high. Forced marriage, particularly of girl children, and violence against women in the family are widespread in many areas of the country."[20]

Laura Bush was caught in another misleading statement shortly after September 11, 2001. In the midst of a conservative agenda to cut social service programs like welfare in favor of religious-based agencies, she said that divorce was declining, while marriages were increasing. She referred to a Houston news report that was retracted four days before her speech before a New York women's group. In fact, a January 2002 AP story pointed out that fewer Americans were taking vows in the self-proclaimed "marriage capital of the world," Reno, Nevada, and more couples were splitting up in Leon County, Florida.

Meanwhile, dogs were almost twice as likely as husbands to get at-

tention from wives, according to a survey by the advertising network
Euro RSCG. [21]

Phony Photo-ops

In many White House photo-ops, Bush and his handlers made sure that
African-American or other minority children were up front and center.
The image projected was that the Bush administration embraced diversity. But the reality often made that image a falsehood, that Bush's seeming support for diversity was quite superficial.

Look at Bush's first cabinet appointments. Five of his 14 cabinet
members were minority—Secretary of State Colin Powell, Education
Secretary Rod Paige, Housing and Urban Development Secretary Mel
Martinez, Labor Secretary Elaine Chao, and Transportation Secretary
Norman Mineta. Bush also appointed minorities to other high-ranking
offices, including Condoleezza Rice as national security adviser, Alberto
Gonzales as White House counsel, and Colin Powell's son, Michael, as
Federal Communications Commission chairman. On the surface, that
record was good, especially compared to previous Republican cabinets,
as it was the most diverse one picked by a Republican president and came
close to Clinton's record seven minority cabinet members. But as an Associated Press article said, "While the younger Bush's Cabinet is visually
diverse, ideologically it is the opposite. Most members hold moderate to
very conservative views, and several face opposition from labor unions
and women's, environmental and civil rights organizations." [22]

Powell, in fact, was the only one who spoke out for affirmative action and was left hanging out to dry several times. For instance, when
Powell publicly criticized Bush's January 2003 decision to argue before
the Supreme Court that the University of Michigan's affirmative action
program was unconstitutional, Rice publicly supported Bush.[23] Some of
Bush's white appointments had records of opposing programs that aid
minorities. For example, Ashcroft worked against racial integration and
the appointment of African Americans to offices as Missouri governor
and attorney general. He also praised former Confederate President
Jefferson Davis and Gens. Stonewall Jackson and Robert E. Lee in remarks to a South Carolina-based magazine.[24]

When confronted about his record on minority inclusion, Bush said
something similar to his line in the 2000 debates: "I've been a tolerant
person all my life." But in 2002, Bush campaigned for at least one Republican senator who had a questionable background regarding minorities.
Besides the aforementioned slurs, Sessions of Alabama prosecuted civil
rights workers on phony voter fraud charges and refused to aggressively
investigate burnings and bombings of black churches. He also once said

he thought Ku Klux Klan members were "okay" until he heard some might have smoked marijuana and charged the NAACP with being "un-American" and "Communist-inspired."[25] Examine what Bush did during the 2000 presidential campaign. He spoke before the segregationist Bob Jones University in South Carolina. He didn't speak out against white supremacists—including Don Black, an ex-Ku Klux Klan grand dragon and the founder of the Internet hate site Stormfront.org—rallying for him in Florida.[26]

Bush supported and benefited from Florida's system of purges that removed thousands of names—about half of them African-Americans—from the voting rolls.[27] He ignored the police roadblocks near Florida black precincts on election day.[28] Then there was the off-radar whisper campaign against Sen. John McCain in South Carolina. Author Ron Suskind wrote in *Esquire* in January 2003 that "what happened has taken on the air of an unsolved crime, a cold case, with Karl Rove being the prime suspect. Bush loyalists, maybe working for the campaign, maybe just representing its interests, claimed in parking-lot handouts and telephone 'push polls' and whisper campaigns that McCain's wife, Cindy, was a drug addict, that McCain might be mentally unstable from his captivity in Vietnam, and that the senator had fathered a black child with a prostitute. Callers push-polled members of a South Carolina right-to-life organization and other groups, asking if the black baby might influence their vote."[29]

The "black baby" turned out to be one the McCains adopted from a Mother Teresa orphanage in Bangladesh. Was this whisper campaign something a "tolerant person" would stomach? And why did the campaigners say McCain fathered a black child with a prostitute when that was an outright lie? As Texas governor, Bush was caught in numerous more lies. Several were related to the horrid 1998 murder of African-American James Byrd in which three white men chained him to a truck and dragged him to death in Jasper, Tx. For one thing, Bush claimed the three defendants were prosecuted under Texas' hate crimes statute, which was untrue. They were really convicted under the state's capital murder statute.[30]

Then, during the 2000 debates, Bush said all three men convicted would be put to death. That was also a falsehood. Only two of Byrd's murderers—John King and Lawrence Brewer—were sentenced to death. The third, Shawn Berry, received life in prison and will be eligible for parole after 40 years.[31] Members of the Byrd family told Salon.com that they weren't surprised Bush got the details of the case wrong.[32] They also said Bush told several more lies, such as that he comforted the family after Byrd's death. Bush didn't even attend Byrd's funeral. Bush spokeswoman Karen Hughes told Salon.com that the no-show was at the Byrd family's request, but family members denied telling him to stay away and noted that other Republicans, such as Sen. Kay Bailey Hutchison, attended the funeral.[33] Bush himself claimed he called family members to offer condolences. But family members said none of them received a phone call from Bush, and he only met with one member after much public pressure.[34] Bush also implied during the 2000 debates that he supported hate crimes legislation. One Byrd family member told Salon.com that Bush told her outright during a meeting that he would not support a 1999 bill to create a stronger hate crimes law, which eventually died.[35]

In fact, the *Washington Post* reported that Bush "maneuvered to make sure a new hate crimes law related to the Byrd killing did not make it to his desk. The new bill would have included homosexuals among the groups covered, which would have been anathema to social conservatives in the state."[36] Bush also claimed to have made strides as Texas governor in increasing minority appointments to state boards and commissions. But that was another falsehood. Such appointments declined about 15 percent under him from the term of predecessor Ann Richards.[37] One of Bush's appointees to the state's Commission on Law Enforcement Officer Standards and Education, Charles Williams, testified in a 1998 court case that terms like "porch monkey" and "black bastard" were not offensive. Williams also argued that when he was growing up, blacks didn't mind being called "nigger." The following year, Bush named Williams chairman of the commission.[38] But after Williams' comments were widely publicized, Bush claimed he didn't know about them. Bush stopped short of calling for Williams' resignation, only saying that he "ought to apologize." Williams eventually resigned.

Finally, before becoming governor, Bush, as part owner of the Texas Rangers baseball team, was blasted by NAACP officials for failing to make sure that a fair portion of contracts for the $194 million taxpayer-subsidized Ballpark in Arlington went to minority companies. The Rangers gave about 5 percent of such contracts to minority firms, compared to as much as 25 percent in Baltimore and other cities, NAACP officials said.[39] It was just another odd development for someone who said he was so tolerant and inclusive.

More Empty Promises

In his 2003 State of the Union address, Bush promised $10 billion in new money to fight AIDS in Africa and the Caribbean over five years. But his 2003 budget proposed only a $550 million increase over the global AIDS money. He found part of the money for his AIDS programs by cutting nearly $500 million from children's health programs. Some said Bush's "War on Terrorism" was misleading in itself because it only targeted Arab terrorists. The campaign ignored white terrorists, such as the ones who committed the 1995 Oklahoma City bombing, who were connected with anti-government groups. In a March 2003 address about Iraq, Bush also painted Iraqi officials with a broad brush in saying, "Peaceful efforts to disarm the Iraqi regime have failed again and again because we are not dealing with peaceful men." But the *Washington Post* reported that Iraq destroyed 817 of 819 medium-range missiles, as well as other chemical or biological warheads, under United Nations supervision.[40]

Vice President Dick Cheney also claimed he supported minority rights. But while in Congress from 1979 until 1989, Cheney opposed measures strengthening laws against housing discrimination and collecting hate crimes data. In addition, Cheney supported apartheid in the racist South African regime, even as it crumbled. Then, Ashcroft claimed in 2001 that there was "no evidence of racial bias in the administration of the federal death penalty." But he conveniently overlooked a Justice Department report released a few months before he took office, which found that minorities were considered for the federal death penalty much more often than whites, accounting for 74 percent of such cases between 1995 and 1999.[41]

"We don't practice anti-gay bias"

Some of the more obvious lies by Bush and administration officials have come when they have dealt with gay rights issues. In 2001, White House officials said that they were not involved with an effort to allow religious charities to practice anti-gay workplace bias. But they later admitted chief aide Karl Rove was involved.[42]

An unnamed White House official also said that Don Eberly, deputy director of the White House Office of Faith-Based and Community Initiatives, had given the Salvation Army "an implicit understanding" that the administration would seriously consider allowing the anti-gay policy.[43] During the 2000 presidential campaign, Bush himself claimed to favor "equal" rights for gays and lesbians, but not "special" rights. But as governor, he supported a Texas law that allowed the state to take adopted children from gay and lesbian couples and place them with straight couples. He also supported a gays-only sodomy law in Texas that criminalized consensual sex in private between two homosexuals. Bush never explained how allowing straight couples—but not gay ones—to take care of adopted children, or allowing heterosexual couples—but not homosexual ones—to practice sodomy in private supported his "equal" rights policy. But that was par for the course for Bush.

NOTES

1. Richard Gehr, "Mouth at Work," *Newsday* (October 8,1990).

2. LeaAnne Klentzman, "Woman files lawsuit against President," *Fort Bend Star* (December 11, 2002).

3. Sarah Wildman, "Closed Sessions: The Senator who's worse than Lott," *The New Republic* (December 30, 2002).

4. Transcript, Commission on Presidential Debates, "The First 2000 Gore-Bush Presidential Debate," October 3, 2000.

5. *Houston Chronicle* (January 18, 2003).

6. Kate Michelman, "Bush's Latest Nominee: Claude Allen, the Triumph of Ideology," *NARAL Pro-Choice America* (October 28, 2003).

7. Patricia Ireland, "George W. Bush: What Does the 'W' Stand For?" *National NOW Times* (Spring 2000).

8. Editorial, "The War Against Women," *New York Times* (January 12, 2003).

9. Transcript, Commission on Presidential Debates, "The First 2000 Gore-Bush Presidential Debate," (October 3, 2000).

10. Jane Spencer, "The 'Abortion Pill': Not Stocked Here," *Newsweek* (June 19, 2001).

11. Karen Tumulty, "Jesus and the FDA," *Time* (October 5, 2002).

12. Transcript, Office of the Press Secretary, The White House, "Press Briefing by Ari Fleischer," (December 10, 2002).

13. 2001 Women's Appointments Project, "Fact Sheet on Women Government Appointees," Women's eNews, a news service by the Fund for the City of New York (November 6, 2000).

14. Jim Cullen, "George II: Back to Business as Usual," *The Progressive Populist* (January 2001).

15. Katrina vanden Heuvel, "Bush's Assaults on Women," *The Nation* (October 7, 2003).

16. David Corn, "The Other Lies of George Bush," *The Nation* (September 25, 2003).

17. U.S. House Appropriations Committee, "Caught on Film: The Bush Credibility Gap," (April 29, 2002).

18. Transcript, Commission on Presidential Debates, "The Second 2000 Gore-Bush Presidential Debate," (October 11, 2000).

19. Transcript, Office of Mrs. Bush, The White House, "Radio Address by Mrs. Bush," (November 17, 2001).

20. Amnesty International, "Afghanistan - 'No one listens to us and no one treats us as human beings': Justice denied to women," (October 23, 2003).

21. Ron Kampeas, "Everything changed? Not really: Many claims of post-Sept. 11 changes in society have little basis in truth," Associated Press (January 17, 2002).

22. Darlene Superville, "Bush selects Cabinet as diverse as Clinton's," Associated Press (January 6, 2001).

23. Scott Lindlaw, "Powell Backs Michigan Affirmative Action," Associated Press (January 20, 2003).

24. Richard Quinn, "Senator John Ashcroft: Missouri's Champion of States, Rights and Traditional Southern Values," *Southern Partisan*, Second Quarter (1998).

25. The Carpetbagger, "Dems confirm plans for Pryor filibuster as Sessions continues charges of bigotry," *The Carpetbagger Report* (July 30, 2003).

26. Donna Ladd, "West Palm Beach: A tale of two cities amid Florida's election madness," *Las Vegas Weekly* (November 23, 2000).

27. Greg Palast, "Jeb Bush's secret weapon," Salon.com (November 1, 2002).

28. Sasha Abramsky, "Voteless in Florida," *Mother Jones* (November 8, 2000).

29. Ron Suskind, "Why Are These Men Laughing?" *Esquire* (January 2003).

30. Alissa J. Rubin, "For Bush and Gore, the Truth Comes in a Variety of Shades," *Los Angeles Times* (October 12, 2000).

31. Terri Langford, "Jasper looks to move on, heal after 3rd verdict: Dragging death, aftermath expected to leave indelible mark on town," *Dallas Morning News* (November 20, 1999).

32. Jake Tapper, "Bush angers slain man's family: The Byrds harbor deep resentments over the Texas governor's treatment of their family and failure to support a hate crimes bill," Salon.com (October 16, 2000).

33. Ibid.

34. Ibid.

35. Ibid.

36. Glenn Kessler, "For Both Debaters, Missteps; Bush Errs on IMF Funds Gore Misspeaks on Tests," Washington Post (October 12, 2000).

37. J. H. Hatfield, *Fortunate Son*. (New York: Soft Skull Press, 2001), p. 219.

38. Jake Tapper, "Are Bush appointees racist? Democrats spotlight a pair of Texas officials who have been dinged for bigoted remarks," Salon.com (October 20, 2000).

39. J. H. Hatfield, *Fortunate Son*, pp. 221-222.

40. Walter Pincus, "U.S. Lacks Specifics on Banned Arms," *Washington Post* (March 16, 2003).

41. Jim Stewart, "Ashcroft: No Death Penalty Race Bias," CBS News (June 6, 2001).

42. Mike Allen and Dana Milbank, "Rove Heard Charity Plea On Gay Bias: White House Denied Senior Aides Had Role," *Washington Post* (July 12, 2001).

43. Ibid.

Ordering the Court With Lies

BY W. DAVID JENKINS III

During the presidential campaign of 2000, candidate George W. Bush remarked that he most admired Supreme Court Justices like Clarence Thomas and Antonin ("Anthony" in Bushspeak) Scalia because they were "strict constructionists." Bush defined a strict constructionist as a jurist who "doesn't use the opportunity of the Constitution to pass legislation or legislate from the bench." To the general public the statement sounded good and Bush's own Texas Supreme Court *was* being touted as moderate not only by his supporters but also by his detractors.

One of the most touted examples of moderate behavior by the TSC was the decision made concerning the Parental Notification Law in which the court ruled in favor of the teenaged girl who had petitioned for the right to an abortion *without* parental notification.[1] This ruling brought on the ire of a Pat Buchanan website, among others from the far right, and helped to perpetuate the lie that Bush was somehow a moderate—even when it came to nominating judges.

Texas governor George W. Bush nominated four Texas Supreme Court judges during his tenure—James A. Baker, Greg Abbot, Deborah Hankinson and Alberto Gonzalez. These four Bush appointments earned their moderate stars by their participation in the decision mentioned above. They based their decision on a mutual distain for "judicial bypass" cases without having to betray their anti-abortion stances.

However, the same court has a reputation for having such a pro-business position that even one of Bush's nominees, Baker, was moved to enter his dissention to a decision concerning limiting class action lawsuits. The opinion of the Texas Supreme Court was so drastic against the rights of ordinary citizens Baker wrote in his dissent that the decision "mocks the Constitutional prohibition of special laws and undermines our special law jurisprudence." Then he also added, quite ominously, "In any event, we all know what is going on here."[2] In other words, corporate interests' first, justice maybe. This was Bush's interpretation of "strict constructionism." And the Texas governor's actions were only the tip of the iceberg.

Americans should have known better prior to that dark November and if the compliant media had done its job concerning the many contradictions between Bush's words as opposed to his actions—his distain for legal procedure and his embrace of legal ideology might have received more mainstream attention. The so-called election of 2000 should have been a glaring red flag for the voting populace.[3]

The participation of at least three of the nine judges in the ruling of *Bush vs. Gore* was dubious at best. Those three judges – Scalia, Thomas and O'Connor—should have received much closer scrutiny as they were all in conflict with several statutes of 28 USC 455 of the Judicial and Judiciary Procedure concerning their blatant conflicts of interest in participating in the court's decision.[4] The conflicts are identified under statutes A and B in 28/455 which state that under certain circumstances "a Justice disqualify[ing] himself in any proceeding in which his impartiality might reasonably be questioned and/or in those circumstances wherein he has a personal bias or prejudice."

O'Connor is a stretch but her public behavior on election night, as it was reported, does shed some light on her obvious predisposition concerning the outcome. O'Connor's election evening exclamation, "This is terrible" —when CBS anchor Dan Rather called Florida for Al Gore before 8 P.M.—clearly indicated her "preference" in the Presidential election.

Scalia's conflict of interest was obvious with two of his sons working in the law firms of Ted Olson and Barry Richard, attorneys representing George W. Bush's legal interest in the cases regarding the 2000 Presidential election—with one son actually working on *Bush v. Gore.*

Scalia also has made public statements since the decision concerning his feelings that the "state should be subservient to the church" or another "divine authority."[5] This would not bear mention if it were not for the fact that many conservatives feel Bush was appointed by God Almighty himself.

Thomas' obvious conflict of interest was apparent because his wife was currently working at the Heritage Foundation reviewing Republican resumés for the Bush administration.

This Supreme Court judge has also decried the "overemphasis on civility" when speaking out against moderates in the right wing. He has made his contempt of conservative timidity quite clear in public speeches on what he considers an "ideological war" which is "cultural and *not* civil."[6]

These alleged strict constructionists then proceeded to "protect" Florida voters by stopping the manual count of over 170,000 votes and handing the election to George W. Bush—even though the national numbers showed he was losing. They derailed the democratic process in a national election and then had the audacity to declare that their decision, *instead of setting a legal precedent*, only applied to *Bush v. Gore!* These are the kinds of judges Bush not only admires but wants to appoint to the federal appellate courts and, quite probably, the Supreme Court.

Bush v. Gore exposed the lie that judges like Scalia and Thomas are "strict constructionists." They made a political decision and have yet to be held accountable—which means they fit right in with the Bush II administration. But, as Justice Stephen Breyer wrote in his dissent, the majority ruling represented "a self-inflicted wound—a wound that may harm not just the court but the nation."[7]

After the Supreme Court handed Bush the keys to the White House, the plan to stack the federal courts with justices who fit the mold of the extreme right was cranked up.

The first order of business was to discontinue the practice of using a special committee of the American Bar Association to screen presidential appointees.[8] This program was originated in 1948 and was first utilized by Eisenhower in 1953 as a means by which potential nominees could be judged by the ABA in order to aid the president and, eventually, the Senate in the judicial confirmation process. The nominees would be rated as "well qualified," "qualified," or "not qualified."[2]

Bush decided to discontinue the practice based upon the reason that it would "grant a preferential, quasi-official role in the judicial selection process to a politically active group." In other words, the administration felt that the ABA, viewed by Bush as a hopeless collection of infamous and liberal trial lawyers, would rule against it over and over because Bush intended to nominate right-wing extremists to the bench. However, if the Bush administration had checked the history of the ABA regarding this process, they would have realized that their reasoning was ridiculous and completely false. Out of the approximately 2,000 nominees rated by the ABA, only 26 have been rated "not qualified"—and 23 of those were nominated by Democrat administrations! So the basis for suddenly discontinuing decades of practice in the judicial selection procedure was a lie, not only to the American people but to the Bush administration itself. However, the future group of judicial nominees was a hint as to why the lie was necessary for the Bush White House.

To set the pace for the future judicial appointments by Bush, there needed to be another lie perpetrated repeatedly by the White House. This was the lie over the "judicial crisis" which Bush cited over and over.[9]

There were a large number of vacancies when it came to federal benches according to Bush—however, he always failed to mention that many of those "vacancies" were *left over* from the Clinton administration.

But once again nobody seemed to pick up on this constantly omitted fact and, of course, the media sure wasn't going to help.

The so-called "judicial crisis" was used as a talking point every time certain members of the Senate Judicial Committee would have a problem with one of Bush's more extreme nominees. Democrats on the committee would start asking tough questions of the nominees and the Republicans would start screaming "foul!" Acting as if they had forgotten the eight years under Clinton, members of the right would accuse the left of playing partisan politics with Bush's nominees.

The Republicans' pathetic ire was laughable and hypocritical, especially when weighed against the list of nominees sent down by the new "sheriff in town." The names read like a list of "wanted" posters. They are members of the Bush Gang of extremists who have no business sitting on *any* bench, let alone the Supreme Court. Consider the following;

PRISCILLA OWEN: Bush was a fan of this lady back when he was in Texas. Nominated to the 5th Circuit Court of Appeals, Owen has a long career as a conservative judicial activist, opposing reproductive rights, environmental protections, and workers' rights. As a lawyer in private practice, Owen did virtually nothing but represent big oil companies. Owen favored big business while serving on the Texas Supreme Court. Owen can also thank Karl Rove for her election to the Texas Supreme Court. Apparently he received $228,000 for "campaign services."[10] Ms. Owen was also accused in an opinion by Alberto Gonzales, the current White House counsel, of engaging in "an unconscionable act of judicial activism" concerning her interpretation of the Texas Parental Notification Statute as applied to abortion cases. Keep remembering, we're talking about "strict constructionists" here.

JEFFREY SUTTON: This guy was nominated to the 6th Circuit Court of Appeals and has strongly supported restricting the ability of Congress to address discrimination against minorities and the disabled. He's also written in favor of declaring the Violence Against Women Act unconstitutional.

CAROLYN KUHL: Now this lady is a piece of work. Nominated to the 9th Circuit Court of Appeals, Kuhl is a former official in Reagan's Justice Department with a long record of opposing reproductive rights, civil rights, and environmental protections. Not only that, but she also has the distinction of being pummeled by the Supreme Court when she tried to restore tax exempt status to Bob Jones University also known as "Racist University". She lost 8-1.

WILLIAM PRYOR: Nominated to the 11th Circuit Court of Appeals, Pryor opposes abortion rights and he called Roe v. Wade "the day seven members of our high court ripped the Constitution and ripped out the life of millions of unborn children." He has argued against the Violence Against Women Act and the Americans with Disabilities Act. Pryor also opposed a Supreme Court ruling that said tying prisoners to hitching posts was cruel and unusual. The Republicans tried to label the opposing members of the Senate to Pryor's nomination as "anti-Catholic!" No, they were anti-extremist, anti-misogynist and anti-sadist.

CHARLES PICKERING: Nominated to the 5th Circuit Court of Appeals, Pickering is a long-time opponent of civil rights protections and has fought for a Constitutional amendment to ban abortion. Pickering authored an article as a law student that described how states could improve laws banning interracial marriage. He has also displayed hostility to Constitutional rights, including the Miranda decision recently upheld by the Supreme Court.[11]

And then we have poor, misunderstood MIGUEL ESTRADA. Now *this* was an interesting exercise in pomposity on behalf of the Bush administration. Here was another hand-picked candidate to be nominated to the Columbia Court of Appeals—also known as a "stepping stone" to the Supreme Court—and the guy had never been a judge. Sure, Miguel had worked in the Solicitor General's Office but he didn't want to answer *any* questions, either actual or hypothetical, concerning his views on important subjects. And he wasn't about to provide the Senate with *any* records pertaining to his work with the SGO. George W. Bush said he didn't have to and that was good enough for him. Of course, it wasn't nearly good enough for the Democrats on the Senate Judiciary Committee and so a filibuster began in response to his and Bush's uncooperative stance.

Then the Republicans on the committee decided to try to label the Democrats as anti-Hispanic—all the while obviously forgetting the names Barquette and Piaz, two Hispanic nominees held up (1,500 days in Piaz's case) by the Republican majority during the Clinton administration because they were "too liberal."[12] The so-called unfair treatment of Estrada, as perceived by the Republicans, infuriated the Right so much that Senate Republicans talked openly about the possible resort to a "nuclear" option to end the filibuster.

On May 9, Senator Frist proposed a resolution to amend Senate rules to reduce the number of votes required to end a filibuster from 60 to a simple majority. In other words, if the Republicans couldn't win by playing by the rules then they wanted to change the rules.[13]

Luckily, Estrada withdrew his name from consideration in the late summer of 2003. But the work of the Democratic opposition is far from over. Both Pickering and Owen have been re-nominated after being defeated once. And then there is the matter of the nomination of Janice Rogers Brown, one of the most archconservatives ever to be considered for a federal bench.

The thing is, if Bush were really so concerned about a "judicial crisis" then he might ease up on such extremist nominations. But the fact is that the claim of a judicial crisis is yet another Bush lie.

Although it is common practice for the minority party to accuse the party in power of "playing politics," it is hypocritical for the Republican majority under Bush to make such a hysterical claim. The 106th Congress under Clinton has the worst record in regards to speed in holding hearings for judicial nominees. As of spring 2003, judicial vacancies are at a twelve-year low. George W. Bush has a 98 percent approval rating as regards his nominees. That's more than 120 judges appointed![14]

If Bush hadn't betrayed the lie that he was a moderate when it came to judicial appointments his approval rating might be even higher. But Bush is anything but a moderate—and the nominees mentioned above are proof of the dark, extremist intentions Bush has for the Federal and Supreme Courts.

The Judicial nomination process is not glamorous. Sure, it can be good for a few headlines for a short time although, overall, it lacks the grandeur of a war or a terrorist attack or even some misguided dim—bulb actor running for governor. But the long-term implications of the wrong person being seated on a judicial bench for life are as severe as any terrorist attack.

The mistakes and irresponsible behaviors remembered and revered as the foundation of the legacy of George W. Bush will also bring difficult questions before the judges who are supposed to be not only our interpreters of our laws but our protectors from injustice. As I write today, the Supreme Court faces appeals of lawyers representing the victims of the Bush/Ashcroft "roundup" after 9/11. The victims include the "detainees" at Guantanamo as well as American citizens being held without charge indefinitely simply because they've been deemed "hostile combatants." Exactly how a court weighted with Bush-appointed ideologues will protect citizen liberties in the face of a never-ending "war" is a question that every concerned American needs to ask without fear of being labeled partisan—let alone unpatriotic.

Americans need to arm themselves with the awareness that George W. Bush is no moderate in any sense when it comes to appointing potential judges who are to act as our interpreters and protectors. That lie, hoisted up almost three years ago, has been exposed as just another empty, misleading campaign promise.

Bush has used a tired old phrase in defense of his misguided nominees that states "the American people deserve justice." Well, he's right—but the truth is that we as a people deserve much better than what he's been proposing.

The possibility of even one of these controversial nominees having a chance of sitting on the Supreme Court should alarm any concerned American—no less alarm than is given to Iraq's future as a self-governing nation or the war on terrorism. We've been forced already to endure disastrous, successive results stemming from the "self-inflicted wound" now scarring this country, a wound that was created through earlier actions of those conservative judges who participated in *Bush v. Gore*. The last thing our country needs is more of the same.

And that's no lie.

NOTES

1. Marc J. Lane, "The Bush Supreme Court: Building Consensus Out Of Political Rancor," Chicago Business.com, *The Lane Report* (December 21, 2000).

2. Molly Ivins, "Texas Judges Show Bush's Philosophy," *Fort Worth Star-Telegram* (October, 2000).

3. Vincent Bugliosi, "None Dare Call it Treason," *Nation* (February, 2001).

4. Alan M. Dershowitz, *Supreme Injustice* (New York: Oxford University Press), 2001.

5. Sean Wilentz, "From Justice Scalia, a Chilling Vision of Religion's Authority in America," *New York Times* (July 8, 2002).

6. Robert Scheer, "A Moderate Wouldn't Make Appointments Like These" *TheNation* (February 20, 2000).

7. Robert Scheer, "Never again will we view the Judiciary as Nonpolitical," *The Nation*, December, 2000.

8. John Andrews, "Bush ends American Bar Assoc. pre-screening of judicial nominees," World Socialist web site (April 2001).

9. Bush speech text February, 2003; Ellen Goodman, "The War Over the Judiciary," *Boston Globe* (May 15, 2003), Ralph G. Neas, "Despite 13-Year Low in Vacancies, Bush Claims a "Judicial Crisis," People For the American Way (May 9, 2002) at <www.commondreams.org/news2002/0509-11.htm>.

10. Nan Aron, "You too can be a judge," *Los Angeles Times* (May 2003).

11. DNC: Supreme Court Watchm, at <www.democrats.org>.

12. NPR's "Talk of the Nation," transcripts (October 2002).

13. Gail Chaddock, "What Estrada's exit means for future battles," *Christian Science Monitor* (September 2003).

14. American Bar Association, at <www.abanet.org/poladv/priorities/judvac.html>.

PART FOUR:
Bush Security and Foreign Policy Lies

A Reckless Foreign Policy

By Bernard Weiner

There are so many lies and deceptions undergirding Bush&Co.'s foreign/military policy that it's difficult to choose the most egregious ones. But let's start with the famous Bush whopper from his 2000 campaign; he was speaking about how the peoples of the world might accept the United States:

> If we're an arrogant nation, they'll resent us. If we're a humble nation, but strong, they'll welcome us. And our nation stands alone right now in the world in terms of power. And that's why we've got to be humble and yet project strength in a way that promotes freedom.[1]

The projection of strength certainly came to be seen, and experienced—with an astounding, bullying arrogance—but the humility was totally missing in action. Also missing was an understanding on Bush's part of anything beyond our borders, thus making him easily rollable for those more conversant with, and possessing a clear agenda with regard to, international affairs—to wit, the neo-cons at the forefront of America's foreign/military policy, led by the likes of Cheney, Rumsfeld, Wolfowitz, et al.

What seems obvious now, in 2004, is that the Bush Administration's foreign/military policy was launched—as with American domestic policy—as a stealth campaign, based on lies and deceptions, designed to calm and obfuscate before unveiling aspects of its true nature.

Domestically, this country—founded on a respect for civil liberties in the face of despotic rulers—drastically changed directions after 9/11 and moved closer to an American brand of fascism under the so-called USA PATRIOT Act.

In foreign policy, the populace should have figured out where Bush&Co. wanted to take the nation just by paying attention to the various key appointments: after interviewing numerous potential candidates for a vice presidential running-mate, Dick Cheney, head of the search committee, selected...Dick Cheney, head of Halliburton; Donald Rumsfeld was named Secretary of Defense, Paul Wolfowitz his chief deputy; James Baker, former Secretary of State, became Bush's consigliere, and exercised great consultative power during the transition phase; Colin Powell, an ambitious military man, took over State. These and other ex-Reagan power-wielders—almost all of whom were part of, or beholden to, the economic powers-that-be—exemplified par excellence the "military-industrial complex" that President Eisenhower had warned us about decades before.

Rumsfeld and those appointed by him at Defense—and urged by him onto the State Department team—were ideologues associated with various right-wing think tanks and committees, most notably the Project for The New American Century (PNAC), a neo-conservative outfit with a hankering for unilateral, aggressive military action abroad.[2]

Though the founders of PNAC and those associated with the organization[3] had not been shy about airing their extreme opinions in print, few outside neo-conservative circles were aware of PNAC and its imperial-like vision—including a desire to effect a policy of "benevolent global hegemony."[4] And so the true dimensions of likely Bush policy slipped under the 2000 campaign radar and the post-election transition phase. Especially since Bush was saying the exact opposite of what was really in the works.

We would be remiss if we failed to mention the next big, associated lie: the assertion by Condoleezza Rice that the Bush-Cheney national-security team had no idea that hijacked airplanes might be used as weapons.[5] The key Bush folks knew of that likelihood well in advance of the 9/11 attacks—thanks not only to briefings they'd received from the outgoing Clinton national-security team about the huge dangers posed by Osama bin Laden, but more specifically because of the voluminous warnings, many quite detailed as to airplanes and possible targets, pouring in from a wide variety of foreign intelligence agencies.[6] However, they chose to do nothing with their foreknowledge.

And why might they have chosen to remain silent about what was about to come down? In a revealing observation in an earlier PNAC document, the authors were sanguine enough to realize that the objective conditions weren't right at that moment for an acceptance of their extremist positions by the American people; that being the case, "the process of transformation, even if it brings revolutionary change, is likely to be a long one, *absent some catastrophic and catalyzing event—like a new Pearl Harbor.*"(emphasis supplied)[7] When 9/11 happened, they took full advantage of the ensuing fright and confusion to unleash their domestic and foreign agendas.

What the Project for the New American Century contributed to this green President and somewhat shaky Administration was a kind of off-the-shelf template of how to move in the world, worked out over the preceding decade by PNAC's idelologue strategists.[8]

This roadmap for how to effect neo-con policy—which became the official National Security Strategy of the United States of America in 2002[9]—can be summarized with one adjective: aggressively, as in "preventive" war, as in permanent war, as in using-nukes-as-offensive-weapons war, as in not letting any other country or organization compete for parity power (not the U.N., NATO, or the EU), as in breaking treaties left and right. And then, of course, lying about what the real goals and motivations are, while inventing rationalizations for such extreme behaviors.

For example, it wouldn't look good for the Bush Administration to admit publicly—based on the PNAC principles underpinning U.S. foreign/military policy—that it wanted to invade Iraq in order to gain a strategic foothold in the Middle East, using Iraq as a demonstration model of what might well befall other Arab countries unless they altered their government/economic/energy structures and policies along lines more amenable to U.S. demands. Former Treasury Secretary Paul O'Neill, who attended National Security Council meetings early in the Bush presidency, has revealed that ten days into the new Administration in 2001, plans were being hatched for how to invade Iraq, along with discussions about how to divvy up the oil revenues internationally in a post-Saddam era.[10]

(A note here about the twin, overlapping strands in the neo-con machine: One faction was more greed-oriented, focusing on control of energy-resources around the globe, and eager to use America's might on behalf of the corporate megafirms that support the party; the other was more idealistically-based, wanting to bring democracy and free-markets to those under autocratic rule, especially in the Arab world—which if accomplished, they believed, in the long run would benefit America and its Middle East proxy, Israel. In short, when the two strands intertwine, it's greed and altruism in one juggernaut package.)

The massive lying/deception/propaganda machine was rolled out to convince the American citizenry and foreign nations that Iraq was about to use its "massive" military might, and its supposed terror weapons, to attack its neighbors and bring ruin to the U.S. and its allies. Wolfowitz alluded to the major problem the U.S. policymakers had in coming up with a public reason that could win over the American citizenry and the foreign allies. In the end, he said, they settled on the imminent danger of Iraq's supposed weapons of mass-destruction (WMD), because they couldn't agree that anything else would work.[11]

And so the lies began about Iraq's alleged WMDs. The threat was so imminent, the Bush spokesmen constantly told us, that there could be no more time wasted for U.N. inspectors to continue their hunt in Iraq. Mushroom clouds might appear over U.S. cities at any moment; within 45 minutes, British sites could be attacked by biochemical-tipped missiles; Saddam Hussein and his "close" al-Qaida allies would be sharing all sorts of dastardly secrets; Iraqi drone plans could attack America's East Coast, and so on.[12] All lies, all the time, in the service of opinion manipulation—and the lying was effective domestically. (However, our foreign allies, and millions of ordinary citizens protesting around the world, smelled something rotten from the very beginning, and would not go along.)

Since we've mentioned the nuclear scare-tactics, let's add one more significant lie in that regard. With British PM Tony Blair at his side at a joint-press conference in the Fall of 2002, Bush said that a report on Iraq's nuclear program by the International Atomic Energy Agency revealed that Saddam could produce a bomb in six months; the IAEA not only denied the existence of any such study but noted that no such finding existed in any IAEA report.[13]

So there were no nuclear reports, no nuclear weapons, no extant nuclear program. But this didn't stop the Bush Administration from lying. "We believe he has, in fact, reconstituted nuclear weapons," Vice President Dick Cheney said as late as March of 2003.[14] Everyone heard him say it on "Meet the Press" on national television, but the need to lie, almost as instinct, is a difficult one to keep buried, and so, despite such assertions by Cheney and others, Rumsfeld told this whopper a few months later: "I don't believe that anyone that I know in the Administration ever said that Iraq had nuclear weapons."[15] These guys were shameless.

In addition to, and interwoven into the Bush lies, there were the lies told by the Iraqi exiles, led by Ahmed Chalabi and his Iraqi National Congress. After years of intimations that he and the INC would be permitted to form a government-in-exile and lead a coup inside Iraq to topple Saddam Hussein, the exiles began to sense the truth of their situation: they would remain forever in exile unless they could return to Iraq under the sponsorship of a formidable U.S. or U.N. military force. If the exiles passed on some whoppers to the U.S. to convince them to invade—well, all's fair in love and war and returning to your homeland.

The exiles knew what the Americans wanted to hear—that the war would be a cakewalk, the U.S. soldiers would be welcomed with kisses and flowers as liberators, and there would be a smooth, calm postwar imposition of U.S. rule—and so they provided those lies. Anything to get their forces back onto Iraqi soil. And the U.S., wanting to believe what the exiles were telling them, since it matched their PNAC vision and gave them more propaganda ammunition to justify an invasion, passed those exaggerated assessments on to others.

Those U.S. citizens who deigned to question these Bush&Co. lies, deceptions and manipulations were dismissed as providing aid and comfort to "terrorists."[16] Or, as in the case of such erstwhile allies like France and Germany—who did the rarely done: publicly chastizing Bush Administration spokesmen—their leaders were threatened and punished.

The Bush system is a closed one: garbage in, garbage out; lies in, lies out. And, since the mass media in America were generally docile, if not downright submissive, the lies tended to multiply in impact, after Fox News and CNN and other cable commentators and rightwing radio talk-show hosts—and Judith Miller at the New York Times—did their agit-prop jobs. The American citizenry, already living in a state of fear and desire for revenge in the years after 9/11, for a long time accepted this with-us-or-against-us view of the world, and tended to swallow the propaganda whole.

The situation began to change when the Occupation phase began in Iraq. A staggering truth began to make its way through even the mass-media propaganda barrage: the Bush Administration, unprepared for anything other than the exile-fed fantasy of a post-war cakewalk, revealed that it had no Plan B.

The fighting army, even though untrained for such tasks, suddenly was ordered to serve as civil police and nation-builders. In reality, the soldiers realized they were little more than targets in a night-time and even daytime shooting/bombing gallery. (Foreign Islamists, who under Saddam were not welcomed, now were entering Iraq to join nationalist fighters in waging guerrilla war against the American Occupiers.) The casualties mounted, new Occupation administrators were moved in and out trying to keep the situation calm enough for long enough to install a U.S.-friendly government and set up the corporate looting-system.

The costs, especially given the rip-offs and fraud involved in such a huge enterprise, were enormous—several hundred billion dollars—while the American economy was in tatters, with social services being cut left and right at home. Voters were starting to ask—and not just liberals and Democrats but Independents and conservative/moderate Republican— why they should bear the bulk of the financial burden of this war, based as it was on lies and deception.

It turned out that not only was Bush&Co.'s foreign/military policy wrong from the git-go, but the Administration was thoroughly incompetent in carrying it out. Not only did a good share of the rest of the world think the Bush Administration incapable of thinking straight, but the international perception was that this was a gang that couldn't even shoot straight. Bumbling, vicious, finger-pointing, political infighting— all these and more were evident in the "post-war" Iraq phase. Internecine warfare erupted, in public, between State and Defense, CIA and the White House, as each tried to deflect the blame for gross policy failures away from itself.

The Bush folks, after sidelining the United Nations in the run-up to the war, found that the situation on the ground had deteriorated to such an extent that it had to return to the U.N., hat in hand, to beg for assistance. The U.S. needed help both in arranging the handover of limited sovereignty back to the Iraqis (hoping that perhaps the Iraqi insurgency might then quiet down prior to the November election in the U.S.), and in trying to squeeze out support funds and troops from the former allies the Bush Administration previously had insulted and humiliated. They learned, surprise!, that many in the international community were happy to see the U.S. bogged down in a Vietnam-like quagmire militarily, and nearly bankrupted by a war it shouldn't have started in the first place.

The Administration's foreign/military policy, unilateralist in the extreme, left the United States pretty much an isolated entity in the world. The U.S., under Bush, was feared but not respected, and had its global image turned 180 degrees within a brief time.

Much of the good will that had flowed to the U.S. after 9/11 from all over the world had evaporated as a result of Bush's lies, deceptions and extremist policies; America was now an international pariah nation, regarded as a kind of arrogant, bullying outlaw—mad cowboys on a tear, shooting first and denouncing any who stood in their way, even to ask questions about the rationale behind the violence. "You're either with us or you're against us"—the Bush&Co. mantra. Few domestically had the guts, or felt they had their backsides covered, to stand up to the onslaught—this was especially so where that opposition should have surfaced: in the Democratic leadership and in the press.

The situation was deteriorating rapidly and the Bush Administration needed a scapegoat. The obvious candidates were Rumsfeld and his Office of Special Plans[17]—the cabal of mostly PNACers Rumsfeld set up under his own wing when the CIA and the other intelligence agencies wouldn't provide him the intelligence he wanted to justify the invasion. But, still clinging to the neo-con strategy and goals, the Administration chose instead to blame the traditional intelligence agencies at the CIA, State and Defense. Bad move. You don't play hardball with the spooks; they're better at the game—and they enjoy playing it.

And so more Bush&Co. lies and deceptions—most having to do with ignoring the pre-invasion warnings and caveats from the CIA—

were provided to the press by those who didn't appreciate the scapegoat role. Perhaps the most damaging was the "yellowcake" lie that Bush used in his January 2003 State of the Union speech, that Iraq was trying to buy that uranium from Niger; the CIA had warned him at least three months earlier that the yellowcake story was based on a crude forgery. But Bush, desperate for political cover for the war he'd already decided on the previous summer, used it in the State of the Union address.

This led Ambassador Joseph Wilson—who had investigated the allegation in Niger and told the CIA upon his return that there was nothing to it—to write a New York Times op-ed essay[18] revealing the insider-truth about the yellowcake tale. Shortly thereafter, "two senior Administration officials," in an act of blatant political revenge and as a warning to other would-be whistleblowers, told six journalists that Wilson's wife was a covert CIA operative. Such relevations are against the law. The coverup on that one is still going on as of this writing.

There is so much sleaze, mendacity and ruthlessness in this Administration that even if impeachment and/or criminal proceedings have not yet been instituted against Bush, Cheney, Ashcroft, et al., it's clear that the Democrats are going to have a field day during the 2004 campaign; they will have a wealth of factual evidence to rely on, detailing the various lies and manipulations that have helped create America's current reckless foreign/military policy, one that not only is putting our young soldiers in great and immediate danger—with more military adventures on the drawing boards if Bush wins, Syria and Iran topping the list—but that is doing great harm to the long-term national-security interests of the United States.

If Bush is defeated in November, the U.S. will find it much easier to mobilize the world in rooting out the actual terrorists, rather than overthrowing more governments and starting more wars; U.S. foreign policy will return to a more sensible middle-course approach, where diplomacy and mutual understanding get things done rather than bullets, missiles and threats of nuclear annihilation. This change toward sanity can be accomplished, but only if we work our asses off to make it happen.

Notes

1. Transcript, "2nd Presidential Debate of the 2000 Campaign," *New York Times* (October 11, 2002).

2. At <www.newamericancentury.org>.

3. Founding members in 1997: Elliot Abrams, Gary Bauer, William J. Bennett, Jeb Bush, Dick Cheney, Elliot A. Cohen, Midge Dector, Paula Dobriansky, Steve Forbes, Aaron Friedberg, Francis Fukuyama, Frank Gaffney,

Fred C. Ikle, Donald Kagan, Zalmay Khalilzad, I. Lewis Libby, Norman Podhoretz, Peter W. Rodman, Stephen P. Rosen, Henry S. Rowen, Donald Rumsfeld, Vin Weber, George Weigel and Paul Wolfowitz. Among those who have affiliated with PNAC over the years since those founders set up the organization: Newt Gingrich, Richard Armitage, John Bolton, Robert Zoellick, Richard Perle, Wayne Downing, Douglas Feith, Michael Ledeen, and so many more. Note: Most of these PNACers are located in positions of great power in the Departments of Defense, State and elsewhere. See also "How We Got Into This Imperial Pickle," at <www.crisispapers.org/Editorials/PNAC-Primer.htm>.

4. William Kristol, PNAC's chairman, and Robert Kagan, intellectual doyen of PNAC, first used this term in their famous article, "Towards a Neo-Reaganite Foreign Policy," in *Foreign Affairs* (July-August 1996).

5. *PBS Newshour* (September 25, 2002).

6. *CBS News* (May 17, 2002).

7. *ABC News Nightline* (March 5, 2003).

8. See the seminal PNAC report: "Strategy for Rebuilding America's Defenses," at <www.newamericancentury.org/RebuildingAmericasDefenses.pdf>.

9. At <www.whitehouse.gov/nsc/nss.html>.

10. *CBS 60 Minutes* (January 11, 2004); *ABC News* (April 1, 2004).

11. Associated Press, "Wolfowitz Comments Revive Doubts Over Iraq's WMD," *USA Today* (May 30, 2003).

12. George Jones, "Blair Hardened Up Iraq Dossier," *Telegraph* (April 7, 2003); Jim Lobe, "Key Officials Used 9/11 As Pretext for Iraq War," *Common Dreams* (July 16, 2003); John McCarthy, "Senators Were Told Iraqi Weapons Could Hit United States: Senator Nelson Aide Says Iraq Information Was Declassified," *Florida Today* (December 18, 2003).

13. When White House press secretary Ari Fleischer was informed that there was no such IAEA report, he then stated "that it was the International Institute for Strategic Studies [IISS] that issued the report saying that Iraq could develop nuclear weapons in six months or less. While it is true the IISS issued a report on Iraq's weapons capabilities...the report said nothing about Iraq being able to develop nuclear weapons in six months or less." Joe Conason, "Scary TV Shows and Real Threats," at <www.salon.com/politics/conason/2002/09/23/bush/print.html>.

14. Derrick Z. Jackson, "Cheney's Misspeaking Streak," *Boston Globe* (September 17, 2003).

15. At <www.slate.msn.com/id/2083532>.

16. Neil Lewis, "Ashcroft Defends Antiterror Plan and Says Criticism May Aid Foes," *New York Times* (December 7, 2001).

17. Julian Borger, "The Spies Who Pushed for War," *Guardian* (July 19, 2003).

18. Joseph C. Wilson 4th, "What I Didn't Find in Africa," *New York Times* (July 6, 2003).

9/11, Bush Lies, and the Puppet Presidency

By Jerry "Politex" Barrett

I. Rice's 9/11 Missile Defense Speech

On September 11, 2001, national security adviser Condoleeza Rice was scheduled to outline a Bush administration policy that would address "the threats and problems of today and the day after, not the world of yesterday" — but the focus was largely on missile defense, not terrorism from Islamic radicals" (*Washington Post*, April 4, 2004).

Condoleeza Rice never gave the speech, of course, because on that day she was in a White House bunker, along with Dick Cheney, in the presence of Richard Clarke, the President's advisor on antiterrorism, who was serving as Crisis Manager in the Situation Room, directing the nation's actions in immediate response to the 9/11 destruction of New York City's World Trade Towers and a portion of the Pentagon.

According to U.S. officials interviewed by the *Washington Post*, the text of Rice's 9/11 speech did not include even one mention of Osama Bin Laden or Islamic extremist groups. Instead, its focus was on Bush's missile defense system that has been desired by Republican administrations since Reagan's, perhaps because the same players, such as Dick Cheney, have been involved in its promotion, both as high-ranking government officials and as high-ranking defense industry businessmen.

As Ivo Daalder, a staff member of Clinton's national security council and presently a foreign policy analyst at Brookings, told the *Guardian* (April 2, 2004) "senior officials in the Bush White House took office with the same foreign policy concerns and outlook they had had eight years earlier working for the first President Bush. 'When they left in January 1993, they hit the pause button. The intervening eight years were missing. They left believing ballistic missile defense was the way to secure America, and came in believing ballistic missile defense was the best way to secure America.'"

The Rice speech was the norm not the exception to the Bush policy since he began his administration eight months earlier. "There were zero references to al-Qaida during these months. That's according to Federal

News Service, which transcribes every presidential utterance. . . . Of course, the president did mention terrorism, terrorists and counter-terrorism 24 times before 9/11. But eight of these comments referred to the Israeli-Palestinian conflict. Another eight involved a range of terrorist threats, including ethnic terrorism in Macedonia and Basque separatists in Spain. In the remaining eight references to terrorism, the new president offered his idea for how to combat it: the Reagan-era missile-defense system formerly known as Star Wars," writes columnist Marie Cocco (*Newsday*, March 30, 2004).

Two days before the 9/11 attacks, Rice told "Meet the Press" that Bush was about "to get serious about the business of dealing with this emergent threat. Ballistic missiles are ubiquitous now." In the Rice speech, she was to reveal that Dick Cheney, former Secretary of Defense, former head of Halliburton, a defense contractor, had been named by Bush "to oversee a coordinated national effort to protect against a terrorist attack using weapons of mass destruction" (*Washington Post*, April 2, 2004).

II. Bush Downgrades Anti-Terrorism

Condi Rice brought a set of understandings, a corporate style, and administrative experiences to her job at the White House, which explains her focus in the months prior to 9/11, asserts Douglas Jehl and David Sanger (*New York Times*, April 4, 2004). She decided that while working as Bush's National Security Adviser, her three concerns would be to concentrate on traditional world power politics, bringing her professional and educational background as a "Europeanist" to the table; paring down the Security Council to make it more operational, delegating authority in the corporate manner; and helping Bush to achieve his campaign pledge of creating a missile-defense system, satisfying both senior-level Republican bureaucrats and defense contractors, the latter being part of the corporate group that put him into the White House. Rice had no missile-defense background, other than the intelligent use of her enthusiasm for supporting Bush's agenda.

Although, "in February 2001, George J. Tenet, the director of central intelligence, told Congress that terrorism was the top threat facing the United States," Jehl and Sanger report that her deputy, Steven Hadley, "deeply connected to the neoconservative wing of the administration," which includes Cheney, Rumsfeld, and Rumsfeld's Defense Department Deputy, Paul Wolfowitz, was assigned the task of overseeing the Bush administration's antiterrorism policy. Prior to 9/11, the neoconservatives in the Bush administration were more interested in Iraq and missile defense than antiterrorism.

Under the Clinton administration, the military came up with a plan to pressure the Taliban to get rid of bin Laden, using military, economic, diplomatic, and political means. In contrast, the Bush administration never acted on the plan, according to David Johnston and Eric Schmitt in the (*New York Times*, April 4, 2004). In June of 2001 Hadley told Wolfowitz to start preparing such a plan, but Rumsfeld, his boss, never ordered new military options.

During the first eight months of the Bush administration, over at the Department of Justice, which funds the FBI, Attorney General John Ashcroft was downgrading terrorism as a priority and slashing the Department's antiterrorism budget. In April of 2000, eight months before the election, Clinton's Attorney General, Janet Reno, gave terrorism her top priority and requested greater funding in that area: "In the near term as well as the future, cybercrime and counterterrrorism are going to be the most challenging threats in the criminal justice area. Nowhere is the need for an up-to-date human and technical infrastructure more critical," she said.

Ashcroft's budget goals memo, written five months prior to 9/11, doesn't include counterterrorism as a strategic goal and, prior to 9/11, Ashcroft ignored the annual FBI request for more translators and counterintelligence agents to deal with a backlog of intelligence, and was attempting to slash both FBI and homeland defense-type counterterrorism funding. Even after 9/11, the FBI requested $1.5 billion in supplemental funding for counterterrorism through Ashcroft, and was only given $530 million by the White House (<www.americanprogress.org/site/pp.asp?c=biJRJ8OVF&b=39039>).

III. Pre-9/11 Dire Warnings With Little Response

The Bush administration's focus in the month's leading up to 9/11 was upon funding and creating a missile-defense system, on Iraq and its imagined "weapons of mass destruction," and the WMD of other "rogue nations." This course of action was taken despite the fact that a proliferation of U.S. intelligence reports increasingly warned of something totally different: attacks on the U.S. from cell-based terrorist groups.

On December 20, 2000, Richard Clarke, Bush's antiterrorism adviser, along with representatives of the FBI, the CIA, and the Clinton State Department, met with Colin Powell to brief him on antiterrorism. Yet, at his confirmation hearings on January 17, 2001, Powell raised around 20 issues during his testimony, and none of them were on antiterrorism or al-Qaida (Associated Press, March 3, 2004).

"The central notion that Mr. Bush did not make terrorism as high a priority as hindsight shows it should have been is one that he himself has admitted. Mr. Bush said as much in an interview with *Washington Post* reporter Bob Woodward for his book on the response to September 11" (*Christian Science Monitor*, April 1, 2004).

In the summer of 2001, intelligence warnings escalated and were, according to CIA director George Tenet, repeatedly communicated to top officials in the Bush White House. *New York Times* writers David Johnston and Adam Nagourney, note:

> Tenet, who briefed Bush on threats almost daily, "was around town literally pounding on desks saying that something is happening, this is an unprecedented level of threat information," said Richard Armitage, the deputy secretary of state, who was quoted in a congressional report last year. But even as the warnings spiked in June and July that year, there appeared to be little sense of alarm at the White House, officials of the Central Intelligence Agency told the commission (*New York Times*, March 28, 2004).

Michael Tomasky observes: "When the Bush administration started hearing more intelligence noises in June and July of 2001, why didn't it — and Rice specifically, since this was her bailiwick — convene the same kind of daily meetings the Clinton administration had when it heard similar noise? The obvious answer . . . is that it wasn't a high priority and that facts could not make it so. And a model existed, then not even two years old, for how to avert catastrophe (*American Prospect*, April 4, 2004).

Further, Bush "officials acknowledged that U.S. intelligence officials informed President Bush weeks before the September 11 attacks that bin Laden's terrorist network might try to hijack American planes" (ABC News, May 6, 2001). On August 6, 2001, Bush "received a one-and-a-half page briefing advising him that Osama bin Laden was capable of a major strike against the US, and that the plot could include the hijacking of an American airplane" (NBC, September 10, 2002).

"On September 4, 2001, a foreign-policy principals group chaired by Rice 'apparently approved' a draft terrorism directive, according to a 9/11 commission report. Among other things, the directive envisioned an expanded covert action program against Al Qaeda (*Christian Science Monitor*, April 1, 2004).

But by then it was too little, too late.

IV. Bush-Cheney Stonewall The 9/11 Commission

After 9/11, the Bush administration dragged its feet on appointing a head of Homeland Security, then it dragged its feet on giving that head

Cabinet-level status, then it stonewalled an independent probe of 9/11, then it agreed on an independent probe, providing it could select its chairman and approve five Republican members, making the 11 member panel a Republican majority. Then it selected Henry Kissinger to head that commission, and all hell broke lose. "By announcing that Henry Kissinger will be chairing the inquiry that it did not want, the president has now made the same point in a different way. But the cynicism of the decision and the gross insult to democracy and to the families of the victims that it represents has to be analyzed to be believed," wrote Christopher Hitchens in one of the more scathing responses to Bush's action (Slate, November 27, 2002).

The *New York Times*' Maureen Dowd added that Cheney's fingerprints were all over the Kissinger nomination: "Only someone as pathologically opaque as the vice president could appreciate the sublime translucency of Henry Kissinger. And only someone intent on recreating the glory days of the Ford and Nixon White Houses could have hungered to add the 79-year-old Dr. Strange —. . . I mean, Dr. Kissinger to the Bush team" (*New York Times,* December 11, 2002).

Kissinger chose not to accept the Bush nomination, not wanting to disclose his consulting firm's client list, which many assumed included members of the Saudi government. Given Kissinger's many conflict-of-interest business ties and the Bush-shaped role of the commission to look at both Clinton's and Bush's relevant pre-9/11 activities with the focus upon recommending future antiterrorist policy, few thought that Bush wanted to fairly examine the facts behind 9/11 and his administration's behavior in the eight months prior to 9/11.

That majority view became strengthened because of the Bush administration's lack of cooperation with the commission in nearly a year and a half since its inception. The White House has pretty much done what it could to slow down the activities of the commission, from refusing to supply the probe with relevant documents to refusing to provide key administration witnesses to establish a relevant narrative. Once the Bush administration managed to slow down the work of the commission to the point where it had to cancel some of its hearings in order to try meet its 18-month report deadline, it attempted to hold the commission to the May 27, 2004 deadline:

> "The commission seems to have turned a corner," said Michael
> Greenberger, director of the Center for Health and Homeland Security . . . "Things are starting to come out that are quite disturbing. . . .
> This is why the Bush administration and the Republicans want this to
> end in May, so it's old news by the time you reach the heat of the elec-

tion cycle" (*Washington Post*, January 29, 2004).

While a new August 2004 deadline was agreed upon, the nation has recently learned of two more Bush roadblocks placed in the way of the 9/11 commission as this book goes to press.

In late February, the White House disclosed that it had withheld over 80% of the 11,000 pages of Clinton papers from the 9/11 commission because they either were "highly sensitive" or they were irrelevant. Federal researchers who looked at the unreleased papers concluded they were relevant, but administration spokesmen indicated those papers would not actually be turned over to the commission. "Mr. Ben-Veniste and other commission members said they were surprised to learn that any Clinton documents had been withheld. 'Since all of the commissioners and most of the staff have security clearances at the very highest level,' Mr. Ben-Veniste said, 'it puzzles me as to what would be withheld on the basis of national security concerns'"(*New York Times*, April 2, 2004).

The implications of this tactic were significant. "Bruce Lindsey, Mr. Clinton's former deputy White House counsel and his liaison to the National Archives . . . said he feared that the commission was making judgments about the Clinton administration's actions in dealing with terrorist threats without full access to its papers . . . [Bush] "officials suggested that similar, highly classified Bush White House documents might also have been withheld from the panel" (*New York Times*, April 2, 2004).

Under increased pressure from both Republicans and Democrats, Bush decided to allow Rice to testify in public and under oath to the 9/11 commission, providing the appearance of an acting White House national security adviser did not set a precedent. He also decided to talk about 9/11 in private and not under oath to the entire 11 person commission, rather than just the Republican chair and the Democratic vice-chair, but insisted that Dick Cheney be there with him. Further, the commission had to agree that it would neither call Rice back nor call upon any other White House member to testify in public.

These are hardly concesssions that lead the public to trust the commission's ability to get to the full truth. This point is emphasized by the editors of the *New York Times*, commenting on the work of the 9/11 Commission:

> Mr. Bush did the right thing only under intense political pressure and after he had already undermined the principles he claimed to be upholding. His reversal came with disturbing conditions attached, wrapped up in a volley of spin. All in all, it leaves the impression of a

White House less interested in helping the 9/11 panel perform its vital task than in protecting the president's political flanks (*New York Times* editorial, March 31, 2004).

Maureen Dowd's version of White House lawyer Al Gonzalez' conditions sent to the commission envisions Cheney as the ventriloquist and Bush as the puppet:

> The Vice President will not address any queries about why no one reacted to George Tenet's daily "hair on fire" alarms to the President about a coming Al Qaeda attack; or why the President was so consumed with chopping and burning cedar on his Crawford ranch that he ignored the warning in an August 6, 2001, briefing that Al Qaeda might try to hijack aircraft; or why the President asked for a plan to combat Al Qaeda in May and then never followed up while Richard Clarke's aggressive plan was suffocated by second-raters; or why the President was never briefed by his counterterrorism chief on anything but cybersecurity until September 11; or why the Administration-in-amber made so many cold war assumptions, such as thinking that terrorists had to be sponsored by a state even as terrorists had taken over a state; or why the President went along with the Vice President and the neocons to fool the American public into believing that Saddam had a hand in the 9/11 attacks; or why the Administration chose to undercut the war on terrorism and inflame the Arab world by attacking Iraq" (*New York Times*, April 1, 2004).

IV. Clarke's Testimony

What Richard Clarke didn't know on 9/11 while he was serving as Crisis Manager in The Situation Room at the White House was that John O'Neill, one of his best friends, was working in one of the World Trade Center towers when they went down. He was killed. Clarke met O'Neill in 1994 when the former White House antiterrorism expert called the FBI for help on the 1993 bombing of the World Trade Center. O'Neill eventually became the FBI's expert on al-Qaeda, but left the FBI two months before 9/11 and became head of security for the World Trade Center.

Some think O'Neill left because he was having a hard time getting officials to focus upon al-Qaeda and other such terrorist groups: "It's clear that the turf battles between O'Neill and diplomats anxious to maintain good relations with Arab states began in the Bill Clinton years. There were signs that problems intensified under the Bush administration." Jean-Charles Brisard and Guillaume Dasquie, the French authors of *Bin Laden: The Forbidden Truth,* claimed to have been told by O'Neill that "the main obstacles to investigate Islamic terrorism were US oil corporate interests and the role played by Saudi Arabia in it." Brisard and Dasquie drew attention to the strong business links between members of the Bush administration and Saudi Arabia through the oil industry, and through defense company the Carlyle Group, between the Bush and Bin Laden families" (Tom Griffin, Asia Times Online, March 27, 2004).

Unlike O'Neill, Clarke has never made any connection between the long history of the Bush family, U.S. corporate oil interests, the Saudis, and bin Laden. While Clarke was higher up in the food chain at the Clinton White House than O'Neill was at the FBI, Clarke's status was lowered in the Bush administration when antiterrorism was put on the back burner. Months before 9/11 he asked to be reassigned to cybersecurity, a post he created. In one of the many interviews that followed his testimony to the 9/11 commission, he noted his dissatisfaction with the Bush administration's downplaying of antiterrorism prior to 9/11, but said he was reluctant to resign because he felt the work he was doing was too important. O'Neill and Clarke were not alone:

> The Bush administration's failure to prevent the 11 September attacks came under even fiercer scrutiny yesterday, when it emerged that two veteran CIA counter-terrorism experts were so frustrated in summer 2001 that they considered resigning and making public their fears about an imminent terrorist strike against US targets (*The Independent,* March 25, 2004).

Clarke began his testimony before the 9/11 commission by addressing the relatives of the victims: "Your government failed you. Those entrusted with protecting you failed you. And I failed you. We tried hard, but that doesn't matter because we failed." Here, Clarke does what "Responsibility Era" Bush is never able to do, he takes responsibility for failure.

Clarke goes on to undercut Bush's strategy to lump his administration with Clinton's in the 9/11 probe so as to minimize the fallout:

> Fighting terrorism, in general, and fighting Al Qaida, in particular, were an extraordinarily high priority in the Clinton administration — certainly no higher priority . . . . The Bush administration in the first eight months considered terrorism an important issue, but not an urgent issue."

The thrust of Clarke's testimony was that the Bush administration ignored the growing threat of terrorism prior to the 9/11 attacks and then did too little to protect the country thereafter, partly because of an obsessive focus on Iraq:

> The reason I am strident in my criticism of the president of the United States is because by invading Iraq . . . the president of the United States has greatly undermined the war on terrorism.

Clarke's testimony and his book detail the groundless fixation on Iraq by Bush and his neocon warriors.

> In his book, *Against All Enemies*, Clarke writes "that because of the administration's fixation on Iraq, he could not get its attention on the rising al-Qaeda danger. . . ." At one meeting, Clarke reports that he told the new deputy defense secretary, Paul Wolfowitz, that al-Qaeda "poses an immediate and serious threat to the United States." Wolfowitz replied that Iraqi terrorism posed "at least as much" danger as al-Qaeda. When the FBI, CIA and Clarke all told Wolfowitz there was no evidence of Iraqi terrorism aimed at the United States, Wolfowitz replied that Iraq was behind the 1993 garage bombing at the World Trade Center — a theory, writes Clarke, that anti-terrorist experts and courts had "investigated for years and found to be totally untrue" (James O. Goldsborough, *San Diego Union-Tribune*, March 6, 2004).

In *Against All Enemies*, Clarke tells us how Bush got him and some aides into a room off the White House Situation Center on September 12, 2001 and, in a tone later termed "intimidating," told Clarke that he wanted any "shred" of evidence that Saddam was behind the 9/11 attacks. On the CBS news magazine "60 Minutes," Clarke described the scene:

> I said "Mr. President, we've done this before. We . . . we've been looking at this. We looked at it with an open mind, there's no connection." He came back at me and said, "Iraq, Saddam . . . find out if there's a connection." And in a very intimidating way. I mean, that we should come back with that answer . . . (CBS, "60 Minutes," March 28, 2004).

That same day, Rumsfeld suggested the U.S. bomb Iraq in retaliation to 9/11. Clarke told Colin Powell, "Having been attacked by al-Qaeda, for us now to go bombing Iraq in response would be like our invading Mexico after the Japanese attacked us at Pearl Harbor" (Richard Clarke in *Against All Enemies*).

V. Bush Lies About Pre-9/11 Activities

On issue after issue, they tell the American people one thing, and do another. They repeatedly invent facts to support their preconceived agenda. Facts which administration officials knew, or should have known, were not true. This pattern has prevailed since President Bush's earliest days in office. As a result, this President has now created the largest credibility gap since Richard Nixon. He Has broken the basic bond of trust with the American people (Sen. Edward Kennedy, Democracy Now! interview with John Dean, April 4, 2004).

So why should Bush and his administration be any different when it attempts to defend itself against critics like former Bush Treasury Secretary Paul O'Neill and Richard Clarke, and reporters and politicians who have been asking questions about 9/11 since it happened. Here's a selection of comments upon recent lies:

Then there are Rice's own inconsistencies in her public statements, the transcripts of which are a gold mine of contradiction and pettifoggery. Did Clarke give the administration a counter-terrorism plan in January or not? One Condi says yes, the other says no. Did that plan include military options? Again, yes and no. Was the plan the administration finally drafted substantially different from what Clarke recommended, or about the same? On all these questions, Rice has contradicted either herself or explanations given by other administration officials (Michael Tomasky, American Prospect online, April 4, 2004).

We speak with former FBI translator, Sibel Edmonds, who was hired shortly after September 11 to translate intelligence gathered over the previous year related to the 9/11 attacks. She says the FBI had information that an attack using airplanes was being planned before September 11 and calls Condoleezza Rice's claim the White House had no specific information on a domestic threat or one involving planes "an outrageous lie" (Democracy Now! March 31, 2004).

Rice apparently reversed herself again in an op-ed column for the *Washington Post* (March 23, 2004): "Despite what some have suggested, we received no intelligence that terrorists were preparing to attack the homeland using airplanes as missiles."

But Edmonds has come forward to testify that specific warnings about Al Qaeda plans to use airplanes as weapons were given to senior U.S. officials during the months preceding the September 11 attacks.

In an interview with the British daily newspaper *The Independent*,

(April 2, 2004) Sibel Edmonds,with top-security clearance, said she has testified about such warnings at a closed session of the 9/11 commission.

> Bush's aides suggested that Clarke had invented the meeting in which Clarke said the president pressured him to find a link between the 9/11 attack and Iraq, ignoring Clarke's insistence that intelligence agencies had concluded that no such link existed. But on Sunday, national security advisor Condoleezza Rice was forced to admit that Bush had pressed Clarke on an Iraq connection. This backed up earlier assertions by former Treasury Secretary Paul O'Neill as to Bush's obsession with Iraq from the very first days of his administration at the expense of focusing on Osama bin Laden and Al Qaeda (Robert Scheer, *Los Angeles Times*, March 30, 2004).

> Cheney claimed Monday that Clarke had been "out of the loop" in the fight against terror, raising the obvious question of why a White House would not involve its counterterrorism chief in major decisions. On Wednesday, Ms. Rice stepped forward to correct the vice president, asserting that, indeed, Clarke "was in every meeting that was held on terrorism" (*Christian Science Monitor*, March 30, 2004).

> White House spokesman Scott McClellan complained last month that when [Rice] testified in private, "only five members showed up" to hear what she had to say. What McClellan didn't tell reporters was that on November 21 — long before Rice met with the five commissioners in February — the White House counsel's office had sent the commission a letter saying no more than three commissioners could attend meetings with White House aides of Rice's rank (*USA Today*, April 6, 2004).

VI. The 9/11 Commission: A Trifecta of Suspicion

In the many months after 9/11, pressure built to have an independent commission formed to look into the events of 9/11. The Bush administration blocked such attempts, but finally agreed to help form such a commission, providing it focused upon antiterrorism activities in both the Clinton and pre-9/11 administrations with an eye to making recommendations to make future antiterrorism activities more effective. In other words, it took the focus away from those who were concerned with the actions of the Bush administration on 9/11 and the implications of those actions.

Margie Burns, one of the contributors to this book, has written:

> The National Security Agency is among the topics not being aired much at commission hearings. But then, there are several such topics.

The Family Steering Committee, composed of relatives of the victims of September 11, has posed a number of significant questions, none of which has been answered, or even mentioned for that matter, during several public hearings. The full range of questions still unanswered exceeds the scope of a single article, but even a short list of the questions pertaining to that day suggests the scope of inquiry" (Asia Times Online, April 1, 2004).

Burns goes on to list questions including Bush's Florida classroom behavior on 9/11, his comments about how he learned of the WTC attack, and his activities during the rest of the day. Pepe Escobar in Asia Times Online provides a selection of specific questions:

1) Why . . . were no F-16s protecting US airspace? . . . Why did fighters not take off from Andrews Air Force base just outside Washington to protect the Pentagon?

2) The pre-September 11 suspicious stock option trades in American Airlines and United Airlines . . . Who profited?

3) What happened to the FBI investigation into flight schools - when it was proved that at least five of the 19 hijackers were trained in US military schools?

4) Why did Bush keep reading a pet-goat story for more than half an hour after the first WTC hit, and 15 minutes after Chief of Staff Andrew Card told him there had been an attack?

5) What really happened to Flight 93? [The black box was not found], unlike Mohammed Atta's intact passport lying in the WTC rubble?

6) What does Rice really know about the very close relations between Mahmoud [Almad, the sending of $100, 000 to hijacker Mohamoud Atta's bank accounts in Florida,] and the top echelons of the Bush administration?" (Asia Times Online, April 8, 2004)o

September 11 has often been referred to as a new Pearl Harbor. On the night of 9/11, Bush wrote in his diary, "The Pearl Harbor of the 21st century took place today" (*Washington Post*, January 27, 2002). This comparison between 9/11 and Pearl Harbor has been known to touch a nerve with some frustrated with the unanswered questions about 9/11, questions that the 9/11 commission is not addressing. The comparision recalls that a group of neocons, including Bush's brother, Jeb, 2000 published a call to arms titled *Rebuilding America's Defenses* through a self-created conservative hawk think tank, the Project for the New American Century (PNAC).

Their proposal was to create a "Pax Americana," a building up of U.S. military might, with bases all over the world, replacing the UN as the central world authority, with the U.S. as a kind of world policeman. Most of the specifics they recommended in the monograph has been instituted by Bush since 9/11. Further, half of the neocon group that produced the monograph are now key members of the Bush administration:

> Paul Wolfowitz is now deputy defense secretary. John Bolton is undersecretary of state. Stephen Cambone is head of the Pentagon's Office of Program, Analysis and Evaluation. Eliot Cohen and Devon Cross are members of the Defense Policy Board, which advises Rumsfeld. I. Lewis Libby is chief of staff to Vice President Dick Cheney. Dov Zakheim is comptroller for the Defense Department" (Jay Bookman, *Atlanta Journal-Constitution*, September 29, 2002).

The authors of the monograph write, "The process of transformation, even if it brings revolutionary change, is likely to be a long time one, absent some catastrophic and catalyzing event — like a new Pearl Harbor (*Rebuilding America's Defenses*, p. 63).

For them, 9/11 turned out to be the "new Pearl Harbor," as far as getting many of their recommendations enacted are concerned. If Bush wins in 2004, two thorns in the side of the neocon hawks and their plan for "Pax Americana," Colin Powell and Condi Rice, will be gone, according to their own statements. One would think their next goal would be to put one of their own in each of these two key policy positions. Some of those who question the actions of Bush and the administration are particularly concerned about the "new Pearl Harbor" aspect of 9/11 and the placement of the monograph's producers in the Bush administration.

Returning to the 9/11 Commission, Bernard Weiner, another contributor to this book writes:

> About the so-called 'independent' 9/11 Commission: The quote marks are used because not only is that word laughable in terms of who Bush appointed and who's in charge, but because White House counsel Alberto Gonzales contacted at least two of the GOP members of the panel right before Richard Clarke's testimony and apparently supplied them talking points for questioning the White House's former counter-terrorism chief. This commission — which, in any case, has concentrated on lower-level intelligence failures all along, rather than on what exactly the executive decision-makers knew, when they knew it, and what they did or didn't do about their knowledge — is designed to be an ineffective truth-seeker" (Crisis Papers, April 6, 2004).

What we have, then, is a trifecta of suspicion concerning the ability of the 9/11 commission to satisfy questions of fact and responsibility for 9/11: Bush's initial selection of Kissinger to chair the committee and conflicts of interest among those selected; the committee's focus upon the Clinton years and the first eight months of the Bush years and its limited task of making recommendations for the future, rather than delving into the actual events of 9/11; and this third cause of suspicion that has yet to be discussed: the commission's selection of executive director.

Philip D. Zelikow, a lawyer from Texas, has a long history of working with members of the Bush administration that would logically be called upon to testify. As Commission critic Paul Sperry puts it, "the commissioners for the most part follow [Zelikow's] recommendations. In effect, he sets the agenda and runs the investigation." It's very likely that Zelikow had input into the commission's decision to limit Rice's testimony to one session, allow Bush and Cheney to testify together and to keep the testimony unrecorded and secret, and to prevent the commission from calling members of the White House to testify in the future. "Former White House terrorism czar Richard Clarke says he briefed not only Rice and Hadley, but also Zelikow about the growing al-Qaida threat during the transition period. Zelikow sat in on the briefings, he says" (Paul Sperry, Anti-War.com, March 31, 2004).

Sperry notes that both Rice and Zalikow were aides to NSA adviser Brent Scowcroft in the first Bush White House, that they co-wrote a book, *Germany Unified and Europe Transformed*, and that, along with Dick Cheney and Paul Wolfowitz, Rice was a member of Zelikow's Aspen Strategy Group. Zalikow was also a member of Bush's 2000 transition team, is a member of Bush's Foreign Intelligence Advisory Board, and has ongoing ties to the Bush White House through his Miller Center of Public Affairs at the University of Virginia.

Confidence in the 9/11 commission's ability to clear up questions about 9/11 took a further hit in early April 2004 during the NBC program "Meet the Press" as reported by *USA Today*:

> The Bush administration would check the report "line by line" to find out if there's anything in there which could harm American interests in the area of intelligence. This sort of vetting is standard for documents that could reveal sources and methods of collecting intelligence. But it raises the prospect of White House censorship and the possibility that the report's release could be delayed beyond the presidential election in November (*USA Today*, April 4, 2004).

VII. Who Is The President?

By his own admission, Bush thinks of himself as a CEO running a corporation. He delegates authority down the line, listens to plans developed up through the chain of command, and makes the final decisions. His decisions, however, appear to be based on conservative ideology, the financial needs of his corporate backers, his political goals, evangelicalism, and his own simplistic, ill-formed visions of the world, rather than the more subtle specifics of the matter at hand. He has called himself a cheer-leader president, one who is the front man for the plans of others. Not a reader, he depends upon the people around him for his daily news of the world and, thus, makes decisions based what he is told about the world from the corporate reps and neocon hawks who surround him. Those senior-level officials who disagree with these keepers of the White House keys are shunted aside, if possible, or who have been pressured to leave, as Colin Powell has said he will do if Bush were to be elected in 2004. With the heavily bureaucratic structure under him, there is little chance that much contradictory information a few levels below him will break through the filter of those who surround him. All of this accounts for the observations about him that have come on the heels of 9/11, both from inside and outside the administration.

> Thomas Kean, chairman of the bipartisan commission investigating 9/11, said: "Although Bush is hardly the first sitting president to face kiss-and-tell tomes, analysts say it's rare to see so many in the first term of an administration, before the president runs for reelection. Even more unusual is the seniority of the authors — aides such as a cabinet secretary, and the administration's top terrorism official."
>
> Many of the current books depict Bush as simplistic and narrow-minded, unwilling to listen to opposing points of view — a portrayal that Senator Kerry is already attempting to exploit in his campaign.
>
> "This is a president who makes decisions almost entirely based on intuition and hunch," says Paul Light, director of the Center for Public Service at the Brookings Institution. "He works with a very small team of highly trusted advisers, and he does not invite dissent" (Liz Marlantes, *Christian Science Monitor*, April 2, 2004).

According to one unnamed insider, even Bush meetings with his cabinet often are geared to protect him from being provided with too much information:

> JOHN DEAN: ...Bush often went to meetings on a script, and I couldn't really say that [before], because I would have revealed one of my sources.

AMY GOODMAN: Explain what you mean.

JOHN DEAN: For example, at a Cabinet meeting, the Secretary would be told before he came to the cabinet meeting what he was expected to say: the subjects that were going to be addressed. They would go around the table in this charade [at a] meeting that really wasn't anything other than a scripted gathering of the Cabinet. It's really extraordinary. Bush would have a few asides, but nothing really of substance to add to these things (John Dean interview, Democracy Now!, April 6, 2004).

Dean went on to say, "Bush [is] a president who is very good at working the campaign trail. He's very good at raising money . . . . He has got a pleasant public personality." Those are Bush's strengths, and that's where he shines. However, when he gets into an interview or goes out on the hustings, embarrassment is often only one sentence away. Bush Watch has called his language difficulty "Bushlexia": "As it has been variously described, it's a combination of dyslexia, attention deficit disorder, apraxia, illiteracy, ignorance, laziness, passive-aggressiveness, inappropriate humor, and an arrogant attitude of privilege" (at <bushwatch.org/english.htm>).

Rather than attempt to change Bush, the White House has placed a positive spin upon his verbal weaknesses, saying Bushspeak is the language of the common man. As such, Bush talked about sophisticated and subtle foreign policy decisions in the language of John Wayne westerns: get 'em dead or alive; the fight against good and evil, etc. And when that rhetoric was inadequate, Bush simply distorted or lied.

Is it any wonder, then, that Bush needed to convince the 9/11 commission that it would be okay for him to appear together with Cheney to give testimoney on 9/11, which the commission did? During the 2000 campaign, when Bush indicated his lack of knowledge early on, sometimes in the language of a political bafoon rather than a presidential candidate, and when the media began to complain about his inexperience, Cheney was the perfect antidote. Bush told reporters, I may be inexperienced, but I'll have people like Dick Cheney to back me up. Now we know what he meant.

In a Salon interview, John Dean explained the theme of his book on the Bush admistration, *Worse than Watergate*:

"It is Cheney, not Rove, who is Bush's backroom brain. He is actually a co-president. Bush doesn't enjoy studying and devising policy. Cheney does. While Cheney has tutored Bush for almost four years, and Bush is better prepared today than when he entered the job, Cheney is quietly guiding this administration. Cheney knows how to play Bush so that Cheney is absolutely no threat to him, makes him feel he is president, but Bush can't function without a script, or without Cheney. Bush is head of state; Cheney is head of government" (John Dean interview, Salon, (March 31, 2004).

The combination of Bush's severe limitations as president and Cheney's neocon hawk ambitions and connections to America's corporations help to explain why the Bush administration was unable to turn from its pre-9/11 emphasis upon missile defense systems and Iraq to fully address the growing, dire warnings leading up to 9/11 that Bush was given.

VIII. Conclusion: Did Bush Do What He Could?

According to Condi Rice, in her answer to commissioner Gorton at the 9/11 hearings on April 8, 2004, if her administration's program to fight terrorism, recommended to Bush on September 4, were put in place on the day after the inauguration, the 9/11 attacks still would have happened. Perhaps that says as much about the limits of the plan as it does the timing of the attacks. Richard Clarke believes that Rice's new corporate bureaucracy system, along with the administration's day-one emphasis upon Saddam Hussein and Iraq, prevented changes in the system, while the warnings of a massive attack on the U.S. grew more dire. During the Rice testimony, commission member Bob Kerrey noted that the administration was warned that terrorists were in training in U.S. flight schools, and if such training were closed down, "this conspiracy would have been rolled up." Fellow member Tim Roemer noted that "Nothing went down the chain to the FBI field offices." Another commission member, Jamie Gorelick, told Rice, "You get a greater degree of intensity when it comes from the top."

The day-after editorial in the *Washington Post* said Rice's contention "that there was no absence of vigor in the White House's response to al Qaeda during its first 233 days in office," was "contradictory and implausible."

The Guardian's editorial on the same day asserted, "The idea that President Bush was fully briefed about al-Qaida, and that the White House understood that it 'posed a serious threat to the United States,' simply does not ring true." To say that a memo entitled *Bin Laden determined to attack inside the United States* did not warn of an impending attack, as Rice did, suggests the administration has begun to lose touch with reality. *The Guardian* editorial noted that Rice "failed to satisfy those watching her testimony that the received image of the pre-9/11 White

House — that it barely feigned interest in foreign affairs — was inaccurate" (*The Guardian*, April 9, 2004).

Richard Clarke, who had been castigated by Rice, Cheney, and other Bush team members, responded quickly to the Rice testimony. "In a telephone interview hours after Ms. Rice completed her testimony . . . Mr. Clarke described a White House operation that had been pointedly and repeatedly warned of a mounting terrorist threat but did little to address it. 'There's broad agreement on the facts,' Mr. Clarke said, 'and a massively different interpretation'" (*New York Times*, April 9, 2004).

One cannot say in hindsight that the Bush administration would have prevented 9/11 if it had concentrated on terrorism instead of Iraq from day one, but it would have had a shot at it, if the Bush administration had not been involved with its own personal agenda. If it had made terrorism its main priority instead of Iraq, which has not proven to have been the threat that the administration told the American people that it was through lies and distortions, it's possible that breaking the log jam of relevant intelligence and an adequately funded staff would have made a difference. Also, as Gorelick pointed out, one should not underestimate the power of the presidency and the reach of the White House and the media to focus both the administration and the American people on what was the "dire" threat of terrorism. None of that, of course, happened.

What did happen, however, is that Bush and his administration gambled with the security of the American people. And Lost. While we cannot expect any administration to succeed all of the time, we do expect all administrations to do everything it can to protect the American people, and this was not the case here.

Confirmtion of Clarke's damaging revelations about the Bush administrations national security efforts came from Gen. Henry H. Shelton, as reported in the *Los Angeles Times*:

> The most damaging remarks came from Gen. Henry H. Shelton, chairman of the Joint Chiefs of Staff until October 1, 2001. Shelton added, 'The squeaky wheel was Dick Clarke, but he wasn't at the top of their priority list, so the lights went out for a few months.' Shelton summed up Rumsfeld's attitude as being 'this terrorism thing was out there, but it didn't happen today, so maybe it belonged lower on the list'" (Daniel Benjamin, *Los Angeles Times*, March 30, 2004).

And then on April 8, 2004 we learned:

> A senior terrorism expert said yesterday that he had delivered a final desperate warning of an inevitable terrorist attack to Condoleeza Rice

five days before al-Qaida struck New York's World Trade Centre and the Pentagon in Washington.

On the eve of the national security adviser's public appearance today to defend the Bush administration's record before the commission studying the September 11 attacks, Gary Hart, a former Democratic presidential candidate who cochaired an earlier three-year public study of the threats to US security in the 21st century, told the Guardian his warning had been ignored.

She [Rice] said: "I'll discuss it with the vice-president," Mr. Hart said; but he felt the response was a brush-off. "All I can say is she didn't feel the degree of urgency I thought was necessary," he said (*The Guardian*, April 8, 2004).

An editorial in the New York Times the day after the Rice testimony sums up much of what has been presented in this essay:

> If Ms. Rice were not set on burnishing the commander in chief's image as the hero of 9/11, she might have been able to admit that Mr. Bush is a hierarchical manager who expects his immediate underlings to run things, and who guessed wrong about what deserved the administration's most immediate and intense attention. The president and his top foreign policy advisers came into office determined to build a missile defense shield, fixated on Iraq as the top problem in the Middle East and greatly concerned about China . . . . Ms. Rice was at her weakest in her testimony before the independent commission investigating the 9/11 attacks when she attempted to portray Mr. Bush himself as a hands-on administrator with a particular concern about terror threats (Editorial, *New York Times*, April 9, 2004).

As we've indicated earlier, Bush is the very opposite of a hands-on president: he willingly serves as a kind of front man for ideological and corporate interests, and his rigid bureaucratic system, along with the rigidity of his thinking, allows the key senior officials around him to carry out the administration's plans, and too much of that comes from the office of the Vice-President. These failings cover all of the activities of Bush and his administration, not just 9/11, and there is absolutely no indication that there would be a change for the better if Bush were to be given a second term by the American people.

The Lies Behind National Security:
America's Un-Patriot Act and the Federal Government's Violation of Constitutional and Civil Rights

BY WALTER BRASCH

Between a diner and an empty store that once housed a shoe store, video store, and tanning salon, in a small strip mall in Bloomsburg, Pennsylvania, is Friends-in-Mind, an independent bookstore.

On the first floor are more than 10,000 books on more than 1,200 running feet of shelves that create aisles only about three feet wide. On top of the shelves are stacks of 10, 15, even 20 more books. On the floor are hundreds more, stacked spine out three- or four-feet high. There are books in metal racks, drawers, and on counters. It's hard to walk through the store without bumping into a pile in the 1,000-square foot store. In the basement are at least 2,000 more books.

"Sometimes I order four or five copies of a title, but often I only order one copy, but I want to have whatever my customers want," says owner Arline Johnson who founded the store in 1976 after working almost two decades as a clinical psychologist and teacher. Unlike the chain stores with magazine and newspaper racks, wide aisles, track lighting, and even a coffee shop, Friends-in-Mind has only books and some greeting cards. Also unlike the chain stores with large budgets for space and promotion to attract hundreds of customers a day, Johnson says she sees "on a real good day" maybe 25 or 30 people; often she sees fewer than a dozen.

In September 1984, she saw someone she didn't want to see. A week after the Naval Institute Press shipped three copies of Tom Clancy's cold war thriller, *The Hunt for Red October*, the FBI showed up. The FBI, which apparently got the information from the publisher, "wanted to know where the books were and who purchased them," says Johnson. She says she told the two men that she couldn't remember to whom she sold two of the copies, but acknowledged she sent one copy to her cousin, who had served aboard a nuclear submarine "and had all kinds of clearances." Johnson says she wasn't pleased about the interrogation—"and my cousin certainly wasn't happy about anyone checking on what he was reading."

The FBI never returned, but occasionally residents in this rural conservative community complain about what's in the store. She's been challenged for selling books about Karl Marx, gay rights, and even dinosaurs. Johnson says she tells the "book police" that "it's important that people learn and read about everything, whether they believe it or not." She also stocks copies of the Constitution and the Federalist Papers. Left-wing. Right-wing. Business. Labor. Anti-establishment. Everything's available in her store. "It's not the government's job to tell me or anyone what they can read," she says. But, over the years, the government has made it "its job."

The most recent series of intrusions upon civil liberties had begun in 1998 when special prosecutor Ken Starr demanded two Washington area bookstores to release records of what presidential playmate Monica Lewinsky had purchased. It was a sweeping allegation that had no reasonable basis of establishing any groundwork in Starr's attacks upon President Clinton. Since then, there have been several cases in which police, operating with warrants issued in state courts, have demanded a bookstore's records.[1]

Then terrorists attacked America on September 11, 2001, and the nation went first into panic and then revenge. In the first weeks after the 9/11 attacks, Americans understandably gave the government wide latitude to seek out and destroy those responsible. The people believed they may have had to temporarily yield a few of their own civil rights to gain their permanent security, a reality that would have shocked and saddened the nation's founders who wrote our keystone documents under terrors we can't even imagine.

The Bush administration had seen the confusion after the attacks as political convenience. Karl Rove, the President's leading political advisor, had even stated that the events of 9/11 would help elect more Republicans in the fall 2002 elections. Within two months of 9/11, drafted in secret under a cloak of "national security," Attorney General John Ashcroft had drawn up then convinced a compliant Congress to pass the USA Patriot Act.[2] The base was the Foreign Intelligence Surveillance Act (FISA). Under that Act, the government may conduct covert surveillance of individuals but only after seeking an order from a special government-created secret court. However, that Court in its first two decades granted every one of the government's more than 12,000 requests. In state actions, individuals have the right to ask local and state courts to quash subpoenas for records. If denied, they may appeal all the way to state supreme courts. There is no such protection under FISA. Not only can't individuals and businesses be represented in that secret court, all parties are bound by a federal gag order prohibiting any disclosure that such an order was even issued. There is no recourse. No appeal.

The Patriot Act, which incorporates and significantly expands FISA, was overwhelmingly approved by Congress,[3] most of whom admitted they read only a few paragraphs, if any at all, of the 150 section 342-page document.[4] The Patriot Act allows searches without "probable cause," "sneak-and-peek" searches with no judicial oversight not just for investigation of potential terrorism cases but also for "any criminal investigation," reduces judicial oversight of telephone and Internet surveillance, and grants the FBI almost unlimited and unchecked access to "any tangible thing" in a company without requiring it to show even minimal evidence of a crime. The Act's sweeping provisions apply not only to homes, businesses, and newsrooms, but also to churches, synagogues, and mosques. Under provisions of the Patriot Act, the federal government can require libraries to divulge who uses public computers or what books they check out, video stores to reveal what tapes customers bought or rented, even grocery and drug stores to disclose what paperbacks or magazines that shoppers bought.

The effect of the USA Patriot Act upon businesses that loan, rent, or sell books, videos, magazines, and music CDs is not to find and incarcerate terrorists—there are far more ways to investigate threats to the nation than to check on a terrorist's reading and listening habits—but to put a sweeping chilling effect upon Constitutional freedoms. Former CBS News anchor Walter Cronkite, interviewed on CNN's "Larry King Live," later called the Patriot Act "disastrously severe."[5]

Nevertheless, President Bush enthusiastically signed the bill, October 26, 2001, commenting that his administration took "an essential step in defeating terrorism, while protecting the constitutional rights of all Americans. . . . [It] upholds and respects the civil liberties guaranteed by our Constitution."[6]

Five weeks after the President signed the bill, John Ashcroft, in testimony before the Senate Committee on the Judiciary, boldly stated: "Since lives and liberties depend upon clarity, not obfuscation, and reason, not hyperbole, let me take this opportunity today to be clear: The Justice Department is working to protect American lives while preserving American liberties."[7]

About 15 months later, again before the Senate Committee on the Judiciary, he re-emphasized his earlier statements:

> I want to assure the Committee that . . . we have carefully crafted our
> post-September 11 policies to foster prevention while protecting the
> privacy and civil liberties of Americans. As I have often said, we at the

Department [of Justice] must think outside the box, but inside the Constitution. I take seriously the concerns of civil libertarians, for I, too, believe that protecting America does not require the sacrifice of those very freedoms that make us Americans.[8]

FBI director Robert Mueller III, acknowledging numerous problems in America's intelligence gathering and analysis, and in announcing a massive reorganization of his agency, claimed the FBI "has been the agency to protect the rights of others." However, the FBI admitted in August 2003 that it had lied in at least 75 instances when it applied for wiretap authorization from the Foreign Intelligence Surveillance Court.[9]

In a speech to the students and faculty of China's Tsinghua University on February 21, 2002, President Bush stated, "I am concerned that the Chinese people do not always see a clear picture of my country. . . . [S]ome Chinese textbooks talk of Americans of bullying the weak and repressing the poor. Another Chinese textbook published just last year teaches that special agents of the FBI are used to repress the working people. Now, neither of these is true . . . [T]hey are misleading and they are harmful." Bush further stated, "Those who fear freedom sometimes argue it could lead to chaos. But it does not. Liberty gives our citizens many rights."[10]

However, those rights are being abridged under the Bush Administration. Of those who voted against the bill, Rep. Earl Blumenauer said he opposed it because of "problems regarding freedom of speech"[11] and Rep. Carolyn Kilpatrick said she planned to vote against it because "vigilance must abide to ensure that our nation does not succumb to terrorism from beyond, but also to ensure that we do not succumb to tyranny from within as well."[12] The only senator to vote against the bill was Russ Feingold, chair of the Constitution, Civil Rights, and Property Rights subcommittee of the Committee on the Judiciary. The nation must "be sure we are not rewarding these terrorists and weakening ourselves by giving up the cherished freedoms that they seek to destroy," Feingold said the day of the vote, emphasizing, "We must redouble our vigilance to ensure our security and to prevent further acts of terror. But we must also redouble our vigilance to preserve our values and the basic rights that make us who we are." Almost every one of the cautions and problems Feingold pointed out in his 5,200 word speech in the Senate would be prophetic. "The Patriot Act crossed the line on several key areas of civil liberties," Sen. Richard Durbin, a member of the Senate's Committee on the Judiciary, stated two years after the bill was enacted into law.[13] Rep. Dennis Kucinich, one of the strongest civil liberties proponents in the House of Representatives, was just as blunt: "This administration has overreached in the area of civil liberties. Government shouldn't have that power. It's not consistent with what we are as a nation."[14] The *New York Times*, in one of its strongest-worded editorials almost two years after the Act first passed, bluntly stated, "Rather than do the hard work of coming up with effective port security and air cargo checks, and other programs targeted to actual threats, the administration has taken aim at civil liberties."[15]

The Patriot Act butts against the protections of the First (free speech), Fourth (unreasonable searches), Fifth (right against self-incrimination), Sixth (due process and the right to a fair and public trial by an impartial jury), and Fourteenth (equal protection guarantee) amendments. How the federal government has implemented the Patriot Act also violates Article I, Section 9 of the Constitution which guarantees the right to petition the courts to issue a writ of *habeas corpus* to require the government to produce a prisoner or suspect in order to determine the legality of the detention. Only in "Cases of Rebellion or Invasion" may the writ of *habeas corpus* be suspended. Nothing during or subsequent to the 9/11 attack indicated either a rebellion or invasion under terms of the Constitution.

The USA Patriot Act, as well as its implementation, has been nothing less than a series of lies the Bush Administration has told the American people. Even the Department of Justice's own web page enhances the lies the Bush administration has told. At the top of the Department's web site is the statement, "The Department of Justice's first priority is to prevent future terrorist attacks."[16] If we believe the Department's official statement, we can only conclude that secondary, less important, responsibilities include investigation and prosecution for racketeering, public corruption, mail fraud, discrimination, and anti-trust violations. Further, Justice's mission statement appears to mute the primary function of the Department of Homeland Security.

In December 2001, Attorney General John Ashcroft lied to the Senate Committee on the Judiciary when he stated that "All persons being detained have the right to contact their lawyers and the families."[17] Using the Patriot Act as a weapon, the government detained more than 2,000 individuals without charging them with any crime, held them in secret locations, didn't release their names, forbade them from having access to legal counsel, or from talking with their families, and claimed that because most of them were "enemy combatants," the Constitution didn't apply to them. The Justice Department even admitted in May 2003 it detained, in secret and without access to legal representation, 50 people it says were "material witnesses," but filed no charges against any of them.[18] About half were held for more than 30 days, according to the Department of Justice. In December 2001, the Department of Justice announced it planned to deport about 6,000 men from Middle Eastern countries. "They were rounded up secretly, jailed secretly, deported secretly," charged Lucy Dalgish, executive director of the Reporters Committee for Freedom of the Press. She called the Administration's actions "excessive," noting that "sometimes there needs to be secrecy in government, but this Administration has gone too far."[19]

Anthony Romero, executive director of the ACLU, said the ACLU had "no problem deporting those who have broken immigration laws, but [the government] should enforce them fairly and uniformly and in a nondiscriminatory way. There are more than 300,000 outstanding deportation orders, but the Justice Department is only focusing on 6,000 of them, based exclusively on nationality and ethnicity."[20]

According to David Cole, legal affairs correspondent of *The Nation* and professor of law at Georgetown University:

> While the September 11 terrorists were training for and coordinating their conspiracy in Florida, the FBI was spending vast resources investigating Mazen Al Najjar, a Palestinian professor from Tampa who spent three and a half years in detention on secret evidence and charges of political association. Al Najjar was released last December when an immigration judge found no evidence that he posed a threat to national security. And while the terrorists were conspiring in New Jersey, the FBI focused its efforts on Hany Kiareldeen, a Palestinian in Newark detained for a year and a half on secret evidence for associating with terrorists. He was freed after immigration judges flatly rejected the government's charges as unfounded; the FBI's principal source was apparently Kiareldeen's ex-wife, with whom he was in a bitter custody dispute and who had filed several false reports about him.[21]

The federal government's "Interview Project" detained thousands of Arabs and Muslims, including U.S. citizens. "The Arab American Institute found that these interviews created fear and suspicion in the community, especially among recent immigrants, and damaged our efforts to build bridges between the community and law enforcement," said Dr. James Zogby, president of the Arab American Institute.[22] The Immigration and Naturalization Service, at the time under the Department of Justice, asked almost 100,000 immigrants, most of them from Arab countries, to register, then deported about 13,000 of them, mostly for minor infractions. Anthony Romero says the ACLU was worried "that there is a growing momentum focusing on a specific community, regarding them as suspicious merely because of where they are from. The government should focus on what they have done, not where they were born. . . . That just fuels the fires of xenophobia against Middle Eastern, Arab and Muslim communities."[23] The interviews, registrations, and detention of Muslims and Arabs is "the most massive case of ethnic profiling since the internment of Japanese Americans during the Second World War," according to Cole.[24]

In *Gherbi v. Bush* (December 2003), the Ninth Circuit Court of Appeals ruled that the Bush Administration was wrong in asserting that U.S. courts held no jurisdiction over the people the government held at Guantanamo Bay, Cuba. In a stringing attack upon the Bush Administration's refusal to acknowledge judicial oversight, the Court ruled:

> [E]ven in times of national emergency—indeed particularly in such times—it is the obligation of the Judicial Branch to ensure preservation of our constitutional values and to prevent the Executive Branch from running roughshod over the rights of citizens and aliens alike. Here, we cannot accept the government's position that the Executive Branch possesses the unchecked authority to imprison indefinitely any persons, foreign citizens included, on territory under the sole jurisdiction and control of the United States without permitting such prisoners recourse of any kind to any judicial forum, or even access to counsel, regardless of the length or matter of their confinement. We hold that no lawful policy or precedent supports such a counter-intuitive and undemocratic procedure. . . . In our view, the government's position is inconsistent with fundamental tenets of American jurisprudence and raises most serious concerns under international law."[25]

"No detainee has been harmed. No detainee has been mistreated in any way," Defense Secretary Donald Rumsfeld said in January 2002, adding, "and the numerous articles, statements, questions, allegations, and breathless reports on television are undoubtedly by people who are either uninformed, misinformed or poorly informed."[26] However, the Justice Department's own inspector general in 2003 reported that the detention of individuals was "indiscriminate and haphazard," and that there were "significant instances" of "a pattern of physical and verbal abuse," including beatings of illegal immigrants, most of them Muslim or Arab, by various employees and officials of the Department of Justice. Included were employees of the FBI, Bureau of Prisons, Drug Enforcement Administration, and Immigration and Naturalization Service.[27] Rep. John Conyers stated that the inspector general's report "shows that we have only begun to scratch the surface with respect to the Justice Department's disregard to constitutional rights and civil liberties."[28] John Ashcroft said "we make no apologies" for detaining almost 800 persons.[29] In December 2003, the Department's internal affairs staff discovered hundreds of videotapes documenting the abuse; the Department of Justice had previously claimed the videotapes didn't exist.[30]

White House Counsel Alberto R. Gonzales once said that proposed tribunals against non-citizens detained at Guantanamo Bay, Cuba, "will be as open as possible."[31] However, there have been no trials, and President Bush had signed an executive order that allows closed proceedings. In January 2004, the Supreme Court, without comment or formal vote, refused to hear an appeal by the Center for National Security Studies (CNSS) and several civil rights and media organizations to release the names of more than 700 persons the government detained, often for more than 90 days without counsel, following 9/11.[31] None were charged with any act of terrorism. The CNSS charged that failure to release the names violated both the First Amendment and Freedom of Information laws. It charged that the federal government had held innocent Muslims and Arabs, refused to release their names, then deported them to avoid acknowledging its own errors. Judge Gladys Kessler of the federal district court of for the District of Columbia agreed with the CNSS suit; a 2-1 split by the U. S. Court of Appeals for the District of Columbia Circuit reversed it.[33] "Until some other court says otherwise, the government can continue the policy of secret arrests that seem,s fundamentally inconsistent with basic American values, and that we know in this case led to a series of abuses," said Steven Shapiro of the ACLU.

Based upon Department of Justice statements, unchallenged by much of the media, Americans felt secure that although non-citizens had no rights and, thus, the government could do what it wanted to them, at least American citizens were safe from intrusion by the government.

"U.S. citizens cannot be investigated under this act," Mark Corallo, official spokesman for the Department of Justice, said a year after the Act was first signed.[34] A few months after that, Corallo said that civil libertarians were "completely wrong" in their accusations that the Act could be used against American citizens.[35] "The public has . . . been misled . . . [The Act] is not directed at U.S. Persons," added Viet Dinh, assistant attorney general and primary writer of the Patriot Act, said in April 2003.[36] A month later, the U.S. attorney for Alaska, parroting official

Department of Justice statements, emphasized that the Patriot Act "can't be [used against] U.S. citizens."[37] They were wrong.

"Nowhere does this statute [FISA] indicate that United States citizens cannot be targeted," the ACLU points out, emphasizing, "In fact, the statute makes it clear that an 'investigation of a United States person' *can* be conducted, so long as it is not based solely on activity protected by the First Amendment. . . . The statute defines 'United States persons' to include both citizens and permanent residents."[38]

However, in the interest of "national security," Ashcroft declared Yaser Esam Hamdi, a 21-year-old American citizen, was an "enemy combatant" and, thus, not entitled to legal representation, that he could be held indefinitely in secret without charges even being filed, and that even *if* a lawyer were to be present, all conversations had to be recorded, a violation of the Fourth Amendment. Any reporter who revealed information about Hamdi's detention could be charged under the Patriot Act. "That sounds idiotic, doesn't it?" asked Judge Robert G. Doumar.[39] The government couldn't provide any evidence that Hamdi had any links to terrorists.[40] Finally, in December 2003, after more than two years, the government allowed Hamdi to talk with his attorney.

In a related case, U.S. District Court Judge Gladys Kessler in August 2002 ruled that the government must release the names of about 1,200 persons it detained following 9/11. None of the 1,200 were charged in connection with the 9/11 terrorism; many were confined solely because they might be potential witnesses. In a 47-page opinion, Judge Kessler declared, "Secret arrests are a concept odious to a democratic society and profoundly antithetical to the bedrock values that characterize a free and open society such as ours. . . . The public's interest in learning the identities of those arrested and detained is essential to verifying whether the government is operating within the bounds of the law."[41] Kessler also ordered the federal government to release the names of any defense attorneys. The Department of Justice, in a piece of fiction worthy of any TV show, claimed that by withholding the names of defense attorneys, even if they wanted their names released to the media and the public, it was really protecting them against the embarrassment of representing terrorists.

Jose Padilla, an American citizen whom the government believed knew something about the al-Qaeda network but had no documented evidence, was arrested by FBI agents in May 2002, then held in a Navy brig in Charleston, South Carolina. For eighteen months, he wasn't permitted contact with his counsel, his family or any other non-military personnel. The Bush Administration argued that to allow Padilla legal counsel would undermine its interrogation and national security, the standard lie the Bush Administration gives whenever it doesn't wish to accept legislative or judicial oversight.

In December, 2003, the U.S. Court of Appeals for the Second Circuit declared the government doesn't have the right to declare a U.S. citizen seized on American soil away from any combat as an "enemy combatant," that it doesn't have the right to deny counsel to that person, and that the Bush Administration has no Judicial or Congressional authority to keep American citizens incommunicado. It ordered the government to release Padilla. In a stinging rebuke to the Administration, the Court ruled:

> As this Court sits only a short distance from where the World Trade Center once stood, we are as keenly aware as anyone of the threat al Qaeda poses to our country and of the responsibilities the President and law enforcement officials bear for protecting the nation. But presidential authority does not exist in a vacuum . . .and this case involves not whether those responsibilities should be aggressively pursued, but whether the President is obligated, in the circumstances presented here, to share them with Congress. . .
>
> Where . . . the President's power as Commander-in-Chief of the armed forces and the domestic rule of law intersect, we conclude that clear congressional authorization is required for detentions of American citizens on American soil because 18 U.S.C. § 4001(a) (2000) (the "Non-Detention Act") prohibits such detentions absent specific congressional authorization. Congress's Authorization for Use of Military Force Joint Resolution, Pub. L. No. 107-40, 115 Stat. 224 (2001) ("Joint Resolution"), passed shortly after the attacks of September 11, 2001, is not such an authorization, and no exception to section 4001(a) otherwise exists."[42]

Refusing to accept the Court's ruling, the Bush Administration declared the Court's opinion to be "troubling and flawed," and declared it would delay and appeal.

Senior officials of the Department of Justice have also claimed the Patriot Act doesn't violate the Constitutional guarantees that law enforcement will detain and arrest individuals only for "probable cause." More than a year after the Patriot Act had become law, LaRae Quy, FBI spokesperson in San Francisco, said "We still have to show probable cause for any actions we take. It's not just an agent descending and saying, 'Hey, I want to go in and see what this person is doing.'"[43] Within a month, Mark Corallo told the media that not only must there be a "probable cause that the person you are seeking the information for is a terrorist or a foreign spy,"[44] but that law enforcement officials had "to convince a judge that the person for whom you're seeking a warrant is a spy or a member of a terrorist organization."[45]

None of the statements was true. "[T]he FBI can obtain records . . . merely by specifying to a court that the records are 'sought for' an ongoing investigation," according to ACLU attorneys. "That standard . . . is much lower than the standard required by the Fourth Amendment, which ordinarily prohibits the government from conducting intrusive searches unless it has probable cause to believe that the target of the investigation is engaged in criminal activity."[46] Before the House Judiciary Committee, John Ashcroft admitted that the standard under the Patriot Act was "lower than probable cause," and that federal officials could go after citizens who were neither spies or members of terrorist organizations.[47]

The Act's official name—Uniting and Strengthening America by Providing Appropriate Tools Required to Intercept and Obstruct Terrorism Act—is itself a lie. The lies the Administration have told about the use of the Patriot Act solely to capture terrorists dates almost to the beginning of the act. "Within six months of passing the Patriot Act," said Dan Dodson, official spokesman for the National Association of Criminal Defense Attorneys, "the Justice Department was conducting seminars on how to stretch the new wiretapping provisions to extend them beyond terror cases."[48] The federal government's implementation of the Act's provisions go well beyond intercepting and obstructing terrorism.

Before the Senate Committee on the Judiciary in December 2001, John Ashcroft had flatly stated, "Each action taken by the Department of Justice, as well as the war crimes commissions considered by the President and the Department of Defense, is carefully drawn to target a narrow class of individuals— terrorists. Our legal powers are targeted at terrorists. Our investigation is focused on terrorists. Our prevention strategy targets the terrorist threat."[49] However, in May 2003, the Department of Justice admitted it used the Act to pursue other non-terrorist activities,[50] and Mark Corallo, trying to justify the Act's use, claimed that "certain provisions could be used in regular criminal investigations."[51]

The Department of Justice cited Section 314 of the Patriot Act as its justification to pursue the owner of a Las Vegas strip club who may have given bribes to local officials. "The attorney general didn't tell Congress he needed the Patriot Act to raid nudie bars," said Laura W. Murphy of the ACLU in November 2003. "The law was intended for activities related to terrorism and not to naked women," said Sen. Harry Reid.[52] "It was never my intention that the Patriot Act be used for garden-variety crimes and investigations," said Rep. Shelley Berkley.[53]

Ashcroft argued there was no distinction between using the tools provided by the Patriot Act to conduct criminal investigations or to pursue terroristic threats. Contradicting Ashcroft, Patrick Leahy, former chair of the Senate Committee on the Judiciary, stated, "We sought to amend FISA to make it a better foreign intelligence tool. But it was not the intent . . . to fundamentally change FISA from a foreign intelligence tool into a criminal law enforcement tool."[54]

These cases, said Gary Peck, executive director of the Nevada chapter of the ACLU, "are exactly why the Patriot Act is a threat to liberties and must be corrected." [55] Peck emphasized, "It's just as the ACLU said from the start. The Patriot Act, which was originally passed off as dealing solely with terrorism, in fact expands government power in areas that have nothing to do with terrorism."[56] The FBI retort was that the Patriot Act "was used appropriately [in its pursuit of the owner of the night club] and was clearly within the legal parameters of the statute."

"If that's true," argued the *Las Vegas Review-Journal*, which has been out front in coverage of Patriot Act issues, "then major portions of this law need to be promptly repealed, unless the [Supreme Court] can get at them and overrule them first."[57] There may have been other instances of the use of the Patriot Act to investigate individuals not suspected of terrorism; however, extensive secrecy has left not only political leaders but all Americans wondering how extensive the Justice Department's stretch of the law is.

President Bush had told the audience at Tsinghua University that "life in America shows that liberty paired with law is not to be feared. In a free society, diversity is not disorder, debate is not strife, and dissent is not revolution."[58] That is accurate, but the President lied to the Chinese students in how his own administration dealt with debate and dissent. In a statement made to *Free Inquiry Magazine* in Fall 1988, Bush had stated, "I'm not sure that atheists should be considered citizens, nor should they be considered patriots," leaving one to wonder how he could claim to be the leader of a country that values diversity, debate, and dissent. Both Ashcroft and Cheney have labeled dissent, even by leaders of both major political parties, to be unpatriotic. Persons opposed to the Bush policies are routinely scrutinized at airport check-ins, according to a report by Paul Harris in London's *Observer*.[59] According to the *Dayton* (Ohio) *Daily News*, "Ashcroft's scowling, swaggering, dyspeptic antipathy for anyone who questions his methods and authority is transforming him and his office into mere caricature."

Under Section 802 of the Patriot Act is a broad and loose definition that permits the government to define any organization opposed to governmental policies as being a terroristic threat to the security of the United States. Persons held under the Bush administration Patriot Act orders are questioned about their political beliefs. FBI agents have entered several mosques, and monitored dozens of anti-war protests to "observe."[60] During the Clinton administration, "fishing expeditions" were prohibited by FBI policy guidelines. The ACLU reports:

> "Ashcroft's guidelines give the FBI a green light to send undercover agents or informants to spy on worship services, political demonstrations and other public gatherings and in the Internet chat rooms without even the slightest evidence that wrongdoing is afoot. . . . The FBI is now very much empowered to conduct investigative 'fishing expeditions' on First Amendment protected activities even though there is no indication of criminal activity."[61]

There is an even greater shadow in the new millennium than during the 1960s and 1970s when the FBI, under J. Edgar Hoover, raided dozens of bookstores, alternative newspapers, and the offices of organizations that opposed the Vietnam War, the Nixon administration, or Hoover himself. Because of Constitutional and civil liberties abuses under the COINTELPRO operation, restrictions were placed against FBI investigations of political activities.[62] John Ashcroft, citing "national security," has loosened those restrictions. Under the Patriot Act, the federal government may again search newsrooms and reporters' records "without proof of probable cause—or even reasonable grounds to believe—that the person whose records it seeks is engaged in criminal activity," according to Lucy Dalgish, of the Reporters Committee for Freedom of the Press.[63] The New York Times reported that the FBI was again monitoring anti-war demonstrations and collecting information about dissidents.

Because of the vagueness of many of the Patriot Act's provisions, "there is an uncertainty that breeds caution among those who might seek to speak, or write, or broadcast freely," says Irwin Gratz, president of the Society of Professional Journalists (SPJ) in 2004-2005. "This 'chilling effect' is the Patriot Act's most pernicious aspect," says Gratz, "because we can never know what information we are denied, or what wisdom we won't have because someone, somewhere, was too scared by the Patriot Act to speak their mind."

"The FBI is dangerously targeting Americans who are engaged in nothing more than lawful protest and dissent," Anthony Romero, ACLU executive director, told The New York Times in November 2003. "The line between terrorism and legitimate disobedience is blurred," he said, "and I have serious concern about whether we're going back to the days of Hoover." Even more frightening, Ashcroft claimed the power of the commander-in-chief shouldn't be challenged, something that should cause even more fear in Americans than anything that happened September 11.

The Patriot Act, claims the Department of Justice, "specifically protects Americans' First Amendment rights."[64] The Society of Professional Journalists, as well as dozens of other associations of journalists, authors, booksellers, librarians, and civil liberties organizations, strongly disagrees. "The Patriot Act attacks the vital principal of a robust public discourse on matters of public interest," says SPJ's Irwin Gratz, "by allowing the government to intrude on private speech through strengthened wiretap provisions and get at the identity of speakers by requiring private business, in certain circumstances to divulge private customer communication."

Some of that investigation involves the federal government probing into the reading habits of Americans. "Terrorism investigators have no interest in the library habits of ordinary Americans," according to an official statement from the Department of Justice."[65] Elaborating upon the statement, Mark Corallo said not only doesn't the Department of Justice "have any interest in looking at the book preferences of Americans [it doesn't] care, and it would be an incredible waste of time."[66] However, the Department of Justice also stated that, "historically, terrorists and spies have used libraries to carry out activities that threaten our national security. If terrorists or spies use libraries, we should not allow them to become safe havens for their terrorist or clandestine activities."[67] Historically, spies and terrorists also used schools, sports arenas, and bedrooms of unsuspecting homeowners. If the government's contention about the use of libraries is to be accepted as a reason for governmental intrusion, then by extension the government would have authority to monitor, with minimal or no judicial oversight, every place where people congregate.

Nevertheless, Assistant Attorney General Viet Dinh told the House of Representatives Judiciary Committee in May 2003 that FBI agents contacted fewer than 50 libraries, and most of them had first contacted the FBI to report suspicious activity.[68] However, about half of the 906 library directors responding to a survey by the Library Research Center of the University of Illinois, October 2002-January 2003, reported their libraries had been visited by federal or local law enforcement personnel to turn over data about their patrons; 219 of them voluntarily turned over data, 225 did not.[69] The Department of Justice tried spinning the facts to account for the lie told by the assistant attorney general. In a June 2, 2003, press release, the Department claimed that what Dinh really stated was that FBI agents contacted the 50 libraries in the course of "criminal" investigations, and that the number of investigations under the guise of terrorism was classified.[70]

Throughout the country, librarians, booksellers, writers, publishers, and numerous civil liberties organizations have spoken out against Department of Justice claims it was protecting not only the nation's security, but also the people's First Amendment rights and rights of privacy.

In one of its strongest resolutions, the American Library Association (ALA) declared it "opposes any use of governmental power to suppress the free and open exchange of knowledge and information or to intimidate individuals exercising free inquiry. . . . ALA considers that sections of the USA PATRIOT ACT are a present danger to the constitutional rights and privacy of library users."[71]

The Santa Cruz, California, public library system was the first in the country to post signs warning its patrons about the government's incursion into their privacy. Neal Coonerty, owner of Bookshop Santa Cruz and president of the American Booksellers Association in 2000-2002, has been outspoken about the Patriot Act. "We don't believe that reading a murder mystery at the beach here means you're plotting a murder," says Coonerty.[72] The South Carolina Library Association condemned the Patriot Act as "a present danger to the constitutional rights and privacy rights of library users ," and called for Congress to take an "active oversight" of the Act and to call for hearings "to determine the extent of the surveillance on library users and their communities."[73] Linda Ramsdell, president of the New England Booksellers Association, and Trina Magi, president of the Vermont Library Association, initiated a letter-writing campaign in Fall 2002 to rally support against many provisions of the Patriot Act.

Among those responding to the call were Michael Katzenberg and Linda Prescott, owners of Bear Pond Books in Montpelier, Vermont, who deleted all titles from the records of their 3,000 Readers' Club accounts. "A citizen's right to free speech explicitly covers the right to read any book," says Katzenberg, "and implicit in that is the right to privacy in which a reader's choice of books is protected from government scrutiny." A story in *Seven Days*, a Burlington, Vermont, weekly newspaper led to an Associated Press story, and reaction from throughout the country. In the first weeks, the owners of the 3,200 square foot independent bookstore received several "very negative" e-mails. However, Katzenberg says that "about 95 percent of more than 300 letters have been very positive." Many of the letters, says Katzenberg, came from readers who switched their on-line purchasing from megastores and chains, which have numerous reasons to track customers' purchases, to smaller independent bookstores because of a fear of the invasion of privacy not by the stores but by government officials.

Arline Johnson at Friends-in-Mind says she doesn't keep computer records, accept credit cards, or even have a store newsletter, all of which can be seized and compromise the Constitutional protections of her customers.

All 50 states have laws or court cases which assure protection of the privacy of library records. But, federal law overrides state laws. Like booksellers, libraries have begun destroying certain records identifying which books patrons borrowed, and have also destroyed logs of who used which computer. Their actions are legal, as long as the shredding is done prior to any government-issued subpoena.

While librarians, booksellers, and authors and journalists are vigorously trying to protect civil rights, many corporations, caught up in the fear of terrorism, have willingly failed to protect their employees' and customers' rights of privacy.

Blue Cross and Blue Shield of Michigan, in its November 7, 2003, issue of *Bluesweek*, an internal company newsletter, proudly declared it ran computer checks on the files of six million individuals it insured.[74] Using key words supplied by the federal government, it isolated the names of 6,000 individuals. Among the descriptors were the names of passenger ships as well as whether the individual had an Arab name. Further investigation showed that none of the 6,000 had any terrorist ties. Aetna checked 13 million records, including about 18,000 in Michigan. Aetna, like Blue Cross and Blue Shield, found no connection. Both companies claim no medical or insurance information was passed along to the government, but say they will continue to search their databases and advise the federal government of names of subscribers who may fit certain profiles.[75]

"At what point did Blue Cross/Blue Shield become an arm of the government, as opposed to a service provider for people?" asked Virginia Rezmierski of the Gerald R. Ford School of Public Policy at the University of Michigan. Rezmierski told the *Detroit News* that although the companies claim what they are doing is being a good corporate citizen, people provide information "under the trust and agreement that we are providing information in exchange for services, not for the company's secondary purpose of being a good corporate citizen."[76] Imad Hamad, director of the Michigan chapter of the American-Arab Anti-Discrimination Committee, acknowledged that governmental agencies "for a legitimate reason" should be able to check on individual records, but "for a well-respected health care provider to try to rush to be considered the most American and run these lists just to play it safe pushes it much too far. It's . . . consistent with the paranoia and fear that we've been dealing with since September 11."[77]

On June 5, 2003, after more than a year of refusing to respond to Congressional requests, John Ashcroft asked the House Judiciary Committee for even more powers.[78] Two months later, with Congressional and public support for the Patriot Act diminishing, John Ashcroft, possibly in violation of federal law that prohibits members of the executive department from publicly lobbying for or against proposed legislation, went on a 10-day 20-city national promotional tour. Each of his 90-minute stops, all bathed by innumerable flags, included a carefully prepared 30-minute speech, 10 minutes with federal officials, and media interviews. Believing most print media journalists would ask tough questions, Ashcroft allowed only local TV reporters to interview him, and then only for three minutes each. In most of his speeches, Ashcroft lied to the American people about reasons for the Patriot Act and its implementation. Reiterating his speech before Congress two months earlier, he claimed that even more powers were needed, including the expansion of secret searches and the increased use of administrative subpoenas without judicial oversight. Any attempt to weaken the Act, said Ashcroft, could allow further terrorist attacks.[79]

"Ashcroft clearly played fast and loose with the facts," wrote *Las Vegas Review-Journal* columnist John L. Smith, "when he made it appear the FBI and other federal law enforcement agencies could investigate the Mafia and other complex criminal organizations, but could not investigate suspected terrorists without the Patriot Act."[80] The already-established Foreign Intelligence Surveillance Act had given the FBI jurisdiction and investigative powers.

In his speech at Tsinghua University, Bush had boldly stated, "Our liberty is . . . overseen by a strong and fair legal system. . . . The president, me, I can't tell the courts how to rule. And neither can any other member of the executive or legislative branch of government. Under our law, every one stands equal, No one is above the law and no one is beneath it." However, obstruction, a reduction of public information, distrust and resentment of the press, and a curtailment of civil liberties have been central to the philosophy of the Bush administration. Vice-President Dick Cheney told the Senate leadership in February 2002 that Bush administration officials would defy all attempts to question them about what they knew before and after the September 11, 2001, attacks. Cloaking itself behind a mantra of "national security," the Department of Justice has refused to comply with federal court orders, and told federal agencies not to comply with Freedom of Information requests if any appeared to be "ambiguous."[81]

"The American people feel that the government is intent on prying into every nook and cranny of people's private lives," declared Rep. William Delahaunt, "while at the same time doing all it can to block access to government information that would inform the American people about what is being done in their name."[82]

The Department of Justice "has simply become a black hole, a room without windows [and] nothing gets out," says Charles N. Davis, executive director of the Freedom of Information Center at the University of Missouri and freedom of information officer for the Society of Professional Journalists. What the Department does release, says Davis, "is tightly managed for maximum propagandistic effect."

Ashcroft also defied the House Judiciary Committee, which directed him to appear before its members to explain how the Justice Department was implementing several provisions of the Patriot Act. "The Justice Department has foiled numerous attempts by lawmakers and civil libertarians to learn how the Administration has deployed new tools granted under the Act," said Nancy Kranich, senior research fellow with the Free Expression Policy Project.[83]

"Rather than inviting congressional involvement [the Bush administration] discourages it—both out of an ideological attachment to executive power and out of an allergy to any kind of legal restraint on its conduct," the *Washington Post* editorialized more than two years after the President signed the Patriot Act.[84]

The *Dayton Daily News* charged that Ashcroft uses "fear-mongering and invective to minimize accountability of federal law enforcement and undermine the authority of the judicial branch of government."

The Justice Department "has largely ignored repeated congressional requests for . . . information, with appropriate safeguards. Constructive oversight by both the Congress and the courts helps ensure that the Justice Department uses its enormous power appropriately both to protect our national security and to uphold individual rights," Sen. Patrick Leahy, at that time chair of the Senate Committee on the Judiciary, stated in August 2002.

The Bush administration's quest for secrecy and hatred for those who question their authority is understandable, considering it had been staring into headlights prior to 9/11. *Newsweek* and numerous other publications reported that the Bush administration, probably for political reasons, discounted the Clinton administration's severe and substantial warnings about terrorist activities. Ashcroft himself opposed an FBI proposal to add more counter-terrorism agents. Numerous memos by the CIA, backed by data from foreign intelligence agencies, were shuffled into a bureaucratic limbo by the Bush administration. More significant, the Bush administration in the months leading up to the 9/11 murders had significant and substantial warnings about the probability that al-Qaeda would use commercial airplanes to conduct terrorist activities.[85] An independent commission, headed by a former New Jersey Republican governor, appointed by President Bush, reported in December 2003 that the 9/11 attacks could have been prevented. "As you read the report, you're going to have a pretty clear idea of what wasn't done and what should have been done; this was not something that had to happen," Tom Keane told CBS News.[86]

With John Ashcroft leading the way, the federal government proposed the Domestic Security Enhancement Act, a draconian set of police powers that would allow the government to investigate all credit card purchases, magazine subscriptions, medical prescription records, travel plans, bank deposits, students' records and grades, and even toll road receipts, among numerous other records, all without judicial oversight, all based upon an "administrative subpoena." The average American, said Rep. Bernie Sanders, "won't even know the government is reading his or her records."[87] Other provisions would have stripped citizenship based upon an individual's association, however remote, with organizations the Justice Department determined to be legal but placed on its list of terrorist organizations; the authorization of secret arrests; an unchecked license for the attorney general to be able to deport any legal permanent resident alien whenever he determines it is not in the nation's economic or foreign policy interest; and to impose gag orders in criminal, not terrorist, cases. Text of the proposed act[88] was leaked to the Center for Public Integrity, which then distributed it to the media in February 2003. Faced by a swelling public outrage, Ashcroft lied to the Senate Committee on the Judiciary, stating that he wasn't seeking those sweeping new powers. But, during the rest of the year, parts of the proposed act began to appear on various bills. During the weekend that Saddam Hussein was captured in December 2003, and overlooked by most major American media which ran two-inch headlines about the capture, President Bush signed additional legislature that gave the FBI even greater powers, including the right to obtain secretly and without a court order, personal records, including all credit card transactions, from all financial institutions. The Congressional authorization had been hidden within an om-

nibus spending bill, and had not come before public debate. The new legislation doesn't "come close to protecting the national security, but [it]
does obscure government decision-making from the kind of oversight
that the public deserves and the kind of oversight that will actually help
us win this war," says James Dempsey, executive director for the Center
for Democracy and Technology.[89]

"If left unchallenged, ands even worse, if expanded," says Charles N.
Davis of SPJ, "the Patriot Act leads us even further from a democratic
government based on civil liberties and the rule of law."

American citizens, "whom the government has pledged to protect
from terrorist activities, now find themselves the victims of the very
weapon designed to uproot their enemies," said Rep. C. L. Otter in the
House of Representatives.[90]

"It becomes increasingly difficult for the American government to
look at its allies, or even enemies overseas, in the eye and defend human
rights, when the U.S. government itself is engaging in efforts that erode
personal privacy, that further racial profiling, that limit judicial review,
that diminish due-process rights," said Anthony Romero.

Chris Finan, president of the American Booksellers Foundation for
Free Expression, said in late 2002 that he believed "we've seen some shift
in the hard-core attitudes of the government's position." His belief that
public opinion will eventually shift "from the panic after September 11 to
allow a reasonable debate of the dangers" is beginning to come true as
dozens of politicians who voted for the Act, as well as millions of Americans who once gave the government their unchecked authority, have begun significant protests.

In May 2003, Philadelphia, with a 1.5 million population, became the
largest of about 200 American cities to condemn the Patriot Act.
Philadelphia's city council resolution called for a repeal of the Act or at
least the provisions that "violate fundamental rights and liberties." In
that resolution, Philadelphia stated it supported the campaign against
terrorism, "but also reaffirms that any efforts to end terrorism not be
waged at the expense of the fundamental civil liberties of the people of
Philadelphia, and all citizens of the United States."[91] Among other
American cities which passed similar legislation are Baltimore, Chicago,
Detroit, and San Francisco. Broward County, Florida, with a population
of 1.6 million, is the largest county to pass similar legislation. The legislatures of Alaska, Hawaii, and Vermont also declared their opposition to
the Patriot Act.

Barbara Comstock, John Ashcroft's director of public affairs and a
former official in the campaign to elect George W. Bush, said "We've had

so much erroneous hysteria out there about our counter-terrorism authority and how it's used."[92] Ashcroft himself was more blunt. In a speech in Memphis, Ashcroft charged: "The charges of the hysterics are revealed for what they are: castles in the air, built on misrepresentation, supported by unfounded fear, held aloft by hysterics."[93] Ashcroft later called statements from the American Library Association and other opponents of parts of the Patriot Act as little more than "baseless hysteria."[94] However, Ashcroft's public affairs officer was forced to modify that statement by saying that what the attorney general really meant was that the nation's librarians were "duped by those who are ideologically opposed to the Patriot Act."

There may be hope for the repeal of some of the sections of the Patriot Act. Rep. Bernie Sanders, with 24 sponsors or co-sponsors, in March 2003 introduced the Freedom to Read Protection Act (HR 1157) that would minimize Section 215. Since then, 117 other representatives added their names as co-sponsors. "One of the cornerstones of our democracy is our right as Americans to criticize our government and to read printed material without fear of government intrusion," Sanders said at the time he submitted his bill. More than three dozen of the nation's largest organizations of librarians, booksellers, journalists, and publishers filed a joint statement that not only declared their support for the Freedom to Read Protection Act but also condemned several sections of the Patriot Act. Both Sens. Barbara Boxer and Russ Feingold have submitted similar legislation in the Senate. During 2003, five representatives and nine Senators submitted separate bills to diminish or repeal several sections of the Patriot Act. In July 2003, the ACLU and six other organizations filed suit charging that Section 215 violates First and Fourth Amendment protections.[95] A coalition of several bookseller, library, and writer organizations filed an *amicus curiae* brief to support the ACLU suit. "The Patriot Act authorizes the FBI to engage in fishing expeditions in bookstore and library records and then bars booksellers and librarians from protesting even after the fact. Such an unprecedented extension of prosecutorial power demands immediate court review," said Chris Finan, upon the filing of the brief to oppose the government's request to dismiss the suit.[96] Within a week of the filing of the ACLU suit, the Center for Constitutional Rights filed suit in Federal District Court, charging that the Patriot Act prohibition against providing "expert advice and assistance" to groups that were identified as terrorists was vague and a violation of First Amendment guarantees for the right of free speech and for association.[97] "Restriction of free thought and free speech is the most dangerous of all subversions," said Supreme Court Justice William O. Douglas in 1952 during the nation's "Red Scare" era. "It is the one un-American act," said Douglas, "that could most easily defeat us."

Rep. C. L. Otter, a conservative Republican, along with Rep. Dennis Kucinich, a progressive Democrat, co-authored a bill in the Summer of 2003 that would have stopped funding of the Patriot Act's "sneak-and-peek" section. Although the House passed the legislation, 309-118, it never moved forward in the Senate. In September 2003, Kucinch introduced legislation that would repeal 10 sections of the bill, among them those that authorized "sneak-and-peek" searches, personal documents searches without a judicial warrant, and the detention of non-citizens without judicial review.

"How much are we willing to change in response to 9/11 attack, to tolerate being watched, our information being joined into databases that create a whole new picture of person that didn't exist before, how much should we accept authorities pushing, probing and demanding?" asked Jim Gilmore, chair of specially-created panel appointed by President Bush to look into civil liberties issues. "If the enemy's going to force us to change what we are as Americans, we should do it with our eyes opened. As a conservative Republican, I'm deeply concerned about this," Gilmore said.[98]

The Patriot Act has a built-in sunset provision; several sections will expire unless Congress renews them before Dec. 31, 2005. However, Judith Krug of the American Library Association isn't optimistic. "It's going to be used as long as they think they can get away with it," says Krug, one of the nation's leading experts in First Amendment rights and civil liberties. Krug says until the people "start challenging the Act in the federal courts, we'll be lucky if we can 'sunset' out any of it."

Although dozens of members of Congress have now spoken out against the excesses of the implementation of the Patriot Act, Congressional oversight of the Act, which was written by the executive branch, has been minimal. "The USA Patriot Act is a grave threat to freedom of expression, to freedom of association and by extension to freedom of information," says SPJ's Charles N. Davis, "for it ushered in a climate of legislative deference and executive power unmatched in American history."

Slightly more than two years after the Act was first passed, the *Washington Post*, in a major editorial, charged:

Congress has stood by in an alarming silence while a fabric of new law governing the balance between liberty and security has been woven by the other two branches of government . . . The parties [Democrat and Republican] are united in their desire not to sully their hands by engaging seriously in deciding the shape of the law. They are content not to do their jobs but instead to let the Bush administration do what it pleases and take the political and judicial heat for it all. . . .

[I]n absenting itself from the policymaking process, Congress does not merely fail to protect American liberty. It also fails to aid the executive branch in fighting terrorism.. . . ."99

If the Patriot Act isn't modified, book publishers will take even fewer chances on publishing works that "might" result in the government investigation; bookstore owners may not buy as many different titles; the people, fearing that whatever they read might be subject to Big Brother's scrutiny, may not buy controversial books or check books out of the library; writers may not create the works that a free nation should read. How ironic it is that a president who says he wants everyone to read, and whose wife is a former librarian, is the one who may be responsible for giving the people less choice in what they may read. Far worse, not only are American rights, including the right of dissent, being trimmed, but every American citizen has become a suspect in the federal government's blatant invasion of individual rights of privacy.

The repression of civil rights under the Bush administration and the lies it has told about the necessity for the Patriot Act have done little to assure our nation's security or to combat terrorism. What they have done is to put far more fear into the American people than any terrorist could. Americans know that one of the great lies is, "Trust us. We're the government and we're here to help you." The greater lie is "We need to restrict your civil liberties and the Constitutional guarantees in order to make you safe." But the truth was spoken by Benjamin Franklin who once argued, "They that can give up essential liberty to obtain a little temporary safety deserve neither liberty nor safety."

NOTES

1. Other cases occurred in Denver and Kansas City (2000), and Cleveland and New Jersey (2001). The American Booksellers Foundation for Free Expression <www.abffe.org> tracks all cases of attempts by law enforcement to seize bookstore records.

2. The Act is identified as P.L. 107-056, 115 STAT. 272. The full text may be found at <www.frwebgate.access.gpo.gov/cgibin/getdoc.cgi?dbname=107_cong_public_laws&docid=f:publ056.107.pdf" It is also available at <www.wpic.org/privacy/terrorism/hr3162.htm>.

3. The vote was 357-66 in the House; 98-1 in the Senate.

4. The House bill is available at: <www.house.gov/judiciary/107-236p1.pdf.>
Also see: Neil A. Lewis and Robert Pear, "Congress, Negotiators Back Scaled-Down Bill to Battle Terror," *New York Times* (October 2, 2001); Neil A. Lewis and Robert Pear, "Terror Laws Near Votes in House and Senate," *New York Times* October 3, 2001); and Robin Toner and Neil A. Lewis, "House Passes Terrorism Bill Much Like Senate's, but With 5-Year Limit," *New York Times* (October 13, 2001). The House vote was 337-79.

5. CNN transcript 091000CN.V22

6. "President Signs Anti-Terrorism Bill," White House news release/transcript <www.whitehouse.gov/news/releases/2001/10/20011026-5.html>.

7. Testimony of John Ashcroft before the Senate Committee on the Judiciary, December 6, 2001 at <www.senate.gov/-judiciarytestimony. cfm?id=121&wit_id=42>.

8. Testimony of John Ashcroft, Senate Committee on the Judiciary; March 4, 2003 at <www.senate.gove/-judiciary/print_testimony.cfm?id=612&wit_id=42>.

9. See, Philip Shenon, "Secret Court Says F.B.I. Aides Misled Judges in 75 Cases," *New York Times* (August 23, 2002) and Philip Shenon, "Congress Criticizes F.B.I. and Justice Department Over Actions Before Secret Wiretap Court," *New York Times* (September 11, 2002).

10. The President's 21-minute speech and response to questions was archived by the Federal Document Clearing House.

11. Earl Blumenauer, *Congressional Record* (October 24, 2001), p. E1922.

12. Carolyn C. Kilpatrick, *Congressional Record* (October 25, 2001), p. E1929.

13. Quoted in an Associated Press wire service article, distributed November 9, 2003.

14. Quoted in Juliet Eilperin, "Kucinich Stresses Civil Liberties," *Washington Post* (December 24, 2003).

15. "An Unpatriotic Act," *The New York Times* (August 25, 2003).

16. See: <www.lifeandiberty.gov>.

17. Testimony of Attorney General John Ashcroft before the Senate Committee on the Judiciary, December 6, 2001 at <www.usdoj.gov/ag/testimony.2001/1206/transcriptsenatejudiciarycommitteee.htm>.

18. See, Transcript of the Hearing Before the Subcommittee on the Constitution of the Committee on the Judiciary, U.S. House of Representatives (May 20, 2003) at <www.house.gov/judiciary/87238.PDF>.

19. Quoted in Cynthia Price, "Homeland Security Versus Right to Information," *NFPW Agenda* (Summer 2003) p. 1. Also see: *Homefront Confidential: How the War on Terrorism Affects Access to Information and the Public's Right to Know*, available from the Reporters Committee on Freedom of the Press and on-line at <www.rcfp.org/homefront-confidential>.

20. Quoted in "Jailed Without Cause," *Newsweek* web edition; January 18, 2002.

21. David Cole, "A Matter of Rights," *The Nation* (September 20, 2001) at <www.thenation.com/doc.mhtml?i=20011008&s=cole>.

22. Testimony of Dr. James Zogby, Senate Committee on the Judiciary (November 18, 2003) at <www.senate.gov/~judiciary/testimony.cfm?id= 998&-wit_id=2873>.

23. Quoted in "Jailed Without Cause," *op. cit.*

24. Quoted in Paul Harris, "Big Brother Takes a Grip on America," *Observer* (September 7, 2003), p. 20.

25. *Falen Gherebi v. George Walker Bush; Donald H. Rumsfeld*, no. 03-55785 United States Court of Appeals for the Ninth Circuit, filed December 18, 2003.

26. News Briefing, Donald Rumsfeld (January 22, 2002).

27. See, *Report to Congress on Implementation of Section 1001 of the USA Patriot Act*, U.S. Department of Justice (July 7, 2003) at <www.usdoj.gov/oig/special/03-07/index.htm>.

28. Quoted in Philip Shenon, "Report on USA Patriot Act Alleges Civil Rights Violations," *New York Times* (July 20, 2003).

29. See Eric Lichtblau, "Ashcroft Seeks More Power to Pursue Terror Suspects," *New York Times* (June 6, 2003).

30. See: "Federal 9/11 Detainee Abuse Caught on Tape; Men Falsely Held as Terrorists Were Beaten, Humiliated," ACLU News release (December 18, 2003) at <www.aclu.org/SafeandFree/SafeandFree.cfm?ID=14616&c=206>.

31. Alberto R. Gonzales, "Martial Justice, Full and Fair," *New York Times* (November 30, 2001).

32. Quoted in Associated Press article distributed January 12, 2004, written by Anne Gearan.

33. See *CNSS v. Department of Justice* 215 F.Supp 2nd 94, 2002, decided August 15, 2002; and 331 F3rd 918, 1003, decided June 17, 2003.

34. Quoted in *Florida Today* (September 23, 2002).

35. Quoted in Diana Graettinger, "Official Counters Patriot Act Critics," *Bangor* (Maine) *Daily News* (April 4, 2003).

36. Speech, National Press Club (April 24, 2003).

37. Testimony of Timothy Burgess before Alaska Senate State Affairs Committee (May 13, 2003).

38. "Seeking Truth From Justice," American Civil Liberties Union, pp. 2-3.

39. See *Hamdi v. Rumsfeld*, 296 F.3d 278.

40. *Yaser Esam Hamdi v. Donald H. Rumsfeld*, 294 F.3d 598 (2002).

41. Center for National Security Studies, et. al. v. U.S. Department of Justice; civil; action No. 01-2500, 217 F. Supp. 2d 58.

42. *Padilla v. Rumsfeld*, docket Nos. 03-2235 (L); 03-2438, U.S. Court of Appeals for the Second Circuit.

43. Quoted in Kevin Fagan, "Arcada the defiant Town ordinance penalizes officials who cooperate with Patriot Act, but law may not stand up in court," *San Francisco Chronicle* (April 13, 2003).

44. Quoted in "Official Counters Patriot Act Critics," *op. cit.*

45. Quoted in *San Francisco Chronicle* (March 10, 2003).

46. "Seeking Truth From Justice," *op. cit.*, pp. 3-4.

47. Testimony of John Ashcroft before the House Judiciary Committee (June 5, 2003).

48. Quoted in "Stretching Patriot Act," *Las Vegas Review-Journal* (September 16, 2003).

49. Testimony of John Ashcroft before the Senate Committee on the Judiciary (December 6, 2001) at <www.senate.gov/-judiciary/testimony.cfm?id=121&wit_id=42>.

50. See: *Report to the House Judiciary Committee on the USA Patriot Act and Related Measures* (May 13, 2003).

51. *Ibid.*

52. Quoted in J. M. Kalil and Steve Tetreault, "Patriot Act: Law's use causing concerns," *Las Vegas Review-Journal* (November 5, 2003).

53. *Ibid.*

54. Statement by Sen. Patrick Leahy, Senate Committee on the Judiciary (September 10, 2002).

55. News release, American Civil Liberties Union (November 5, 2003).

56. Quoted in "Patriot Act knows no limits," *Las Vegas Review-Journal* (November 5, 2003).

57. "Patriot Act knows no limits," *op. cit.*

58. George W. Bush, "President Bush Speaks at Tsingua University" (February 22, 2002) at <www.whitehouse.gov/news/releases/2002/02/20020222.html>.

59. See, "Big Brother Takes a Grip on America," *op. cit.*

60. Report to the Congress, Department of Justice (May 21, 2003).

61. "Seeking Truth From Justice," *op. cit.*, p. 8.

62. See: Brian Glick, *War at Home: Covert Action Against U.S. Activists and What We Can Do About It*; Jim Redden, *Snitch Culture: How Citizens are Turned Into the Eyes and ears of the State*; Nelson Blackstock, *COINTELPRO: The FBI's Secret War on Political Freedom*; Ward Churchill and Jim Vander Wall, *COINTELPRO Papers: Documents From the FBI's Secret Wars Against Domestic Dissent.*

63. News Release, Reporters Committee for Freedom of the Press (August 20, 2003) at <www.rcfp.org/news/documents/20030820ashcroft.html>.

64. "Dispelling the Myths," Department of Justice at <www.lifeandliberty.gov/subs/u_myths.htm>.

65. *Ibid.*

66. Judith Graham, "Librarians Protest Potential Snooping; Patriot Act Makes Access to Records too Easy, They Say," *Chicago Tribune* (April 4, 2003).

67. "Dispelling the Myths," *op. cit.* at <www.lifeandliberty.gov/subs/u_myths.htm>.

68. See, "Transcript of the Hearing Before the Subcommittee on the Constitution of the Committee on the Judiciary, U.S. House of Representatives" (May 20, 2003) at <www.house.gov/judiciary/87238.PDF>.

69. See *Public Libraries and Civil Liberties: A Profession Divided*, The Library Research Center, University of Illinois at Urbana-Champaign (Leigh S. Estabrook, director) at <www.lis.uiuc.edu/gslis/research/civil_liberties.html>.

70. "Statement of Barbara Comstock, director of public affairs, on DOJ Testimony Regarding Libraries," news release, U.S. Department of Justice; June 2, 2003.

71. For the full resolution, see <www.ala.org/Template.cfm?Section=IF_

Resolutions&Template=/ContentManagement/ContentDisplay.cfm&
ContentID=11891>.

72. Quoted in "Are They Watching What You Read?" *Monterey County* (Calif.) *Herald* (September 29, 2003).

73. *Resolution on the USA Patriot Act and Related Measures That Infringe on the Rights of Library Users*, South Carolina Library Association (March 13, 2003) at <www.scla.org/docs/patriotactresolution.html>.

74. See "Blues do part for National Homeland Security," *Bluesweek* (November 7, 2003).

75. See Amy Lee, "Blues, Aetna help hunt terrorists," *Detroit News* (November 16, 2003).

76. *Ibid.*

77. *Ibid.*

78. See Adam Clymer, "Justice Dept. Balks at Effort to Study Antiterror Powers," *New York Times* (August 15, 2003).

79. See: "Eric Lichtblau, Ashcroft Says Efforts to Weaken Terrorism Law Will Place Americans at Greater Risk," *New York Times* (August 20, 2003).

80. John L. Smith, "The attorney general and the Patriot Act," *Las Vegas Review-Journal* (August 31, 2003).

81. See Adam Clymer, "Government Openness at Issue As Bush Holds On to Records," *New York Times* (January 3, 2003).

82. Quoted in Susan Schmidt, "Ashcroft Wants Stronger Patriot Act," *Washington Post* (June 6, 2003).

83. Nancy Kranich, "The Impact of the USA Patriot Act: An Update," Free Expression Policy Project (2003).

84. Editorial, "Silence on the Hill," *Washington Post* (January 5, 2004).

85. See David E. Sanger, "Bush Was Warned bin Laden Wanted to Hijack Planes," *New York Times* (May 16, 2002); John King, "Bush briefed on hijacking threat before September 11," CNN broadcast (May 16, 2002); Jason Burke and Ed Vulliamy, "Bush knew of terrorist plot to hijack US planes," [London] *Observer* (May 19, 2002); Torcuil Crichton, "Britain warned US to expect September 11 al-Qaeda hijackings," *London Sunday Herald* (May 19, 2002); Associated Press, "9/11 report, Rice remarks in conflict: Investigators say Bush got specific data on threats," originally transmitted July 29, 2003; "Ashcroft Flying High," Washington Bureau, CBS-TV News (July 26, 2001); Patrick E. Tyler and Neil Macfarquhar, "Traces of Terror: the Intelligence Reports; Egypt Warned U.S. of a Qaeda plot, Mubarak asserts," *New York Times* (June 4, 2002); Dana Priest and Dan Eggen, "9/11 Probers Say Agencies Failed to Heed Attack Signs," *Washington Post* (September 19, 2002).

86. Quoted in "9/11 Chair: Attack Was Preventable," CBS News (December 17, 2003)at <www.cbsnews,com/stories/2003/12/17/eveningnews/printable589137.s html>.

87. Bernie Sanders, "Patriot Act Overreaches," *USA Today* (September 23, 2003).

88. A copy of the confidential draft memo of January 9, 2003, is available at <www.publicintegrity.org/dtaweb/downloads/Story_01_020703_Doc_1.pdf>.

89. Interview with James Dempsey by Bob Garfield, "Snooping in the Dark," On the Media, WNYC-AM/National Public Radio, aired January 9, 2004.

90. See *Congressional Record* (July 22, 2003), p. H7290.

91. "Resolution Against the USA PATRIOT ACT and Other Executive Orders for the City of Philadelphia, Pennsylvania," resolution 020394 at <www.philly peace.org/patriotact/resolution.html>.

92. Quoted in Eric Lichtblau, "Justice Dept. Lists Use of New Power to Fight Terror," *New York Times* (May 21, 2003).

93. Quoted in "Kucinich Stresses Civil Liberties," *op. cit.*

94. See "Ashcroft Mocks Librarians and Others Who Oppose Parts of Counterterrorism Law," *New York Times* (September 16, 2003).

95. See *Muslim Community Association of Ann Arbor, et. al. v. Ashcroft and Mueller*, U.S. District Court, Eastern District of Michigan.

96. "Free Speech Groups Support Patriot Act Change," News release, American Booksellers Foundation for Free Expression (November 3, 2003) at <www.abffe.org/11-3-03pressrelease.html>. The *amicus curiae* brief is accessible at <www.abffe.com/amicus_brief.pdf>.

97. See *Humanitarian Law Project v. Ashcroft*, U.S. District Court, Central District of California, CV-98-01971-ABC.

98. Michael Moran, "Domestic spying vs. secret police: FBI walking tough, thin line on domestic surveillance," MSNBC, (September 2, 2003) at <www.msnbc.msn.com/id/3071395/>.

99. "Silence on the Hill," *op. cit.*

Why "National Security" is a Misnomer

BY MARGIE BURNS

Experts in every branch of security currently give us to understand that the term "national security" is something of a misnomer. The White House and the administration have claimed that our national security has been strengthened under their handling. However, these claims are false; both news reports and security experts have revealed ongoing breaches of security over the past two years. "National security" is in most respects no better now than it was before 9-11, and is often worse.

Homeland Security

The crown jewel of the Bush White House's claims regarding national security is the Cabinet-level "Department of Homeland Security," created in fall 2002. Among a series of distortions and half-truths, the White House has repeatedly taken credit for creating the Department of Homeland Security, when in fact the White House opposed the legislation until forced by Congress to accede to it, with some impetus from opinion polls indicating public support for the broad concept. The administration came around on the agency only after passage of legislation protecting re-insurers and other large insurance companies from litigation connected to terrorism. Direct beneficiaries of the bill were major insurance carriers for the World Trade Center, including HCC Insurance (formerly Houston Casualty Company), with Marvin P. Bush, youngest brother of George W. Bush, on its board of directors. Bush is still listed as a company advisor; his departure from the HCC board was announced the same day as passage of the liability legislation.[1] This connection, though documented in regulatory filings and other public records, has never been mentioned publicly by the White House.

Having acquiesced, the White House told two *Washington Post* reporters that "homeland security" had been largely the brainchild of Vice President Cheney. According to White House Chief of Staff Andrew Card in this sole interview, the oddly-named "homeland security" edifice developed in response to the 9/11 attacks.[2]

This is not so. Adopting instead the obfuscation-and-pork-barrel approach, the administration created the odd "homeland security" entity, justified by rightwing think tanks and pushed strenuously by publications from the Reverend Sun Myung Moon's media empire well before 9/11.[3]

In a quiet campaign, this package was actually already in place, prepared in think tanks and communications media awaiting a "second Pearl Harbor" to justify further militarizing the world's one superpower. The "Institute for Homeland Security," self-described as a think tank, was actually formed in the northern Virginia suburbs of DC in October 1999. The institute in turn is part of a corporation called ANSER, short for Analytic Services, Incorporated, a mainly one-client shop catering to federal agencies in the military and the intelligence community, especially the CIA. The DOD in 1998 listed ANSER 58th among top contractors.[4]

The Institute's self-described mission is "To provide executive education and public awareness of the challenges to homeland security in the 21st century." As "a nonprofit public-service research organization examining a new set of national security challenges," it produces workshops, programs for executive-level policy makers, a weekly Homeland Security Newsletter, a Homeland Security opinion poll on its web site, and the Journal of Homeland Security, established October 2000 and featuring "articles by senior government leaders and leading homeland security experts."[5]

With "field offices and operating locations throughout the world," according to its annual report, Analytic Services began as a research center for the Air Force, closed as a federal entity in 1977, and has garnered federal contracts and patents ever since. In March 2002, the federal government listed ANSER as a "cognizant agency": "Any State, Local, or Non-Profit agency expending more then [sic] $25,000,000 in total federal awards in a single Fiscal year" (based on FY 2000: $74,456,395 for ANSER).

Aviation Security

The nation has also been falsely told that the new department coordinates information and intelligence to produce a unified response to security threats. The nation has also been falsely told that such unified response is in place, including specifically tightening up aviation security.

It is natural for a grateful and bruised nation to believe these claims. Let's take a closer look at these falsehoods.

With regard to aviation security (AVSEC, in the argot), the best-regarded experts agree on one melancholy proposition: owing largely to top-level managerial problems in the administration, security breaches in aviation are at least as problematic now as they were before 9-11, and are often worse.

Particularly splashy incidents have made periodic headlines. In August 2003, homesick young man Charles McKinley shipped himself to the Dallas suburb of DeSoto, Texas, via airports in three cities, without being caught. In what was promptly dubbed "Cargo Class," McKinley successfully avoided detection at airports in New York, Wayne, Indiana, and Dallas before being delivered to his parents' yard, where he released himself from the shipping box in front of a startled deliveryman. Had McKinley waited a few minutes, he would not have been caught at all.[6]

In September 2003, college student Nathaniel Heatwole emailed authorities that he had left bags containing contraband items, including box cutters, on two Southwest Airlines planes. Although Heatwole told the feds which planes he had hidden the items aboard, they were not found until five weeks later, partly because Transportation Security Administration (TSA) officials did not forward the emails to the FBI. This lapse directly contradicts repeated White House statements that the new security entities are set up to share information and coordinate efforts.[7]

In the saddest airport-related incident, on October 15, a Houston police officer reported that Kyle Fix, a security screening supervisor at Bush Houston Intercontinental Airport, flagged him down and confessed to killing his wife, Dominique. Her body was found by police at the family home in Houston. The TSA has stated that Fix began work at Intercontinental in 2002, after passing several background checks.[8]

Little of this surprises insiders with lengthy experience in civil aviation. Lack of space constrains treatment of this large topic, but AVSEC Cassandras, all bearing armloads of documentation, anecdote, and sometimes videotape to support their claims, and bristling with credentials, include FAA whistleblower Bogdan Djakovic, formerly with the FAA's "Red Team" of undercover airport security inspectors; former FAA inspector Steve Elson, a special agent trained in counterterrorism and another "Red Team" member; NASA special agent in counterintelligence/counterterrorism Kieran T. (Kerry) Spaulding, formerly an FAA special agent; Brian F. Sullivan, retired FAA special agent for the New England Region; and Billie Vincent, former Director, Office of Aviation Security, FAA.[9]

These and other aviation security specialists have pointed out for over two years that federal security-tightening measures focused on ordinary commercial passengers leave a gaping "back door" regarding cargo handling, ground crews, private charter planes, unauthorized personnel, and airport perimeters.

This is not to say that the focus on screeners has resulted in adequate security regarding the mundane tasks of screening baggage, carry-ons and passengers. Minor incidents of passengers' carrying weapons or dangerous objects on board flights, without being stopped or detected by screeners, are frequently reported. Worse, the overwhelming majority of security breaches are not reported, and most are not even discovered. A General Accounting Office study in fall 2003 reported numerous failed undercover tests in which airport security checks let through flamboyantly contraband knives, box cutters, guns, and bombs.[10]

Former "Red Team" member Steve Elson says in an extensive interview that he has repeatedly found airport security measures failing even the most elementary tests. Now retired from the FAA but volunteering as an aviation-security consultant, Elson has repeatedly demonstrated airport security breaches, sometimes in front of television reporters. His attempts to carry lead-lined film bags through airport screening, for instance, have succeeded 95 percent of the time. As Elson points out, "if you don't look in [the lead bag] or under it, you fail." The significance of lead bags is that they foil an X-ray machine and could easily conceal weapons or other contraband; thus a ninety-five-percent failure rate on this simple tactic does not augur well for complex tactics. Elson himself, in the interview, sketches several ongoing security breaches, all easily and inexpensively correctible.[11]

Training of the mostly-new squad of federal screeners is an ongoing sore point. In confidential correspondence, personnel engaged to train screeners say that screening students have been allowed to skip part of the required 40-hour training, to cheat on exams, and even to get a passing grade when they fail.

Only a few of the screener problems have surfaced in news reports. One off-the-record anecdote, sent to me by an aviation security specialist who prefers not to be named, featured screeners at Houston Bush Intercontinental Airport caught having sex in the airport's chapel. Screeners at Norfolk International Airport, in Virginia, have complained covertly that an official there abuses his authority over subordinates in ways including unwanted sexual touching and advances, abusive language, and arbitrary promotions and firings.

Fundamental to the situation is the basic security structure itself. Rush-staffing a newly created Transportation Security Administration, in the also-new Department of Homeland Security, with no adequate organizational blueprint, was an almost insurmountable challenge. Resulting

problems include high turnover, lack of training, poor morale, and gaping loopholes in a gigantic "security" apparatus that generates sizeable
contracts but little confidence among those who know it best.

In Kerry Spaulding's words, "This agency (TSA) was formed from a
corrupt and failed group of incompetent people who, in reality, have
little or no knowledge of operational security requirements. This sense
of arrogance, lack of successful leadership models, and grossly absent
practical experiences in applying [operations security] in a dynamic environment such as commercial aviation operations has been the norm for
this bunch."[12] Existing problems are compounded by the fact that, despite public statements about "information sharing" and "coordinating,"
accountability is routinely passed among agencies like the proverbial hot
potato. When I attempted to ask the TSA questions about problems on
the morning of September 11, 2001, for instance, the agency responded
through a spokesperson that since the TSA did not exist then, I should
direct my questions to the FAA. When I got in touch with the FAA,
however, the department responded that all questions regarding security
must go through the TSA.

Generally, "transparency" and "accountability" seem to be lip service. When I tried to ask the pertinent agencies questions regarding individual responsibility or even job descriptions, I was told through
spokespersons that government agencies cannot comment on or discuss
any "personnel matter." One frustrated employee, who declines to be
named, sums up administration policy on security problems as "Fix it,
don't find it."

While ongoing security breaches in civil aviation are by no means
the whole picture, the breadth and amplitude of the problems in aviation
reflect and illustrate similar problems in the nation's nuclear industry,
petrochemical and chemical industries, borders and ports. The GAO has
produced a series of reports documenting problems (the usual phrasing
is "challenges still remain") in these areas.[13]

The Sad Results

Whatever combination of overlapping agendas created an unwieldy new
cabinet department, several results should by now be apparent. Briefly
stated, they are as follows:

- "National security" is, as ever, the justification for any draconian
  invasion of privacy and/or civil liberties. Invasions of privacy or
  extensions of police-state powers into individual liberties in the
  home or workplace are presented as one side of a clash of cat-

egorical imperatives, in which necessary freedoms are pitted against also-necessary security and safety.

- Seldom does "national security" suffice actually to improve the condition or quality of first responders or the everyday nuts-and bolts of genuine security. Nor, if you notice, has "national security" sufficed to justify the firing of any pertinent official in the CIA, the FAA, or the office of the National Security Advisor, which might as well be vacant. There have been no such firings.

- Never does "national security" avail to curb policies that are sweeping breaches of security, such as corporate "outsourcing" to offshore entities. Even a security company, for example, that enjoys contracts with the US military is not prohibited from contracting with the militaries of other countries. The same laissez-faire attitude is applied to "free trade" arrangements that relax every cross-national regulation including security regulations.

- Neither has "national security" yet been used to support sane and prudent policies that might genuinely promote security, such as pursuing genuine diplomacy and other peaceable means to defuse tensions. Rather, the White House has often chosen to throw gasoline on the flames.

- Nor has "national security" resulted in any investigation of the Bush family's security-sensitive business links with the ruling cliques of Saudi Arabia and Kuwait, in spite of ample evidence in the business press and elsewhere that those links have persisted since at least the 1980s and have influenced some highly questionable policies.

- "National security," however, has unquestionably generated big contracts. Indeed, one can make sense of almost any Bush pronouncement by inserting the phrase "big contracts" at the pertinent juncture: "This Department of Homeland Security will foster a new culture throughout our government, one that emphasizes [big contracts]." Or, "We have dramatically improved information sharing among our intelligence agencies, and we have taken new steps to protect our critical infrastructure [big contracts]." Et cetera.

This strangely laissez-faire indifference to consequences, when big business is involved, obtains even when the business involved is security. Back in 1985, then-Assistant Secretary of Defense Richard Perle complained to a Senate panel about some Warsaw Pact companies, "By operating as legitimate businesses, these commercial officials can legally obtain credit information on vulnerable American executives and firms, visit military sites, acquire sensitive technology and recruit spies."[14] Now, when cyberspace has expanded these insecurities exponentially, the same complaint could be registered. But it never is. US banks and other financial entities buy protective software from the same vendors as foreign banks, the US military engages contractors engaged by foreign militaries, the federal government and the states are served by shared private contractors on sensitive sites, and nobody raises a concern.

The Bigger Picture

While there is no single remedy, good policy would promote the public good over the private (and often secret) benefit of administration cronies including business associates and even family members. Such an approach necessitates genuine streamlining and transparency in federal agencies—cutting redundancies, eliminating some layers, and forcing prioritizing and accountability in others.

Instead, we have an administration aggressively covering up 9-11 and preventing genuinely expert research into it, even when such research might rebut the most nonsensical theories. White House stonewalling on 9-11 investigation continues while the White House milks those dreadful events for all possible political benefit domestically, simultaneously advancing an agenda of US colonialism in the Middle East, generating big contracts for friendly companies and their management, and making money off the twin industries of "defense" and "security" for close relatives of George W. Bush.

These actions are unlikely to proceed from any good motive, but they do comprise a strategy of sorts. The rational working hypothesis here would be that this strategy is neither totally conscious nor totally unconscious. Individuals do not usually wake in the morning thinking, 'What harm can I do today?' On the other hand, the individuals making key decisions in these matters are not being directed in a trance either. But however loosely or tightly defined the over-all strategy, one of its key tactics is the all-purpose counterattack of "conspiracy theory."

One big problem in the public discourse, regarding national security, is a given: the large divide between those citizens who were always spy- and police-minded, and those of us who were not.

Social alignments are powerful in the life of the nation. Those of us who were not particularly spy buffs before 9-11, or crime-and-punishment types, or heavily security-oriented, intuitively shy away from the grim topics now being manhandled in the corridors of power. Just as some citizens feel vaguely that they are too classy for "politics," those who love the life of the mind tend to avoid the dark underside of intrigue and glamorized violence, including what the current administration is doing in our name.

This avoidance is reinforced by other natural deterrents to discourse: unwillingness to incite further harm to innocent Muslims; nauseated saturation with the terms "terrorist" and "terrorism"; disinclination to be called nervous Nellies by someone like George F. Will; and perhaps some intimidation generated by thuggish 'Team Bush' and its blind lobby-fed hacks.

These divisions have now proven to hurt the polity without helping security, but they still persist, especially with the none-too-subtle threat of being labeled "conspiracy-minded," now used just as the old accusations of "conspiracy" (Commie conspiracy, etc.) were used, to discredit any threat to the status quo. The shorthand threat and interchangeable terms "conspiracy," "conspiracy theory" and "conspiracy theorists" share, among them, one and only one key signification: loss of status.

It's a surprisingly effective tactic, for one so simple. If you venture to suggest that the simultaneous hijacking of four jumbo jets, culminating in the deaths of three thousand innocent people and including the skyjackers' crashing into the Pentagon, might call for some investigation not left entirely to the individuals responsible at the time, you're probably going outside your comfort zone in the first place, peering into the abyss of something so bloody and bizarre. Worse, you're in imminent danger of turning into the Mel Gibson character in the movie Conspiracy Theory (viewed recently by Bush, right around when he began using the word "revisionist"), going off to work in a skullcap and a uniform with your name embroidered over the pocket.

This cartoonish fantasy is hardly "class," but it does impinge on some terrified concern with money, gentility, and especially status. Thus it packs a disproportionate wallop among exactly the people who should know better, and whom we desperately need to know better, including journalists and other writers, college faculty and researchers, and political candidates and office holders.

It is important to point out administration lies. Citizens should be free to address genuine public safety and public health issues without either being recruited for World War III or being lied about, and threats of name-calling, implied or explicit, are threats of lying. An administration pretending to build up "defense" and "security," while damaging both, has an interest in discrediting political opponents and disarming critics.

NOTES

1. <www.hcch.com/content/press_releases/2002/nov_22_02nov_22_02_body.htm>.

2. <www.globalpolicy.org/wtc/liberties/2002/0609secrecy.htm>

3. See Moon's right-wing flag ship publication *Insight on the News*, on the web at

4. <www.anser.org>

5. <www.homelandsecurity.org>

6. <www.thesmokinggun.com/archive/crateguy1.html>

7. <www.cnn.com/2003/LAW/10/20/airline.scare>.

8. <www.abclocal.go.com/ktrk/news/101503_local_wifemurder.html>.

9. See <www.whistleblower.org/article.php?did=456&scid=26>; <www.osc.gov/documents/press/2003/pr03_07.htm>; <www.pbs.org/newshour/bb/transportation/jan-june02/aviation_1-24.html>; and <www.worldnetdaily.com/news/article.asp?ARTICLE_ID=26614>.

10. <www.transportationsec.com/ar/security_tsa_fire_focused>.

11. CBS News (September 4, 2002).

12. Quoted in Margie Burns, "Aviation Security, Texas Style," at <www.populist.com/04.1.burns.html>.

13. See <www.gao.gov>.

14. William Welch, "Pentagon Official Says Soviets 'Looting' U.S. Technology," Associated Press (October 23, 1985).

Diagnosing Our Leaders, Avoiding Bogus Wars

By Heather Wokusch

Much has been made of the psychological challenges of our Commander in Chief and his parade of lies leading to the invasion of Iraq, but one fundamental question remains: Why did we buy this crap in the first place?

Transcending history is the simple truth that behind every pathological liar of a leader sits a co-dependent public enabling further lies and destruction.

So we either let the war on Afghanistan and the war on Iraq spiral into a never-ending war on terror that serves no one but weapons manufacturers and corrupt politicians trying to justify re-election, or we seek help. Immediately.

But leaving this relationship won't be easy. Every dysfunctional union has its mutual perks, and in this case, the Bush administration's macho, narcissistic posturing fills a need in the American public. Conveniently, it also helps create that need.

So how do we throw the bums out and move on? And how do we make sure we're never suckered into another quagmire of a war?

Diagnosing Our Leaders

The first step is taking a closer look at who we're up against and why; the whole Iraq mess is a good place to start. We now know the Bush administration's behavior leading up to the invasion was characterized by:

- Lying and breaking promises
- Picking fights
- Impulsiveness, not planning ahead
- Recklessly disregarding the safety of others
- Conning others for personal gain

If you put these symptoms into the DSM IV[1] (a psychological diagnostic manual) you get back something like Antisocial Disorder with a twinge of Narcissism, or in other words, a personality type best known for three overriding cravings: money, power and control. People like this take authority by creating an environment of fear, isolation and unpredictability. They limit information flow, use others' confusion and panic for self-advancement, and can't tolerate independent or disobedient people who threaten their worldview.

In other words, these people are scam artists with a fascist streak.

Fits the Bush administration so far. But how do we stop enabling the bad behavior of our so-called leaders? How do we devise a roadmap to peace and good government for the USA?

Here's an action plan; add your own ideas and keep pushing until we've won our democracy back.

10-Step Plan for Rescuing the USA and Avoiding Future Bogus Wars

1. Face the real reasons Iraq was invaded

Targeting Iraq had little to do with Hussein's alleged WMD and everything to do with a covert US push for global hegemony—at least that's the approach of a conservative US think-tank called the Project for a New American Century (PNAC).

PNAC calls for a global Pax Americana based on superior US military capability, and its roster of affiliates reads like a White House "Who's Who" (Vice President Cheney, National Security Adviser Rice and Defense Secretary Rumsfeld, among others). The PNAC mission statement, entitled "Rebuilding America's Defenses,"[2] was written in September 2000 and seems downright creepy in light of developments ever since.

The report recommends a massive increase in weapons expenditures so America "can fight and win multiple, simultaneous major theater wars."

It calls for the US Army to defend "American interests in the Persian Gulf and Middle East" and states that while "the unresolved conflict with Iraq provides the immediate justification, the need for a substantial American force presence in the Gulf transcends the issue of the regime of Saddam Hussein."

The report ominously acknowledges "some catastrophic and catalyzing event— like a new Pearl Harbor," as enabling the PNAC vision to be realized more quickly.

Sound familiar?

In addition to its blueprint for world domination, however, the Bush administration had other reasons to attack Iraq.

When bombs started devastating Baghdad in March 2003, the US economy was in trouble. Millions of jobs had been lost under Bush's reign; business investment and manufacturing levels were down. Consumers were saddled with record amounts of debt, and the US trade deficit was causing headaches. A distraction was needed.

There were also concerns about oil and future oil profits. A report prepared for Cheney's energy task group in April 2001 warned, "The energy sector is in critical condition . . . Gulf allies are finding their domestic and foreign policy interests increasingly at odds with America's strategic considerations . . . Iraq has become a key 'swing' producer, posing a difficult situation for the U.S. government."[3]

And of course, the corporate scandals rocking Wall Street were striking suspiciously close to the White House. How convenient that headlines over Harken, Halliburton and Enron et al seemed to disappear after the invasion started.

Domestic problems and a Dr. Strangelove approach to foreign policy don't justify invading another country. Period. The upcoming presidential elections, combined with the administration's plummeting polls, spell more rally-around-Bush invasions (Iran? Syria?) unless we make some serious changes fast.

2. Confront the lies

Who can forget the barrage of official statements vaguely linking Hussein with the 9-11 attacks, followed by the much later admission by Bush that in fact no link existed?

Another scam used to justify the invasion of Iraq linked Hussein with devastating nukes:

- Bush, Oct 7 2002: "The evidence indicates that Iraq is reconstituting its nuclear weapons program . . . Iraq has attempted to purchase high-strength aluminum tubes and other equipment needed for gas centrifuges which are used to enrich uranium for nuclear weapons." Bush adds that Hussein has had many meetings with Iraqi nuclear scientists, "a group he calls his 'nuclear mujahideen' . . . his nuclear holy warriors."[4]
- Cheney, March 16 2003: "We believe [Saddam] has, in fact, reconstituted nuclear weapons."[5]

Yet somehow after the invasion of Iraq had begun, the administration's story radically changed and the earlier "mushroom cloud" hysteria vanished.

- Cheney: "I did misspeak. We never had evidence that [Saddam] had acquired a nuclear weapon."[6]

- Defense Secretary Rumsfeld: "I don't know anybody in any government or any intelligence agency who suggested that the Iraqis had nuclear weapons."[7]

This backtracking would be almost laughable if over 180 Congress members hadn't cited Iraq's nuclear threat as key to passage of a resolution authorizing use of force against Iraq. In other words, we went to war over a lie. That's not laughable—that's impeachable.

3. Put the costs in perspective
As of March 2004, the amount of money spent on the invasion and its aftermath could instead have been spent back home:
-    providing 32,090,266 children with health care
-    hiring 1,426,030 school teachers
-    building 1,069,524 additional affordable housing units
-    offering 1,898,964 four-year scholarships at public universities[8]

According to a study by Yale University economist William D. Norhaus, "With $166 billion spent or requested, Bush's war spending in 2003 and 2004 already exceeds the inflation-adjusted costs of the Revolutionary War, the War of 1812, the Mexican War, the Civil War, the Spanish American War and the Persian Gulf War combined."[9]

Consider also that apart from the billions being spent in Iraq, Bush has requested more billions for developing homegrown WMD, which of course must be used in order to justify the costs of building and testing it, which leads to even more wars requiring more money for weaponry, and so on.

But the true costs to our country lie in dead and wounded service members, with families torn apart due to long deployments overseas. And of course, there's the death and havoc we impose on civilian populations abroad, not to mention the increased security risk for ourselves.

4. Stop war profiteering
Let's see now. The US provisional authority somehow can't account for billions of dollars of Iraqi funds earmarked for that country's reconstruction.[10] Meanwhile, the US vice president holds 433,333 unexercised stock options in/receives large payments from Halliburton, a company soaking American taxpayers via no-bid contracts in post-war Iraq. The US president's father is heavily connected to Carlyle, a company striking it filthy rich from exclusive contracts in his son's ongoing War on Fill-In-The-Blank.

If any of us pulled this kind of conflict-of-interest scam we'd be thrown in the slammer. Why do we let Our Leaders get away with it?

5. Pick your information sources carefully

Much of the media stopped reporting balanced or accurate news about Iraq even before bedding down with the US military during the invasion.

For example, even though a majority of Americans didn't support invasion without UN approval, only 3% of the sources on U.S. network newscasts represented an anti-war perspective.[11] (How many military officers do you remember seeing interviewed on TV? How many peace activists?)

In addition, most Americans were found to have held at least one of these three mistaken beliefs:

- "Weapons of mass destruction have been found in Iraq"
- "Clear evidence exists of links between Iraq and al Qaeda"
- "World public opinion favored the US going to war with Iraq"

80% of those relying on FOX held at least one of the three wrong beliefs, compared to 23% relying on PBS or National Public Radio. Not surprisingly, 86% of those who held all three mistaken beliefs backed the war, compared with only 25% of those who believed none.[12]

Bottom line: The American public was conned into war through fake stories, like the Jessica Lynch fairytale, but rarely shown the true face of battle: dead Iraqi civilians and maimed veterans. In an unbelievably cynical move, the Pentagon has even banned showing the homecoming of coffins for fallen soldiers.

And in true Orwellian fashion, the US government is now controlling history. After being caught fudging its web site (by changing "combat" was over in Iraq to "major combat") the White House has altered its Iraq directories to prevent search engines from indexing and archiving material, thus making history easier to erase.

The need for accurate reporting is critical for each of us, but how does Bush stay informed? Here are excerpts from an interview on FOX news in late 2003:

FOX: How do you get your news?
Bush: I get briefed by Andy Card and Condi in the morning. They come in and tell me. In all due respect, you've got a beautiful face and everything.

I glance at the headlines just to kind of a flavor for what's moving. I rarely read the stories and get briefed by people who are probably read the news themselves. But like Condoleeza Rice, in her case, the

national security adviser is getting her news directly from the participants on the world stage.[13]

Bush later added, ". . . the best way to get the news is from objective
sources. And the most objective sources I have are people on my staff
who tell me what's happening in the world."

What's scarier: Bush's grammar, or the concept of "Condi" as an objective source?

6. Set your bullshit detectors on red alert

Like any good propagandist, Bush has a knack for turning complex issues
into cartoons. Recall his analysis of 9/11: "America was targeted for attack
because we're the brightest beacon for freedom and opportunity in the
world."

Bush's September 2002 speech to the United Nations was similarly
dim: "If we meet our responsibilities, if we overcome this danger ... the
people of Iraq can shake off their captivity. They can one day join a
democratic Afghanistan and a democratic Palestine, inspiring reforms
throughout the Muslim world."[14]

Bush repeated this knight-in-shining-armor optimism on March 20
2003, as the US launched air strikes on Baghdad, insisting he had initiated war "to disarm Iraq, to free its people, and to defend the world from
great danger."[15]

In other words, Bush was dropping bombs on Iraqi civilians in order
to save them.

And what would the Iraqis' reaction to this assault most likely be?
Days before the invasion began, Deputy Defense Secretary Paul
Wolfowitz said, "Like the people of France in the 1940s, the Iraqis view
us as their hoped-for liberator."[16] This rosy assessment was echoed by
Cheney, who insisted "we will, in fact, be greeted as liberators," then
went on to predict the conflict would "go relatively quickly . . . weeks
rather than months."

Of course, the reality on the ground has turned out to be something
completely different. Thousands of Iraqi civilians ended up dying as a
result of the US-led invasion, and almost a year after the war supposedly
ended, US soldiers are still being slaughtered in revenge attacks. Iraq is
economically and socially shattered, and the country has become a mag-
net for anyone with a grudge against the States.

But the news isn't all bad. In late 2003, US newspapers were flooded
with upbeat letters-to-the-editor written by soldiers based in Iraq, reporting positive developments like "the quality of life and security for

the citizens has been largely restored."

One catch: The letters were fakes, planted by the Army to put a happy face on the grim realities of occupation. It became obvious that something fishy was going on when 11 different newspapers ended up running the exact same letter, supposedly written by different soldiers, on the same day. Even more embarrassing, none of the soldiers whose names appeared on the letter had actually written it. Instead, their Army superiors had just handed them a copy to sign for propaganda purposes.[17]

The theme is clear. Both before and after the invasion of Iraq, the Bush administration whitewashed reality, and by "embedding" the media and military (every lewd connotation applicable) their job was made much easier. But the public deserves more than platitudes and wishful thinking as a basis for war, and had damn well better insist on it next time.

7. Think globally

The Bush administration has thumbed its nose at important international agreements ranging from non-proliferation to climate change. It has questioned the relevance and credibility of the United Nations, and resorted to dirty tricks against its members: before the UN's crucial Iraq vote in March 2003, for example, the US conducted a covert surveillance campaign against countries defying American interests, including bugging the home and office phones of Security Council delegations.[18]

Is this any way for our country to be behaving? "Why do they hate us?" is self-explanatory when our government acts like an abusive jerk.

In March 2003, Bush justified ousting Hussein by saying, "These are the actions of a regime engaged in a willful charade (and trying to) defy the world."[19]

Bush could be describing his own regime's actions.

8. Demand solid proof for future WMD claims

Bush administration members didn't only lie about Iraq's nukes; they also lied about the existence of other WMD, and their lies were so detailed you just had to believe them. A sampler:

- January 28 2003, Bush: Our intelligence officials estimate that Saddam Hussein had the materials to produce as much as 500 tons of sarin, mustard and VX nerve agent ... U.S. intelligence indicates that Saddam Hussein had upwards of 30,000 munitions capable of delivering chemical agents.[20]

- Feb 5 2003, Secretary of State Powell: "Our conservative estimate is that Iraq today has a stockpile of between 100 and 500 tons of chemical weapons agent. That is enough to fill 16,000 battlefield rockets."[21]

- March 30 2003, Rumsfeld refers to Iraq's WMD: "We know where they are. They're in the area around Tikrit and Baghdad and east, west, south and north somewhat."[22]

It turns out these claims were bald lies meant to prod the public into war. Rumsfeld later gave the bizarre excuse, "Sometimes I overstate for emphasis," as justification for lying.[23] How can we ever trust what he says again?

But the biggest WMD scam involved the bogus claims about Hussein's trying to buy uranium in Niger. UK Prime Minister Tony Blair got the ball rolling in September 2002, when he released a 50-page report on Hussein's WMD, including the revelation that Iraq "had sought to acquire uranium in Africa that could be used to make nuclear weapons."[24] Bush ran with Blair's report, warning, "The danger to our country is grave. The danger to our country is growing. The Iraqi regime ... is seeking a nuclear bomb, and with fissile material, could build one within a year."[25]

Condoleeza Rice called Iraq's arms declaration a "12,200 page lie" for among other reasons, not addressing "Iraq's effort to get uranium from abroad."[26]

In his 2003 State of the Union address, Bush lodged the same charges with 16 important words: "The British government has learned that Saddam Hussein recently sought significant quantities of uranium from Africa."[27]

Soon after, Rumsfeld said the Hussein regime "was working on several different methods of enriching uranium, and recently was discovered seeking significant quantities of uranium from Africa."[28]

The climax came with Powell's UN address on February 5, 2003. Powell insisted, "Every statement I make today is backed up by sources, solid sources. These are not assertions. What we are giving you are facts and conclusions based on solid intelligence." He then gave scary scenarios about "Iraq's attempt to reconstitute its nuclear weapons program" and warned that "Saddam Hussein is determined to get his hands on a nuclear bomb."

Unfortunately, all of the claims about Hussein's weapons adventures in Niger were either directly misleading or downright lies. The root of it all, Blair's paper, was a sham based on crudely forged documents, and although intelligence experts had warned Bush against the Niger-uranium story, his administration used it anyway. As for the UN address, Greg

Thielmann, a well-placed WMD expert later accused Powell of purposely deceiving the public, calling the speech "one of the low points" in Powell's career.[29] How can we ever trust *any* of these con artists again?

9. Clean house

According to the US Constitution, " The President, Vice President and all civil Officers of the United States, shall be removed from office on impeachment for and conviction of treason, bribery and other high crimes and misdemeanors."[30]

Lying to Congress and the American people to con them into a bogus war should qualify as grounds for impeachment, but the boot can't stop at Bush. President "Halliburton" Cheney, anyone? Cheney now stands as the most corrupt American vice president since Spiro Agnew, but immeasurably more dangerous than Agnew ever was. This whole corrupt warmongering administration has to go — and straight to International Criminal Court.

10. Start fresh

The crucial issue here is not that Bush administration members lie or even why they lie, but why the hell we have let them get away with it. We've got to set higher standards for our democracy before it's too late.

NOTES

1. *Diagnostic and Statistical Manual Fourth Edition*, American Psychiatric Association, 2000

2. "Rebuilding America's Defenses: Strategy, Forces and Resources for a New Century," a report of The Project of a New American Century, September 2000, at <www.newamericancentury.org>.

3. "Strategic Energy Policy: Challenges for the 21st Century," James A. Baker III Institute for Public Policy at Rice University (April 2001) at <www.bakerinstitute.org/Pubs/studies/bipp_study_15/study15.pdf>.

4. George W. Bush, "President Bush Outlines Iraq Threat" (Oct. 7, 2002) at <www.whitehouse.gov/news/releases/2002/10/20021007-8.html>.

5. Meet the Press, NBC (March 16, 2003). As noted in "U.S. Officials Make It Clear: Exile or War," *Washington Post* (March 17, 2003).

6. Meet the Press, NBC (September 14, 2003).

7. Department of Defense, "News Briefing" (June 24, 2003) at <www.dod.mil/transcripts/2003/tr20030624-secdef0301.html>.

8. At <www.costofwar.com>.

9. William D. Norhaus, "The Cost of the Iraq War Put in Perspective" The Baltimore Chronicle (September 19, 2003).

10. "Iraq: the missing billions. Transition and transparency in post-war Iraq," *Christian Aid* (October 23, 2003) at <www.christian-aid.org.uk/indepth/310iraqoil/index.htm>.

11. "FAIR study finds democracy poorly served by war coverage," *Fairness & Accuracy in Reporting* (May/June 2003) at <www.fair.org/extra/0305/war study.html>.

12. "Misperceptions, The Media and The Iraq War," PIPA/Knowledge Networks (October 2, 2003) at <www.pipa.org>.

13. FOX News (Sept.23 2003) at <www.foxnews.com/story/0,2933,98111,00.html>.

14. George W. Bush, "President's Remarks at the United Nations General Assembly" (September 12, 2002) at <www.whitehouse.gov/news/releases/2002/09/20020912-1.html>.

15. "President Bush Addresses the Nation" (March 19, 2003) at <www.whitehouse.gov/news/releases/2003/03/20030319-17.html>.

16. "Wolfowitz Says Disarming Iraq Is 'Second Front' in War on Terror," speech to a Veterans of Foreign Wars conference (March 11, 2003) at <www.usembassy.state.gov/tokyo/wwwh20030313a2.html>.

17. "Orwellian Strategy Used to Sell the War," *San Francisco Chronicle* (October 16, 2003).

18. "Revealed: US dirty tricks to win vote on Iraq war," *Observer* (March 2, 2003.

19. George W. Bush, "War on Terror," Presidential Radio Address (March 8, 2003) at <www.whitehouse.gov/news/releases/2003/03/20030308-1.html>.

20. George W. Bush, "State of the Union Address" (January 28, 2003) at <www. whitehouse.gov/news/releases/2003/01/20030128-19.html>.

21.Colin Powell, "United Nations Address" (February 5, 2003) at <www.edition.cnn.com/2003/US/02/05/sprj.irq.powell.transcript.06/index.html)

22. Donald Rumsfield, from "This Week", ABC, (March 30, 2003).

23. Donald Rumsfield, National Press Club speech (September 10, 2003).

24. *Iraq's Weapons of Mass Destruction: The Assessment of the British Government*, 6 (Sept. 24, 2002)

25. George W. Bush, "Remarks by the President on Iraq," The Rose Garden (September 26, 2002) at <www.whitehouse.gov/news/releases/2002/09/20020926-7.html>.

26. Condoleeza Rice, "Why We Know Iraq Is Lying" (January 23, 2003) at <www.whitehouse.gov/news/releases/2003/01/print/20030123-1.html>.

27. George W. Bush, "State of the Union Address" (Jan. 28, 2003).

28. Department of Defense, "News Briefing" (January 29, 2003) at <www.dod.mil/transcripts/2003/t01292003_t0129sd.html>.

29. "The Man Who Knew," CBS News (October 15, 2003) at <www.cbsnews.com/stories/2003/10/14/60II/main577975.shtml>.

30. Article II, Section 4 of The Constitution of the United States of America

PART FIVE:
Summary

50 Most Telling Bush Lies

A list selected by the contributors to this book and Bev Conover, edited by Steven Scholl.

1. Bush and his administration lie about Iraq's alleged weapons of mass destruction (WMDs). The threat was so imminent, the Bush spokesmen constantly told us, that there could be no more time wasted for U.N. inspectors to continue their hunt in Iraq. Mushroom clouds might appear over U.S. cities at any moment; within 45 minutes, British sites could be attacked by biochemical-tipped missiles; Saddam Hussein and his "close" al-Qaeda allies would be sharing all sorts of dastardly secrets; Iraqi drone planes could attack America's East Coast, and so on.

Fact: All lies, all the time, in the service of opinion manipulation. And the lying was effective domestically. However, our rapidly dwindling list of foreign allies, and millions of ordinary citizens protesting around the world, smelled something rotten from the very beginning, and would not go along (Associated Press, "Wolfowitz Comments Revive Doubts Over Iraq's WMD," *USA Today*, May 30, 2003; George Jones, "Blair Hardened Up Iraq Dossier," *Telegraph*, April 7, 2003; Jim Lobe, "Key Officials Used 9/11 As Pretext for Iraq War," *Common Dreams*, July 16, 2003; John McCarthy, "Senators Were Told Iraqi Weapons Could Hit United States," *Florida Today*, December 18, 2003).

2. So there were no nuclear reports, no nuclear weapons, no extant nuclear program. But this didn't stop the Bush Administration from lying. "We believe he has, in fact, reconstituted nuclear weapons," Vice President Cheney said as late as March of 2003. Everyone heard him say it on "Meet the Press" (March 16 telecast) on national television, but the need to lie, almost as instinct, is a difficult one to keep buried, and so, despite such assertions by Cheney and others, Rumsfeld told this whopper a few months later: "I don't believe that anyone that I know in the Administration ever said that Iraq had nuclear weapons."

Fact: These guys are shameless. (Derrrick Z. Jackson, "Cheney's Misspeaking Streak," Boston Globe, September 17, 2003. The above quote from Rumsfield comes from his testimony at a hearing of the Senate's appropriations subcommittee on defense, May 14, 2003).

3. Bush's "16 words of deceit" claiming that Saddam tried to buy uranium (yellowcake) from Niger. "The British government has learned that Saddam Hussein recently sought significant quantities of uranium from Africa" (2003 State of the Union Address).
Fact: The documents on which Bush based this claim were already known to be forgeries — bad forgeries at that. Furthermore, former Ambassador Joseph Wilson, who had been sent to Niger by the CIA to check out whether Saddam had tried to buy yellowcake (milled uranium) from that country, had already made his detailed report saying there was no truth to the allegation (Joseph C. Wilson 4th, "What I Didn't Find in Africa," New York Times, July 6, 2003).

4. Bush lies about Saddam's weapons of mass destruction: "Our intelligence officials estimate that Saddam Hussein had the materials to produce as much as 500 tons of sarin, mustard and VX nerve agent. In such quantities, these chemical agents could also kill untold thousands. He's not accounted for these materials. He has given no evidence that he has destroyed them" (2003 State of the Union Address).
Fact: The entire world now knows that this is the biggest of his lies, a willful act of deception that was the pretext for sending American soliders into harm's way, draining federal coffers of funds for domestic and legitimate foreign relations needs, straining long-standing relationships with traditional allies, and perpetuating hatred and fear of the United States around the world. Despite the reports of the United Nations weapons inspectors that Saddam was cooperating and their inspections had not turned up any weapons, Bush persisted in the lies about Saddam's weapons of mass destruction, even claiming that Saddam had purchased aluminum tubes for this nuclear program, over the protests of experts who said such tubes were not suitable for such a project, and that he had built unmanned drones capable of dropping chemical or biological weapons on the U.S. The drones turned out to be short-range reconnaissance that weren't capable of reaching Iraq's neighbors, much less the U.S., and were incapable of carrying anything. As the WMD lies crumbled, Bush, while continuing the hunt for WMD, began speaking of WMD programs. In his 2004 State of the Union Address, the WMD became "weapons of mass destruction-related program activities."

5. Bush and his team lie in an attempt to link Saddam Hussein to al-Qaeda. With nuclear arms or a full arsenal of chemical and biological weapons, Saddam Hussein could resume his ambitions of conquest in the Middle East and create deadly havoc in that region. And this Congress and the America people must recognize another threat. Evidence from intelligence sources, secret communications, and statements by people now in custody reveal that Saddam Hussein aids and protects terrorists, including members of al-Qaeda. Secretly, and without fingerprints, he could provide one of his hidden weapons to terrorists, or help them develop their own (2003 State of the Union Address).

Fact: Before the invasion, Bush and members of this cabinet repeatedly lied about Saddam harboring al-Qaeda operatives and stated that he might supply them with chemical, biological or nuclear weapons. Several State Department intelligence officers, including Greg Thielmann, who had worked for State's Bureau of Intelligence and Research, plus a United Nation's terrorism committee, refuted those lies. (The Man Who Knew," CBS News, October 15, 2003; and Juan Cole, "Iraq and al-Qaida (Again)," Informed Comment, August 22, 2002).

6. Bush insistently links Saddam to the September 11th attack of the World Trade Center and Pentagon by al-Qaeda. "In his prime-time press conference last week [March 2003], which focused almost solely on Iraq, President Bush mentioned September 11 eight times. He referred to Saddam Hussein many more times than that, often in the same breath with September 11" (*Christian Science Monitor*, March 14, 2003).

Fact: This was a not so subtle propaganda ploy to implant in many Americans' minds that Saddam bore some responsibility for the September 11 attacks. Masterfully, Bush told the media that there was no evidence that Saddam was involved, but by continuing to make references to Saddam and September 11, up to 70 percent of the American people, according to various polls, believed there was a connection ("US public thinks Saddam had role in 9/11," *The Observer*, September 7, 2003).

7. The Bush Administration claims that Saddam Hussein had other WMDs. The Bush administration didn't stop at claiming Hussein had devastating nukes; it also gave detailed accounts of his other chemical and biological WMD. In the months preceding war Bush claimed, "Our intelligence officials estimate that Saddam Hussein had the materials to produce as much as 500 tons of sarin, mustard and VX nerve agent," and Secretary of State Powell insisted, "Iraq today has

a stockpile of between 100 and 500 tons of chemical weapons agent" (State of the Union Address 2003; also see Colin Powell's United Nations Address, February 5, 2003).

Fact: Of course, nothing of the kind has been found.

8. Bush War claims that Iraq was invaded for the benefit of Iraqis. When bombs started dropping on Baghdad in March 2003, Bush claimed the war was "to disarm Iraq" and "to free its people" (President Bush Addresses the Nation, March 19, 2003).

Fact: While thousands of Iraqi civilian casualties and the subsequent ham-fisted U.S. occupation have proven him wrong, it's unfair to say there have been no post-war beneficiaries. Dick Cheney's Halliburton, for example, has made a fortune from no-bid contracts, and the US provisional authority has somehow misplaced billions of dollars of Iraqi money earmarked for reconstruction. Bush himself has benefited not only from his poseur fly-boy Commander role, but also from the fact that nasty questions about the troubled US economy and White House connections to corporate scandals have faded with wartime distraction (Mike Allen and James V. Grimaldi, "Halliburton Probe Is Growing Worry for Bush, Hill Republicans," *Washington Post*, July 20, 2002; also see "Iraq: the missing billions: Transition and transparency in post-war Iraq," *Christian Aid*, October 23, 2003).

9. After a short conflict, U.S. forces would be warmly welcomed by the Iraqis. Rosy scenarios about post-war Iraq were professed by top administration officials such as Deputy Defense Secretary Wolfowitz, who said, "Like the people of France in the 1940s, the Iraqis view us as their hoped-for liberator." Vice President Cheney echoed the "liberators" theme, predicting the conflict would last "weeks rather than months" (Wolfowitz Says Disarming Iraq Is "Second Front" in War on Terror, speech to a Veterans of Foreign Wars conference, March 11, 2003).

Fact: Iraq remains a political disaster under U.S. occupation and the Bush nation-building plan seems to have an astounding ignorance of the perils involved in dealing with a deeply divided Iraqi society. Divisions between Kurds, Shi'ites and Sunnis are complex. Attacks on U.S. and coalition forces now occur daily while attacks on civilians who appear to be working with U.S. interests are escalating. Unrest is growing and it looks as though George W. Bush's fantasy of a short interim between invasion and founding of a truly democratic Iraq will not materialize. Remember that his father promised a democratic Kuwait following his foray into Iraq in 1991. (Juan Cole, "The Risks of Peace and The Costs of War," *Journal of the International Institute*, Winter 2003.)

10. In 2003, Bush claimed that the nation's top economists forecast substantial economic growth if Congress passed the president's tax cut.

Fact: "The forecast with that conclusion doesn't exist. Bush and White House Press Secretary Ari Fleischer went out of their way . . . to cite a new survey by 'Blue-Chip economists' that the economy would grow 3.3 percent this year if the president's tax cut proposal becomes law. That was news to the editor who assembles the economic forecast. 'I don't know what he was citing,' said Randell E. Moore, editor of the monthly *Blue Chip Economic Forecst*, a newsletter that surveys 53 of the nation's top economists each month. 'I was a little upset,' said Moore, who said he complained to the White House. 'It sounded like the *Blue Chip Economic Forecast* had endorsed the president's plan. That's simply not the case'" (*Newsday,* February 24, 2003).

11. "A balanced federal budget remains a high priority of the president" (Bush administration budget director Michael E. Daniels, Jr. (New York Times, February 4, 2003).

Fact: "The budget differs from those of other recent presidents in two important ways. Nowhere does Mr. Bush make balancing the budget an important goal. And he makes no claim that the era of big government is over, or even nearing an end. "This is a president of big projects and big ideas," his budget director, Mitchell E. Daniels Jr., said today . . . Paying no heed to the notion of a balanced budget, Mr. Bush advocates deep tax cuts on top of the large ones enacted two years ago. By contrast, when big deficits began to appear after President Ronald Reagan drove tax cuts through Congress in 1981, Mr. Reagan approved offsetting tax increases . . . Mr. Daniels said this morning, "A balanced federal budget remains a high priority for this president." But unlike the submissions of recent predecessors, this budget describes no plans to reach that goal" (*New York Times*, February 4, 2003).

12. "Bush opened his final radio address of 2002 with these lies: 'In 2002, our economy was still recovering from the attacks of September the 11th, 2001, and it was pulling out of a recession that began before I took office.' Bush concluded 2002 with the same dishonesty that defined his economic policy throughout the year-a mendacity that ranged from denying the tax cut had anything to do with the re-emergence of the deficit to arguing that the terrorism insurance bill would create 300,000 construction jobs" (Daniel Gross, *Slate*, December 30, 2002).

Fact: There is no evidence that the economy was in recession when

President Bush took the oath of office on Jan. 20, 2001:

"[To define a recession,] economists rely on the. . . measurements of the National Bureau of Economic Research, the official arbiter of recessions and expansions. NBER has been run since 1977 by Harvard economist Martin Feldstein, an architect of the Bush tax cut and an intellectual mentor to many prominent Republican policy-makers.

"The current President Bush is probably not conversant with NBER's 'recession dating procedures.' But it's a sure thing his economic and political advisers are. So shame on them for feeding him dishonest lines" (Daniel Gross, Slate, December 30, 2002).

13. Bush lies about the the value of "a trillion."
Fact: "Call it a 'Bush trillion.' It's a sum that is either much more or much less than $1 trillion—whichever is convenient—but one that George W. Bush thinks he can get away with calling 'a trillion dollars' in speeches. During the campaign Mr. Bush, to emphasize his moderation, claimed that he was matching a trillion dollars in tax cuts with a trillion dollars of new spending. In fact he proposed less than half a trillion in new programs, and now he proposes no real increase in spending at all. The tax cut, on the other hand, turns out to be $1.6 trillion, except that it's really $2 trillion once you count the interest costs. And it will be $2.5 trillion if it is accelerated, something Mr. Bush has urged but not factored into his numbers, and if a major wrinkle involving the alternative minimum tax is ironed out. Meanwhile Mr. Bush has come up with another trillion, this time his 'trillion-dollar contingency fund.' It comes as no surprise that the actual number in his budget is only a bit more than $800 billion. And more than half of that consists of funds that Medicare was supposed to be setting aside for the needs of an aging population. So maybe we also need to define a 'Bush contingency,' as in: 'Gee, people might get older, and they might have medical expenses. We can't be sure—but it could happen'" (Paul Krugman, *New York Times*, March 7, 2001).

14. Global warming has not been proven and needs further study.
Fact: Global warming is an accepted fact by scientists in the United States and throughout the world. "Further study" has simply provided more confirming evidence and refinements (National Academy of Sciences: "Leading Climate Scientists Advise White House on Global Warming," Press Release, June 6, 2001; Paul Harris, "Bush Covers Up Climate Research," *The Observer* (UK), September 21, 2003).

15. The air in downtown Manhattan immediately after 9/11 was safe.
Fact: The EPA said otherwise in a report prepared shortly after the at-

tacks on 9/11. In that report, New Yorkers were warned of the health dangers posed by the dust and particulates resulting from the collapse of the World Trade Center towers (Marie Cocco, "White House Deceit Covered Up 9/11 Truths," *Newsday*, August 28, 2003; Juan Gonzales, "It's public be damned at the EPA," *New York Daily News*, August 26, 2003).

16. Bush's EPA Administrator Christy Todd Whitman claimed the nation has made significant progress in protecting water resources, implying that such 'progress" was occurring under the Bush administration.
Fact: This claim by Whitman, ended with the words: "in the last 30 years." On the face, this is true. But the statement was intended to convey the falsehood that this "progress" was continuing and would continue under the Bush Administration. In fact, the Administration has proposed to remove 20% of the wetlands from federal protection, and the easing of air pollution standards will reverse recent progress in reducing acid rain pollution in the northeastern waterways. (Osha Gray Davidson, "Dirty Secrets," *Mother Jones*, September/October 2003; Ted Williams, "Down Upon the Suwannee River," *Mother Jones*, September/ October 2003).

17. Oil development will not harm the Arctic National Wildlife Refuge.
Fact: In 2002, the US Geological Survey released the findings of a twelve year study, which concluded that oil exploration would in fact adversely affect the habitat of the area. Interior Secretary Norton then ordered a "reassessment" which, after one week, contradicted the USGS conclusions ("US Rejects Study by its Own Arctic Scientists, *Seattle Post-Intelligencer*, March 20, 2002).

18. Bush will protect our forests with his "Healthy Forests Initiative."
Fact: In April, 2003, Governor Davis of California requested $430 million of emergency funds to remove dead and diseased trees from the acutely threatened southern California forests. The request was denied the day before the devastating fires broke out in the San Bernardino mountains. "Healthy Forests" is, in fact, an invitation to the logging industry to take healthy trees from the national forests (Robert Salladay and Zachary Coile, "Bush ignored pleas for funds that could have prevented Clifornia fires, *San Francisco Chronicle*, October 31, 2003; Edward O. Wilson, "Bush's Forest Plan Worse than Fire, *Newsday*, August 29, 2003.)

19. Environmental regulations damage the economy and costs jobs.
Fact: On the contrary, the Office of Management and Budget reports that "the health and social benefits of enforcing tough new clean-air regulations during the past decade were five to seven times greater in economic terms than were the costs of complying with the rules" (Eric Pianin, "Study Finds Net Gain From Pollution Rules," *Washington Post*, September 27, 2003).

20. Bush lied about Bioterrorism. Smallpox and anthrax were deliberately chosen to reinforce propaganda designed to justify preemptive war against Iraq by such charades as Secretary of State Colin Powell dramatically holding aloft a vial of faux anthrax bacillus proclaiming "if this were filled with anthrax such as Saddam Hussein has hidden, it could kill millions." Eventually the administration focused on smallpox as the bioweapon of choice. Bush and the Republican Congress negotiated a deal to stockpile 250 million doses of smallpox vaccine-enough to vaccinate the entire U.S. population.
Fact: The six-member crew sent to Iraq with the specific assignment to search for any sign of smallpox, officially stated in its report, "we found no physical or new anecdotal evidence to suggest that Iraq was producing smallpox or had stocks of it in [its] possession" (Secretary Colin Powell, Presentation before U.N. Security Council, February 5, 2003; D. Linzer, "Team pox finds no smallpox in Iraq," September 19, 2003, Associated Press).

21. Bush lied about AIDS Prevention: In his January 2003 State of the Union address, George Bush announced the Emergency Plan for AIDS Relief, a five-year, $15 billion initiative to turn the tide in the global effort to combat the HIV/AIDS epidemic. In July, he asked Congress for only $2 billion with specific stipulations requiring that one-third of the AIDS prevention funds be spent on the Sexual Abstinence until Marriage Program.
The promises made to fight the AIDs epidemic that has killed 7.5 million Africans since 2001 are unfulfilled because the Bush Administration underfunded its own program by $1 billion the first year and placed unrealistic restrictions on funds provided. The *Wall Street Journal* recently reported that Bush intends to further step back from his commitment to fight AIDS and poverty in developing countries (AIDS/HIV Prevention Program, www.whitehouse.gov; N. D. Kristof, "When Prudery Kills," *New York Times*, October 8 2003; *Wall Street Journal*, December 10, 2003).

22. Bush is the self-described "Education President" and his campaign promotes his tenure as Texas Governor, when Bush created an education miracle.
Fact: Bush's "Texas miracle" was at best a "mirage." Two separate studies have concluded that Texas test score improvements weren't reflected when students took national tests (the NAEP and the Stanford Achievement Test). Moreover, Texas test scores were artificially raised by encouraging low-performing students to leave school and cooking the books to alter the dropout rates (Diana Jean Schemo and Ford Fessenden, "A Miracle Revisited: Gains in Houston Schools: How Real Are They?" *New York Times*, December 3, 2003; Molly Ivins and Lou Dubose, *Bushwhacked*, New York: Random House, 2003, pp. 72-96).

23. Bush's "budget for next year [2004] boosts funding for elementary and secondary education to $53.1 billion. That's a 26-percent increase since I took office."
Fact: The $53.1 billion figure actually represents Bush's total proposed education budget, whereas the elementary and secondary education components are only $34.9 billion. Moreover, not only is there no increase in 2004 overall education spending over 2003, but elementary and secondary education are actually cut by close to a billion dollars (George W. Bush, Sept. 28, 2003, Tennessee speech; David Corn, "Capital Games," *The Nation*, September 15, 2003.)

24. Bush reforms promote children's reading programs and literacy.
Fact: Bush made Even Start literacy program cuts and teacher training cuts and he proposed to de-federalize Head Start. Moreover, states have been lowering their education standards in order to avoid NCLB sanctions (George W. Bush, Hyde Park Elementary, Jacksonville, Florida, September 9, 2003; Senator Christopher J. Dodd, "Bush Has Left Education Reform Behind," *Hartford Courant*, May 12, 2002).

25. In the 2000 Presidential campaign, Al Gore was slandered as a "serial liar" and a "self promoter." Examples? He claimed, among other things, to have "invented the internet," and to have "discovered the Love Canal toxic waste site."
Fact: The "lies" were made by the GOP campaign. Gore never made such claims, and one is hard-pressed to find any examples of deliberate lying in his public record (Molly Dickerson: "Who's lying, Gore or the media?" TomPaine.com, October 8, 2000; Robert Parry, "He's no Pinnochio," *Washington Monthly*, April, 2000; Eric Boehlert, "Gore's too-willing executioners," Salon, October 27, 2000).

26. Bush: Said he found Gore's tendency to exaggerate "an issue in trying to defend my tax relief package. There was some exaggeration about the numbers" in the first debate.
Fact: "No, there wasn't, and Bush himself acknowledged that the next day on ABC's "Good Morning America" when Charlie Gibson pinned him on it" (Salon, October 12, 2000).

27. The decision of Bush v. Gore was beyond reproach.
Fact: The Supreme Court issued a political decision in December 2000 that awarded a presidential election to the candidate who was clearly losing. The decision was made in order to "protect" the voters of the state of Florida by prohibiting the count of every vote. At least three justices were in violation of several statutes contained in 28 USC 455 of the Judicial and Judiciary Procedure in regards to conflict of interest (Alan Dershowitz, *Supreme Injustice*, Oxford University Press, 2001; Vincent Bugliosi, "None Dare Call it Treason," *The Nation*, February 2001).

28. Condoleezza Rice, Bush's national-security advisor, asserted that Bush/Cheney and their national-security team had no idea that hijacked airplanes might be used as weapons.
Fact: The key Bush folks knew of that likelihood well in advance of the 9/11 attacks—thanks not only to briefings they'd received from the outgoing Clinton national-security team about the huge dangers posed by Osama bin Laden, but more specifically because of the voluminous warnings, many quite detailed as to airplanes and possible targets, pouring in from a wide variety of foreign intelligence agencies. However, they chose to do nothing with their foreknowledge (Margaret Warner Interview with Condoleeza Rice, "Rice On Iraq, War and Politics," on "The NewsHour with Jim Lehrer," September 25, 2002; "What Bush Knew Before Sept. 11," CBS News Report, May 17, 2002).

29. Justices Anton Scalia and Clarence Thomas are "strict constructionalists."
Fact: Scalia and Thomas, Supreme Court justice that Bush admires, are two of the most outspoken ideologues on the far right. Justice Thomas has publicly declared the need for an ideological war in defense of a far right agenda and the need for conservatives to cease what he perceives as an "overemphasis on civility." Scalia holds deep religious convictions and stated openly that a person's religious beliefs should be the basis in all decisions and that "the State should be subservient to the Church." He once remarked in a speech that any judge who opposed the death penalty on moral grounds should "step down" (Robert Scheer, A Moder-

ate Wouldn't Make Appointments Like These," *The Nation*, February 20, 2000; Sean Wilentz, "From Justice Scalia, a Chilling Vision of Religion's Authority in America," *New York Times*, July 8, 2002).

30. The Democratic opposition in the Senate is "playing politics" over "qualified" nominees.
Fact: Although it is common practice for the minority party to accuse the party in power of "playing politics," it is hypocritical for the Republican majority under Bush to make such a claim. The 106th Congress under Clinton has the worst record in regards to speed in holding hearings for judicial nominees. As of this writing Bush has had 168 of his nominees approved and only 4 have been blocked. One of GOP's largest complaints is the alleged "unfair" treatment of Bush nominee, Miguel Estrada. A member of several right-wing activist groups, Estrada was consistently vague concerning his positions on many subjects during his confirmation hearings. The conflict over his nomination only grew when the White House rejected any release of opinion papers to the Senate Committee which Estrada may have written. The Democratic minority was expected to accept Estrada's "qualifications" on the basis that Bush and the Republican senators said he was "qualified." When Democrats refused to blindly go along and confirm Estrada, the Republicans accused them of "playing politics" and being anti-Hispanic—even though prominent Hispanic organizations such as the Puerto Rican Legal Defense and Education Fund and the Congressional Hispanic Caucus opposed Mr. Estrada's nomination (John Rossomando, "Senators Allege Politicizing of Judicial Appointments," *Christian Science Monitor*, July 2, 2001; Gail Russell Chaddock, "What Estrada's exit means for future battles" *Christian Science Monitor*, September 5, 2003; see also the American Bar Association web site at <www.abanet.org/poladv/priorities/jud>).

31. In 2001, White House officials said that they were not involved with an effort to allow religious charities to practice anti-gay workplace bias.
Fact: But they later admitted chief aide Karl Rove was involved. An unnamed White House official also said that Don Eberly, deputy director of the White House Office of Faith-Based and Community Initiatives, had given the Salvation Army "an implicit understanding" that the administration would seriously consider allowing the anti-gay policy (*Washington Post*, July 12, 2001).

32. Bush claims: "I strongly respect the separation of church and state" (Press Conference by the President, February 22, 2003).

Fact: Bush has challenged the separation between church and state like no other President in modern times. The Bush administration has screened nominees to ensure that they share the President's evangelic world view despite a Constitutional prohibition against religious tests for any public office, made judgments about which faiths are legitimate or not and failed to adhere to Constitutional limitations in implementing the Faith-Based Initiative (Joaquin Cabrejas, "Bush, The New Face of the Religious Right, *American Humanist Association*, pp. 18-19, 2002); Wendy Kaminer, "Faith-Based Favoritism," *The American Prospect*, April 9, 2001; Alan Cooperman, "White House Aide Angers Pagans," *Washington Post*, December 8, 2003).

33. President Bush cancelled $34 million in funding to the U.N. Population Fund on the basis that the money was being used for forced abortions in China.
Fact: Bush's decision ignores the findings of both a UN and State Department study that found no evidence the funds were being used for this purpose. Bush relied on this false claim to justify his pandering to the Christian Right (Joaquin Cabrejas, "Bush: The New Face of the Religious Right," American Humanist Association, 2002).

34. There exists "widespread bias against faith-based organizations ["FBO's"] in Federal social service programs" which includes violating FBO's "fundamental civil right" to discriminate in hiring based on religion, sexual preference and other grounds if "important to its religious identity" ("Protecting the Civil Rights and Religious Liberty of Faith-Based Organization: Why Religious Hiring Rights Must Be Preserved," *White House Office of Faith-Based and Community Initiatives*, 2003 and "Centers for Faith-Based and Community Initiatives, Unlevel Playing Field: Barriers to Participation by Faith-Based and Community Organizations in Federal Social Service Programs," January 29, 2001).
Fact: "FBO's have qualified for millions in federal grants and experienced FBO's stated "quite unequivocally . . . that we have not encountered restrictive conditions as a result of our religious orientation and our religious affiliation" (The Pew Forum on Religion in Public Life, *Lift Every Voice: A Report on Religion in American Public Life*, 2001). Independent studies confirmed the absence of barriers to FBO's participation in government programs" (Ira C. Lupu and Robert W. Tuttle, "Government Partnerships with Faith-Based Service Providers: The State of the Law," *The Roundtable on Religion and Social Welfare Policy*, 2002). There also is "no hard evidence that hiring requirements are keeping [FBO's] from apply-

ing for government contracts" (Jane Eisner, "Far from Promised Land, Faith Initiatives Are Starving," *Philadelphia Inquirer*, July 6, 2003).

35. Bush says: Investing some Social Security money "under safe guidelines . . . gets a better rate of return than the paltry 2 percent that the federal governmen gets for you today."
Fact: According to Paul Krugman that rate of return "ignores a multitrillion-dollar debt [created from taking that money out of Social Security] that somebody has to pay" and Bush has not accounted for (*New York Times*, September 13, 2000).

36. "Bush also got himself onto shaky ground when he accused the Clinton–Gore administration of failing to deliver a middle-class tax cut."
Fact: "The [Clinton] administration negotiated a budget bill with the Republican Congress in 1997 that included a children's tax credit that reduced taxes for the middle class." (E.J. Dionne, Jr., *Houston Chronicle*, October 18, 2000).

37. Bush: "Bush said the number of uninsured Americans has been rising for seven years."
Fact: "The number declined in 1999 for the first time since the Census Bureau began collecting data in 1987, according to a federal report last month. About 42.5 million people, or 15.5 percent of the population, lacked insurance in 1999, compared with 44.2 million, or 16.3 percent, in 1998, the Census Bureau reported" (*Washington Post*, October 18, 2000).

38. "Bush, who opposes a national health insurance program, says the Clinton administration pushed such a plan in 1993."
Fact: "While the Clinton administration did propose an overhaul of the nation's health care system, it would not have been a national health care system like the government-run programs in other countries. Instead, it would have required employers to offer workers insurance, or pay into a fund to cover them, while creating a system of purchasing pools for businesses and individuals to buy coverage" (*USA Today*, October 18, 2000).

39. Bush: "You can quote all the numbers you want but I'm telling you we care about our people in Texas. We spent a lot of money to make sure people get healthcare in the state of Texas" (Transcript, Commission on Presidential Debates, "The Second 2000 Gore-Bush Presidential Debate," October 11, 2000).
Fact: Gore had correctly noted that Texas ranks 49th out of the 50 states

in healthcare in children with healthcare, 49th for women with healthcare and 50th for families with healthcare.

40. Bush: said he favored "equal" rights for gays and lesbians, but not "special" rights.
Fact: "Bush has supported a Texas law that allows the state to take adopted children from gay and lesbian couples to place the kids with straight couples." Salon, 10/12/00. "Bush supports hate crime protections for other minorities! So Bush doesn't believe that gays should have the same "special" rights in this regard as blacks, Jews, Wiccans and others. Employment discrimination? Again, Bush supports those rights for other Americans, but not gays. Military service? Bush again supports the right to military service for all qualified people—as long as they don't tell anyone they're gay. Marriage? How on earth is that a special right when every heterosexual in America already has it? But again, Bush thinks it should be out-of-bounds for gays. What else is there? The right to privacy? Nuh-huh. Bush supports a gays-only sodomy law in his own state that criminalizes consensual sex in private between two homosexuals (*New Republic*, October 13, 2000).

41. Bush: "Bragged that in Texas he was signing up children for the Children's Health Insurance Program (CHIP) as "fast as any other state."
Fact: "As governor he fought to unsuccessfully to limit access to the program. He would have limited its coverage to children with family incomes up to 150 percent of the poverty level, though federal law permitted up to 200 percent. The practical effect of Bush's efforts would have been to exclude 200,000 of the 500,000 possible enrollees" (*Washington Post*, October 12, 2000).

42. Bush: "We ought to do everything we can to end racial profiling."
Fact: "The Texas Department of Public Safety has just this year begun keeping detailed information about the race and sex of all people stopped by its troopers, the sixth year Bush has been in office" (Salon, October 12, 2000).

43. Bush: "Some of the scientists, I believe, Mr. Vice President, haven't they been changing their opinion a little bit on global warming?"
Fact: "Bush's dismissive comments about global warming could bolster the charge that he and fellow oilman Dick Cheney are in the pocket of the oil industry, which likewise pooh-poohs the issue. [While] there is no

consensus about the impact of global warming, . . . most scientists agree that humans are contributing to the rising global temperature. "Most climate experts are certain that global warming is real and that it threatens ecology and human prosperity, and a growing number say it is well under way," wrote *New York Times* science writer Andrew Revkin" (Salon, October 13, 2000).

44. Bush: "We're one of the first states that said you can sue an HMO for denying you proper coverage."
Fact: Here is a typical lie of ommission: "He did not say that he strongly considered vetoing the bill that subjected HMOs to malpractice suits and eventually, facing the prospect of having his veto overridden, allowed the measure to become law without his signature" (*Washington Post*, October 18, 2000).

45. Bush stated that prescription drug coverage should be "an integral part of Medicare."
Fact: "An odd description of his plan, which is notable for encouraging private-sector choices that may be outside the Medicare system." (*Washington Post*, October 18, 2000)

46. Bush: "Bush boasted that since he has been governor, violent crime in Texas has gone down."
Fact: "Just this week, the latest federal statistics, comparing 1999 with 1998 crime, show that all crime increased in 12 large Texas cities" (*Boston Globe*, October 18, 2000).

47. Bush on jobs: "President Bush released a personally signed report promising that his economic plan would create 2.6 million new jobs by 2004."
Fact: "When data suggested that this would no be possible, he 'distanced himself' from the report and 'declined to endorse the jobs estimate' publically during an Oval office appearance. Now, with a new jobs report showing that his economic program continues to fall short, the president has resorted to outright dishonesty. Specifically, the president deployed Labor Secretary Blaine Chao to Capital Hill last week [early March 2004] to claim that he never actually signed the report. She told lawmakers that the president 'doesn't sign this report'" (*The Daily Mis-Lead*, March 9, 2004).

48. Bush lies on the 2004 presidential campaign trail, distorting John Kerry's voting record in the Senate.
Fact: "Voters are entitled to a minimum level of honesty . . . on that score, Mr. Bush's initial [campaign ad] attacks fall short. For example,

the respective views of the two candidates on the proper use of intelligence in the war on terrorism are a legitimate — indeed a critical — issues in the first election of the president after September 11, 2001. Yet Mr. Bush's attack on a Kerry proposal nine years ago to cut the intelligence budget does more to distort than to illuminate. When Mr. Kerry prposed a $1.5 billion cut over five years in the intelligence budget, the United Sates was reaping the "peace dividend" from the Cold War, and the center of congressional debate was not whether cuts could be made but how much could be cut from Pentagon and CIA spending. Mr. Kerry's proposed 1 percent cut was not 'gutting,' as Mr. Bush alleged." (Editorial, *Washington Post*, March 14, 2004).

49. Further lies along the early campaign trail came when the Bush team created fake news reports to tout the Bush administration's controversial new Medicare law.

Fact: "Federal investigators are scrutinizing television segments in which the Bush administration paid people to pose as journalists praising the beneifts of the new Medicare law . . . The videos are intended for use in local television news programs. The materials were producded by the Department of Health and Human Services, which called them video news releases, but the source is not idenitfied. Two videos end with the voice of a woman who says, 'In Washington, I'm Karen Ryan reporting.' But the production company, Home Front Communications, said that it had hired her to read a script prepared by the government. . . One question is whether the government might mislead viewers by concealing the source of the Medicare videos, which might have been broadcast by stations in Oklahoma, Louisiana and other states. Ferderal law prohibits the use of federal moeny for "publicity of propaganda purpose" not authorized by Congress" (*New York Times*, March 15, 2004).

50. The lies that led to the invasion of Iraq bring down Bush's Spanish ally and weaken the already weak "coalition" forces. The new Spanish prime minister is outspoken in his estimation of Bush.

Fact: "Spain's incoming Socialist Prime Minister, JoseLuis Rodriguez Zapatero, the unexpected victor in . . . [the] general election, launched a withering attack on Tony Blair and George Bush yesterday over their decision to go to war in Iraq. Announcing that the 1,300 Spanish troops currently stationed in Iraq would be pulled out by summer, the quiet spoken leader declared: 'You can't organize a war with lies. Mr Blair and Mr. Bush must do some reflection and self-criticism,' he added in remarkably frank comments for the next prime minister of Europe's youngest democracy and the fifth largest economy." (*Independent*, March 16, 2004).

Bush and the American Experience

BY KENT SOUTHARD

Not that I'm asking you to care especially, but it's been an eventful last few years for me. First, I managed to unblock memories of child abuse —funny how the human mind works, how the child tries to survive un-bearable treatment by pretending it didn't happen, and packing it into a little A-bomb timed to detonate in middle age. Apparently post-divorce, and through circumstances beyond the control of my dear Mom, I had the type of childhood which typically produces serial killers and/or right-wing radicals. It was a mighty struggle, but through force of character and the grace of God, I managed to avoid both those fates.

Next there were the layoffs—my employer, which never had a layoff in its hundred-year history since its founding by Alexander Graham Bell, laid off two-thirds of the company, yours truly included. De-regulation of the telecom industry had allowed the speculative building of vastly more network capacity than can probably be used in my lifetime, and a lot of major players got seriously over-extended in their debt. Hundreds of thousands of careers were ruined, trillions of investor's dollars vapor-ized—remember this whenever some conservative goes on about "the superior and efficient allocation of resources by the free market."

And lastly, the woman I loved was lost to cancer. You work for years to not settle, to be worthy of true love, and then you finally meet your completely perfect soul mate and there seems to be a clock ticking. The last months, you spend a lot of time in sterile hospital rooms, talking about how good the food is and what's on cable. Various personnel come and go like so many busboys, and you can't help but hate having this pre-cious individuality set down amid this indifferent routine. And then fi-nally, she's back home, in some strange medical bed, and there are only minutes left. And then, in early afternoon, there are none.

So, like I say, I've got things to deal with. But there's something more, something that's overshadowed everything else in my life, some-thing of greater importance. To all those that carry America in their hearts, the actions of the U.S. Supreme Court on behalf of George W. Bush were a rending of the fabric of history: "There's no such thing in the constitution as the right to vote for president," said Antonin Scalia the first time the Florida case came before the court, and a week later he acted on those words, stopping the vote count in such an expressed way as to make a continuation impossible. In one motion, the complete nature of the Bush coup was revealed—not only did might make right, at home and soon abroad, but it was announced that they did not recognize the legitimacy of the democratic principle itself. Later, Scalia would be quoted as saying 'democracy observes the divine authority of government.'

It was as if the ground beneath our feet vanished into thin air, the solid ground we assumed had been the bedrock of our country. Somehow, through the infernal mechanism of the 'conservative' movement's opinion making machine of pundits and broadcast empires, they seem to have taken ownership of the concept of American 'exceptionalism.' Why this would be so is a mystery, when the powers they represent have stood steadfast against every expansion of liberty ever accomplished in our history. They have no right to claim ownership, for their hearts seem completely blind to what America truly is. America is the first country in human history to have liberty and democracy as its reason for existence —and without them, we don't have our country.

Words have meaning, conservative pundits like to say, and so they do —but we need to realize the meanings this conservative movement gives to words have nothing to do with how the rest of us traditionally understand them. Freedom, liberty, and democracy, to conservatives, only refer to the power that accrues to money. This is something Kevin Phillips talks about, if you've ever heard him interviewed. Kevin Phillips, as a young man in the Nixon administration, invented the GOP's Southern Strategy, wherein the party of elite money crafted its popular appeal (once directed at the educated middle class) around the obdurate resentments and reactionarism of the Old South. He thought himself quite the clever young man at the time, but now he says he didn't realize the Republican party's "needle always seems to gravitate towards big money and its wants."

So the agenda brought with such naked force by the Bush coup is apparently a familiar, if latent one, in American history. Two hundred years ago, when the presidency of Thomas Jefferson turned back Alexander Hamilton's Federalist movement, we assumed the issue had been settled in favor of democracy. Hamilton thought the country should be run as a dictatorship on behalf of the rich; and so the modern conservative movement gives the Federalist name to their legal society —membership in which seems a requirement for Bush's judicial appointees.

Our top Marine general of the early 20th century, Gen. Smedley Butler, closed his career with a book entitled *War is a Racket*. Butler compared himself to Al Capone, candidly listing all the countries he had subdued on behalf of which corporate interests.

The shock of the Bush administration lies in its embodiment of all that's worst in our history, and it's careful and explicit repudiation of all that's best.

Much shock ensues also, of course, due to the surpassing strangeness of the person of George W. Bush himself. In one sense he's of a fairly common type, at least in the circles he was born into—a country club alcoholic from a young age, filled with brittle and unearned opinion, whose all-encompassing sense of entitlement would seem to preclude even the slightest self-doubt. (His brothers are all some version of the same thing.) The public Bush oscillates between a salesman's schmooze and an unfathomable bitterness; early in the administration before he was as tightly edited visually as well as verbally, we could catch glimpses of extreme pathology. Sitting next to Clinton on Inauguration Day, Bush's feet continually bounced on the floor like a spastic. Other times he sways as if in a breeze unfelt by others, or his face can register what can only be described as "being out to lunch." He often seems possessed of a surreal serenity, most often when circumstances would least warrant it—like when he's about to invade Iraq against the opinion of the entire world. Bush brings to mind the critic John Simon's description of Doris Day" a "personality untouched by human emotions, her brow unclouded by human thought."

(I rather imagine that with George W. Bush, we have our first Prozac President. In fact, I imagine the whole administration's on it or something similar. The common rap on this stuff, to which I can add my personal experience, is that "it takes away your depth." It puts a cheezy sheen in your mind, whatever's in it. You could be Jeffrey Dahmer and not change your behavior a bit, because on Prozac there are no worries, regardless.)

The shock produced by the Bush administration has been deepened by the fact of the complicity of our national media. From the 2000 campaign itself, where no attention was paid to such available scandals as Bush's crooked business deals and military desertion; to the theft of the election itself; to the self-evident fraudulent accounting behind his tax cuts; to the black hole of secrecy surrounding 9/11; to the readily available truth regarding Saddam Hussein's 'weapons of mass destruction' - the trademark experience of life in America under the Bush administration is that this White House lies through its teeth about absolutely everything, while the national media does little to challenge it. The few of our better newspapers may report the truth, here and there, but they don't headline it. A few Internet web sites, most notably Bushwatch, have collated these news sources to produce a truthful narrative of Bush's lies — a narrative absent from the broadcast world where most people get their news. It is to the great credit of so many people of this country that they have mounted a stiff resistance, if only in their minds and backbone, in the face of such a strategic onslaught of pure propaganda.

But perhaps the final shock produced by the Bush experience, and maybe the biggest, is how so many of our fellow citizens fervently embrace the Bush agenda in all its fascistic anti-American totality, even when confronted with the truth. None of the Bushphenomena, the bald lies, the naked aggression, and brute force, could have been possible without a receptivity for it.

I wouldn't be the first to suggest that what we're witnessing is the continuation of the culture wars of the 60's. In most important ways, it seems time has hardly moved at all since then. It seems to me the essence of that time was that corporate domination of our society began to be felt at the personal level absolutely everywhere, and there was no longer any escape from it. When Henry Ford first set up his production line he found he was losing workers after only a couple of weeks, because the boredom and sheer character-draining tedium of the work was such that a worker would simply quit and return to the family farm. By the '60s, there were no longer any family farms to return to in any appreciable numbers; and increasingly, there were no longer any family businesses. Corporate employment became the complete context of our life. (Forty years on, we seem to shop in 'Big Box' stores or not at all; independent recording studios of distinction and historical import, such as A&M are brought up and shattered. Publishers close out their 'small press' labels, while Clear Channel has enacted the first rule of all revolutionaries: take over the radio stations—never again will a generation be radicalized by anit-war anthems heard on the radio. Corporate dominance seems total—and now in the Bush economy, the corporations have had a 'recovery' unfelt by us mere workers and citizens. Surveys of home employment show an increase in the number of the self-employed, and perhaps among the most resourceful of us, that's true. But it also reflects a lot of former professionals who are now $200 a month 'consultants.')

Conservatives point to the social rebellions of the '60s as the cause of the breakdown in our families and social fabric—but they've got it exactly backwards. It was the corporate world that demanded that the father give the corporation primary loyalty over his family, that came to reward an attitude of neglect towards wife and family. It wasn't the counter-culture that created our current male paradigm, that perfectly mirrors the legal "personhood" of the corporate entity itself—claiming all the rights of citizenship but none of the responsibilities. Current alleged "Christian" movements, such as Promise Keepers, keep this model intact—the thrust is all towards returning the male to his position of "authority," which his family is supposed to automatically respect, regardless of whether he actually performs his duties to his family.

It's said that under the Soviet totalitarian occupation of Eastern Europe, "free love" was experienced as a form of personal freedom, an experience of personal protest. I feel something similar took place here in the '60s, with the exception that our totalitarianism was corporate in nature. I went to a poetry reading a few years back, a poetry slam, just to see what was out there. It struck me that each and every poet, and virtually every poem, dwelled on the experience of discovering one's sense of inviolable self through sex. It occurred to me that the left in our country, or at least much of the counter-culture that rose in opposition to our corporate domination, has remained a bit stuck in that particular moment of self-discovery. (I'm not saying the country didn't need a little loosening up—the soul and dark heart of the conservative movement seems to have been shaped by lightless repression and sexual hysteria.)

It was at my 10th college class reunion in the mid-'80s that I noticed something about my fellow boomers—an odd thickening that seemed out of place in supposedly educated people only in their early 30s. It was of a quality different from the mere addition of a few pounds, though that was in plain evidence, too. There was a sudden and startling opacity, a rigid inflexibility. The willful blindness of this mindset is illustrated by an exchange a few years later with someone I'd known from schooldays: this individual, otherwise a very fine fellow, told the story of how back at private school, he and his brothers used to drive around the black parts of that midwest city, giving people the finger and shouting "Fucking Nigger!" He said when a brother tried this in Los Angeles, a black man got out of his car with a gun. I commented "It's just not safe to be a racist in LA." Later I heard from this guy that I was "really opinionated."

This obduracy has become much the national style, and the perfect fit for George W. Bush.

It seems to me that the rebellions of the '60s were of such a shapeless and inarticulate quality, helped along by an education system that seemed to work against articulation, that they were doomed to failure. It was as if the country was striving to escape the gravitational pull of corporate conformity and domination, but lacking the understanding to do so, we couldn't achieve orbit and fell back. And so the response became to embrace that corporate conformity, blindly and fiercely.

And so we have the curious level of political debate in this country, devoid of intelligence, logic, or seeming point. We are of a generation that has only known dimly perceived rebellion and rigid, unthinking conformity. We have an administration of corporate power that quite literally, day in and day out, makes no sense; yet any question of it is framed as being un-American.

To save ourselves and our country, we need simply to return to our individual and national character, what our country is supposed to be about: individual liberty, freedom, and democracy; with the understanding that our government is formed with our consent, and exists to protect us from despotic power, both foreign and domestic. Otherwise, there is nothing to prevent America from fulfilling Winston Churchill's vision of a future world under Nazism, "a new dark age, made more sinister by the lights of perverted science."

ABOUT THE CONTRIBUTORS
(In order of the chapters)

JERRY "POLITEX" BARRETT (www@bushwatch.com), General Editor of Bush Watch (www.bushwatch.com) and co-editor of four books on literature and/or film, received his M.A. from the University of Connecticut and was founder and Director of the Film Studies Program at the University of Delaware.

DAVID LOY (loy@shonan.bunkyo.ac.jp), a social critic and author of numerous books and articles, is a Professor of Philosophy on the Faculty of International Studies at Bunkyo University, Japan.

TREVOR REDNOW (www@bushwatch.com) is a psuedonym for a senior business executive at a Fortune 500 company.

LISA KADONAGA (kadonaga@uvic.ca) holds a Ph.D. in Geography from the University of Victoria (British Columbia, Canada), where she now teaches and contributes political essays on the Internet.

DR. ERNEST PARTRIDGE (gadfly@ipg.org), a philosopher with a specialty in moral philosophy and environmental ethics, has taught at the University of California, the University of Colorado, and as the Hulings Professor of Environmental Ethics at Northland College. He is the editor of The Online Gadfly (www.igc.org/gadfly) and co-editor of The Crisis Papers (www.crisispapers.org).

THE BREW (brew@thedailybrew.com subject line: Re: The Daily Brew) is a psuedonym for a West Coast attorney, author, and former adjunct professor of law and finance at a PAC-10 university who is a political activist and publishes The Daily Brew (www.thedailybrew.com/).

NATHAN NEWMAN (nathan@newman.org), holds a Ph.D in Sociology from University of California, Berkeley and a J.D. from Yale, is a lawyer specializing in labor law and policy, and provides a Web site of opinion (www.nathannewman.org/) containing a full list of his publications.

CHERYL SEAL (Cherdav44@aol.com) is a freelance writer and Internet political commentator best known for her exhaustive analyses of explosive topics (eg. "Smoking Gun: The 9/11 Evidence that May Hang G. W. Bush"). She is also a professional science abstractor and the author of a book on the plight of the American forest.

SARA DEHART, MSN, PhD. (dehart.ss@verizon.net) Associate Professor Emeritus, University of Minnesota is a freelance writer and democracy activist, living in the Seattle, Washington area.

BENNET KELLEY (BKelley@BushLies.net) is an attorney with an Internet company in Los Angeles. He was Co-Founder and National Co-Chair of the Democratic National Committee's Saxophone Club. Kelley publishes

BushLies.net and his commentaries have been published in the *Los Angeles Daily Journal*, *MediaDailyNews* and on the web and include "A Republican Case Against Bushism" and "The Case for Televised Mid-Term Debates."

MADELEINE BEGUN KANE (MadKane@MadKane.com), a "recovering lawyer" and musician whose humorous Web site musings (www.mad-kane.com) have been published in numerous newspapers and print magazines and in many anthologies. Kane is a National award winning humorist (National Society of Newspaper Columnists), whose political song parodies are popular "sing-alongs" at anti-Bush demonstrations. We caught her on a day when she wasn't "recovering."

KEVIN SHAY, a freelance writer based in Washington, D.C., has written an electronic book, "We Will Not Get Over It: Restoring a Legitimate White House."

W. DAVID JENKINS, III (DUMOD@aol.com) lives in upstate New York, works in the mental health field, publishes political essays throughout the Internet, and edits his own political Web site, W.David Jenkins, III (wdjiii.tripod.com/wdjiii3/index.html).

DR. BERNARD WEINER (crisispapers@comcast.net) has taught American politics and international relations at Western Washingon University and San Diego State University, was a writer/editor with the *San Francisco Chronicle* for nearly twenty years, has published widely in leading progressive journals, has authored four volumes of poetry and numerous plays, and currently co-edits The Crisis Papers (http://www.crisispapers.org).

WALTER M. BRASCH, Ph.D., (brasch@ptd.net) a journalist/social activist and professor at Bloomsburg (Pa.) University, is author of 13 books and writes a syndicated column, which has won more than 60 major media awards during the past two decades.

DR. MARGIE BURNS (margie.burns@verizon.net), with a background in Renaissance literature and Shakespeare, is a Texas native and Washington, DC-based freelance writer.

HEATHER WOKUSCH (heather@heatherwokusch.com), a Californian with a background in clinical psychology, has spent many years in Asia and Europe, works as a free-lance writer and cross-cultural trainer, and has been featured across the web and in periodicals internationally (www.heatherwokusch.com).

KENT SOUTHARD (cheapbmr@pacbell.net), a military "brat," college graduate, and veteran of the telecom "lay-off" wars, has provided a full bio of himself in his writings over the years at Bush Watch. (http://bushwatch.org/kent.htm).